LIFE CONDUCT IN MODERN TIMES

Philosophy and Medicine

VOLUME 89

LIFE CONDUCT IN MODERN TIMES

KARL JASPERS AND PSYCHOANALYSIS

by

MATTHIAS BORMUTH

University of Tübingen, Germany

 Springer

A C.I.P. Catalogue record for this book is available from the Library of Congress.

ISBN 1-4020-4764-9 (HB)
ISBN 978-1-4020-4764-9 (HB)
ISBN 1-4020-4765-7 (HB)
ISBN 978-1-4020-4765-7 (e-book)

Published by Springer,
P.O. Box 17, 3300 AA Dordrecht, The Netherlands.

www.springer.com

Printed on acid-free paper

The translation of this book was made by
Susan Nurmi - Schomers

TO HANS HEIMANN
THE FIRST READER

TABLE OF CONTENTS

ACKNOWLEDGEMENTS

This work could not have been produced without the help of various individuals and institutions and the great measure of ideas, financial assistance and moral support which they provided. Most prominently, I would like to mention Dr. Hans Saner. As the executive of Karl Jaspers' estate, he pointed out thematic aspects worth pursuing at the onset of the project and later on, he drew my attention to various facets of Jaspers' philosophy and biography.

I am indebted to Prof. Urban Wiesing for the productive, intellectually stimulating climate of the Institute for Ethics and History of Medicine at the University of Tübingen. My conversations with Prof. Reiner Wiehl, the eminent Jaspers scholar and President of the Karl Jaspers Foundation, enhanced my perspective on the tradition of the liberal *bourgeoisie*, within which Jaspers placed himself.

Without a six-month research grant from the German Literary Archives in Marbach, it would not have been possible to uncover crucial sources in letters and manuscripts of Jaspers' literary estate. A three-year scholarship from the German Research Society (*Deutsche Forschungsgemeinschaft*) which enabled me to participate in the graduate program entitled "Ethics in the Sciences and Humanities" at the University of Tübingen, gave me the opportunity to engage in intense study of Jaspers' psychiatric and philosophical thought, Max Weber's sociology and the medico-ethical discussion relevant to issues addressed in my investigation. My thanks go to these institutions and their staff for their valuable support.

The recently deceased Prof. Johannes Cremerius and Prof. Walter Bräutigam enhanced my perspective on psychoanalysis; both of them collaborated closely with Alexander Mitscherlich and came to hold leading positions in academic psychoanalysis. The writings of Wilhelm Hennis and the opportunity I had to engage in personal conversations with him concerning the sociology of life conduct inspired my study of Max Weber. In Tübingen, Georg Hartmann made extremely knowledgeable suggestions for reading in the philosophical sphere which proved to be crucial for my research approach. The countless conversations with Prof. Werner Janzarik and Prof. Michael Schmidt-Degenhard, the most prominent representatives of psychopathology in Heidelberg who succeeded Karl Jaspers and Kurt Schneider, invested the psychiatric dimension of my study with the necessary historical orientation.

In Tübingen I had the great fortune to find in Prof. Hans Heimann, an *emeritus* of the Psychiatric Clinic, a colleague keenly interested in my project who followed the emergence of the manuscript chapter by chapter on an almost weekly basis. Without his ongoing, committed readership I would have hardly ventured to open up my study to the pronounced interdisciplinary orientation it ultimately adopted. The fact that Heimann was not only one of the first psychopharmacological researchers in Switzerland but also soberly advocated psychopathological and psychotherapeutic positions corresponds in a singular way with the ideal upheld by Jaspers, namely to view psychiatry as a methodologically dualistic discipline devoted to mind and nature alike. A letter written by the existence philosopher in 1950 in which he comments on Heimann's methodological approach as outlined in an article entitled "The Influence of Karl Jaspers on Psychopathology" gives an indication of such an affinity. The letter is addressed to Jacob Klaesi, the Director of the Psychiatric Clinic at the University of Bern-Waldau; here Jaspers writes, "I am enormously delighted about the work of your first assistant, Dr. Heimann. He understands my 'Psychopathology' in the sense crucial to me, namely as a methodological mindset. Today I am convinced, even more so than in my early years, that unprejudiced perceptions and openness to potential insights from all corners can only be gained in this way. Please relay my deeply felt thanks to Dr. Heimann."

The fact that my book can be made accessible to an English-speaking readership some few years after its publication in German is attributable to the interest which Dr. Corinna Delkeskamp-Hayes took in my cultural-scientific investigation. She brought me together with Prof. Tristram H. Engelhardt, who deemed my study illuminating enough from an ethico-medical vantage point to accept it for publication in the "Philosophy and Medicine" series. My thanks go to both for their commitment to the project on its way to completion. The staff of Springer contributed to its smooth execution.

I am indebted to my colleague from the Institute for Ethics and History of Medicine in Tübingen, Dr. Susan Nurmi-Schomers, for having taken upon herself the task of translating my book, rendering my thoughts in her North-American tongue and infusing them with new expressiveness. My gratitude goes to her for this. My father, Karl-Heinz Bormuth, read the manuscript upon completion. I am deeply indebted to him and my mother for all their support. The German original would not have come to such a successful completion without the help of German-speaking friends who acted as avid readers of the original. I wish to thank Ágotha Bu, Dr. Peter Geiss, Dr. Annette Hilt, Dr. Peter Goßens, Oliver Grassmück, Eleonore Hochmuth-Pickert, Dorit Krusche, Berenike Lisker, Susanne Michl, Dott. Moira Paleari, Diethild Plattner, Petra Plättner, Dr. Larson Powell, Dr. Dirk Oschmann, Silke Ruoff, Christina Schneider and in particular Dr. Ulrich Bülow; in his function as *primus inter pares*, his critical reading of the manuscript relieved it of certain tedious passages.

The English translation constitutes an abridged version of the German original. Some sections on the history of psychoanalysis and medicine have been removed, and for the sake of systematic coherence, certain biographical excursions have been deleted as well. In all other respects the English translation corresponds to the German edition of 2002. In closing may I express my hope that the fundamental question of life conduct in modernity, which Karl Jaspers raises in philosophical terms shaped by Max Weber's thought, awakens the interest of an English-speaking readership.

Matthias Bormuth, July 2005

CHAPTER 1

INTRODUCTION

> We read, but we are also read by others. Interferences of
> these readings. Forcing someone to read himself as he is read
> (slavehood). Forcing the others to read me as I read myself
> (conquest).
>
> Simone Weil[1]

Karl Jaspers was born in Oldenburg in 1883, grew up in a liberal-minded banker's family, studied medicine and was granted a chair in philosophy at the University of Heidelberg in 1922.[2] The decisive factor in this appointment was Jaspers' 1919 monograph *Psychology of World Views (Psychologie der Weltanschauungen)*, which founded so-called 'existence philosophy'.[3] What is less known is that in 1913 Jaspers had already published an epoch-making methodological systematics, his *General Psychopathology (Allgemeine Psychopathologie)*, which had established him as an authority in the field of psychiatry in the German-speaking world.[4] As a result of this as well as the fact that Jaspers addressed questions concerning physicians' self-identity[5], Jaspers is now celebrated as one of the "classic figures of medicine".[6]

---

[1] Weil (1990), pg. 134.

[2] Karl Jaspers (1883-1969) worked as a psychiatrist in Heidelberg starting in 1909, and from 1914 on he held a position as a *Privatdozent* for psychology in the Department of Philosophy after having completed his *Habilitation*. In 1920 he was granted an assistant professorship and in 1922 a chair in this department. In 1937 he was forced to retire because his wife was Jewish. In 1945 he was reinstated. In 1948 he took a position at the University of Basle, where he taught until 1961.

[3] Cf. PWV, pp. IX-XII and Arendt (1948), p. 73f.

[4] Jaspers published the monograph in 1913 as thesis for the *Habilitation* and published revised editions in 1920, 1923 and 1946.

[5] Cf. GP 4, pp. 624-686. Fundamental reflections on the physician-patient relationship are also to be found in the *Philosophy* from 1932, which established Jaspers' fame as an existence philosopher.

[6] Cf. Blankenburg (1991) and v. Engelhardt (1986). A critical editon of his correspondance concerning psychiatry and the natural sciences, co-edited by Dietrich von Engelhardt and the author of this study, will appear soon. In addition, two volumes of letters which address purely philosophical and cultural issues will be published (at Benno Schwabe Publishers in Switzerland) under the supervision of the general editor of the project, Prof. Reiner Wiehl, *emeritus* of the Department of Philosophy at the University of Heidelberg.

Since the 1963 publication of his book in English translation, it has become well-known in the English-speaking world.[7] In 1997, a new edition of the *General Psychopathology* was published by Johns Hopkins University Press in Baltimore. As Paul R. McHugh remarks in the foreward, its methodological approach is "indispensible" for psychiatry.[8]

In the various editions of the *General Psychopathology* Jaspers treats Sigmund Freud and his psychoanalysis[9] in an increasingly critical vein. His 1931 cultural-philosophical essay *Man in the Modern Age (Die geistige Situation der Zeit)* condemns Freud's psychoanalysis as a questionable ideology, and after 1945 he attacks its basic tenets once again in individual, polemical articles. In 1954 Jaspers tells us that even as a young psychiatrist he had put up "inner resistance" to Freud and that this had been for reasons which transcended purely scientific matters. What Freud had attempted to establish in the "medium of science" was perceived by Jaspers as a "reprehensible" philosophy which he aimed to challenge with "thought from completely different origins".[10] In a letter to Carl Friedrich von Weizsäcker, who defended psychoanalysis in his response to Jaspers, we read: "The devil is at the root of this. For this reason there can only be complete rejection."[11] Without a doubt, Jaspers' increasingly critical view of psychoanalysis can be attributed to the emergence of his own philosophy. The aim of this book is to trace the development of Jaspers' critique of psychoanalysis as it presented itself in various journalistic writings and to elucidate the arguments, motives and contexts which shape it from the time of its first formulation in the context of Jaspers' psychiatric work down to its final critical expression by Jaspers the political philosopher. This study is to be understood as an historical reconstruction of conditions which induced Jaspers to take a critical view of psychoanalysis. The sociology of Max Weber, a figure whom Jaspers held in high esteem, will serve as a methodological framework for this study. In Jaspers' *Psychology of World Views* we read:

> Max Weber's writings on the sociology of religion as well as his political works analyze the psychology of world views in a new way in the sense that they fuse together what would seem to have been impossible to conjoin before, namely historical research of the most concrete kind and systematic thought.[12]

In other words, Jaspers is fascinated by Weber's attempt to grasp the motivational significance of value convictions and ideas in terms of social action. Jaspers

---

[7] The translation project was carried out by the Department of Psychiatry at the University of Manchester. As E.W. Anderson, the author of the foreward to the first English edition informs us, Willy Mayer-Gross, a Jewish colleague of Jaspers in Heidelberg, had introduced Jaspers' psychopathological approach to England after 1933. Cf. GP 4, pg. XIIIf.
[8] Paul R. McHugh is the Director of Psychiatry and Behavioral Sciences of Johns Hopkins Medical Institutions. Cf. GP 4, pg. Xf.
[9] To find out more about Freud's biography, consult Freud (1925), Gay (1988) and Lohmann (1998).
[10] PWV, pp. IXf.
[11] Copy of letter from Karl Jaspers to Carl Friedrich von Weizsäcker, August 8, 1953, JLE-GLA.
[12] Cf. Jaspers (1919), pg. 14.

was in fact the first to view Weber immediately after his premature death in 1920 not only as a national economist, a jurist, a sociologist, an historian and politician, but also to publicly emphasize his role as a philosopher.[13] With a strong sense of conviction he writes, "[...] for many of us, Max Weber is a philosopher. It is not appropriate for this great man to be committed to a single profession or science. If he was a philosopher, perhaps he was the only philosopher of our times and was a philosopher in a sense in which no one else could be termed as such today."[14] His quite extensive 1932 monograph entitled *Max Weber – A German in Political Thought, Research and Philosophizing* (*Max Weber. Deutsches Wesen im politischen Denken, im Forschen und Philosophieren*) affirms this assessment. As Jaspers writes, "Max Weber did not teach a philosophy; he was a philosophy."[15] Thus it hardly comes as a surprise that in 1949, when Jaspers is at the zenith of public recognition as a philosopher and psychiatrist, he should look back and acknowledge the decisive role which Max Weber had played for him. As he writes, "I am indebted to Max Weber not only for my *Psychopathology* of young years, but also for providing me with the means to formulate my philosophy."[16] To be sure, a few years before his death in 1969, new insights into Weber's biography disillusioned Jaspers' perception of Weber's exceptional ethical integrity.[17] Despite apparent discrepancies in positions on theoretical values which came to alienate Jaspers, he remained convinced of and fascinated by Weber's unique scientific contribution and his uncompromising intellect.[18]

My investigation of Max Weber's sociological writings shows that the assumed affinity towards Webers's thought on the part of Jaspers does not evidence itself when it comes to certain crucial nuances, however. Instead, when writings of these two figures are looked at from a congruent perspective, subtly different readings present themselves. In other words, Weber's sociology involves concepts and evaluations which are not to be found in Jaspers' thinking, but despite this fact they are close enough to the perspective of the latter's work in psychiatry and the approach of his existence philosophy to provide the framework for a discerning and profound examination of his critique of psychoanalysis. In particular, three aspects of Weber's sociology promote an understanding of Jaspers' position. First of all, Weber's work supplies us with a sociological theory of modernity which serves as a point of reference for Jaspers' existence philosophy, making his critique of psychoanalysis comprehensible. Second of all, Weber's postulate of 'value freedom' offers us a metascientific framework within which we can reconstruct Jaspers' arguments and the aporias they present. Thirdly, in the course of such a reconstruction, Weber's

---

[13] Cf. Jaspers (1921), pg. 32.

[14] Cf. Jaspers (1921), pg. 32.

[15] Cf. Jaspers (1932a), pg. 94.

[16] Copy of letter from Karl Jaspers to Willy Hellpach from April 22, 1949, JLE-GLA.

[17] The exact circumstances of this process of disillusionment, which Dieter Henrich has examined, will be elucidated later. Cf. pp. 58-62 of this monograph.

[18] For according to Jaspers, Weber allowed himself no metaphysical refuge like the ones he believed to have discovered in Nietzsche's and Kierkegaard's writings. Cf. letter from Karl Jaspers to Hannah Arendt from April 29, 1966, in AJC, pp. 635-639; cf. AJB, pp. 671-673.

sociological concept of ambitious intellectual 'life conduct' is assigned a special role, for it couples ideas and social action in such a way as to help us grasp a main aspect of Jaspers' existence philosophy, namely its implicit ethics and motivational dynamics. Jaspers' reservations concerning Freud's psychology are to be primarily attributed to his own interest in a concept of life conduct founded on existence philosophy; this is the thesis put forth and argued by this study.[19] As regards psychoanalytically oriented medicine Jaspers writes: "Wanting to entrust a physician with the prescription of one's life conduct is an escape from seriousness to convenience on the part of some modern human beings."[20]

The concept 'life conduct' implies that in taking actions, the individual can choose goals of action which seem purposeful to him so that his life practice is invested with a certain degree of systematization within the context of its guiding constructs of meaningfulness. This was found to be the case particularly in the realm of the religions which Weber had investigated sociologically. But Weber had discovered a tendency to place social action within the framework of religious patterns of meaning and to establish specific similar patterns of life conduct on the part of secularized intellectuals and philosophers as well.[21] To be sure, a meaningful use of the concept of life conduct in the context of modernity presupposes that individuals have certain room for making voluntary decisions about possible goals of actions. And it is this dependency of the concept of life conduct on the freedom of the individual to make his own decisions which allows us to fully comprehend Jaspers' approach, as the individualistic aspect of existence philosophy – a central component of it – constitutes an appeal against modern mass society. Weber's diagnosis is sobering. In allusion to Nietzsche he speaks of the "last stage of this cultural development" as an age inhabited by "[s]pecialists without spirit, sensualists without heart".[22] Jaspers seizes upon this diagnosis of human beings dictated by goal-oriented rationality and capable of no more than trivial consumption during their leisure time. In doing so he speaks of "philosophical life conduct", individual self-reflection and decisions, writing: "And if [the modern human being] just begins to encounter himself, the giant of this world wants to pull him back into the all-devouring machine which produces empty work and empty pleasure."[23]

This book has seven main chapters. The first addresses Jaspers' critique of psychoanalysis as it is formulated primarily in the first editions of the *General Psychopathology* published in the years 1913 and 1920. For this reason it remains essentially focussed on the psychiatric perspective. The second chapter gives a sketch of Jaspers' existence philosophy on the basis of his 1931 cultural-philosophical treatise entitled *Man in the Modern Age* (*Die geistige Situation der Zeit*), as this work also formulates Jaspers' conception of modernity; and moreover, it illustrates how Jaspers positioned the concept of life conduct informed by his existence philosophy

---

[19] Jaspers speaks of "philosophical life conduct". Cf. Jaspers (1950a), pp. 92-100.
[20] Jaspers (1953a), pg. 38.
[21] Cf. *Wirtschaft und Gesellschaft* (*Economy and Society*), pg. 275.
[22] Cf. Weber (1904/05), pg. 182; cf. Weber (1976), pg. 204.
[23] Cf. Jaspers (1950a), pg. 92f.

during this period, which is of crucial importance for this investigation.[24] Jaspers' understanding of Weber's postulate of value freedom and the implications it had for his critique of psychoanalysis are addressed in the third chapter. This section of the book also focusses on *Man in the Modern Age*. The fourth chapter returns in part to the psychiatric perspective in that it concerns itself with the 1941/42 edition of the *General Psychopathology*.[25] Not only did the emerging existence philosophy alter the fundamental concepts of the *General Psychopathology;* it also changed Jaspers' notions of psychotherapy and psychoanalysis to a considerable degree. National socialism also influenced Jaspers' perspective on psychoanalysis. His assumption that psychoanalysis had become a mere historical phenomenon after having been forced to dissolve as an institution is proven wrong by the fact that a psychoanalytically oriented institute devoted to the study of psychosomatics was established in Heidelberg after the war. Jaspers was involved in the founding of the institute, acting as an expert consultant. The fifth chapter investigates the arguments against psychoanalysis put forth by Jaspers within the context of its potential reinstitutionalization. Jaspers' direct adversaries were the psychosomaticist Viktor von Weizsäcker and his assistant Alexander Mitscherlich. In the sixth chapter the debate over psychoanalysis carried out among these figures, which had previously only been conducted within the walls of the university, will be illuminated in the public form it ultimately took on. In his articles "Critique of Psychoanalysis" ("Zur Kritik der Psychoanalyse")[26] and "Physician and Patient" ("Arzt und Patient")[27] from 1950 and 1953 respectively, Jaspers responds to lectures on psychosomatic medicine and psychoanalysis published by von Weizsäcker and Mitscherlich in 1949. What irritates Jaspers most is the important role played by interpretation on the part of the physician in the new school of psychosomatics. Moreover, he attacks Mitscherlich's idea of introducing obligatory training analysis for all physicians working in the area of psychotherapy at universities. In the following years, Jaspers' critique of psychoanalysis adopts an increasingly pronounced socio-political slant, as the seventh chapter documents on the basis of his series of lectures entitled *Reason and Anti-Reason in our Time (Vernunft und Widervernunft in unserer Zeit)*.[28] In particular, the debate on totalitarianism which was conducted during the 1950's will be illuminated as the historical framework in which Jaspers' critique unfolds. Jaspers' student Hannah Arendt made significant contributions to this debate.[29] Arendt was also the one to report to Jaspers of the important role which psychoanalysis had begun to play in the U.S.A. in the 1940's, witnessing this development as an emigrant. In

---

[24] The book was the first philosophical work to be published – after *Psychology of World Views* in 1919 – by Jaspers after teaching as a philosopher for almost 10 years preliminary to the *Philosophy*. Cf. MMA, pg. 4 and the letter from Karl Jaspers to Ernst Mayer from April 16, 1930, JLE-GLA.

[25] Cf. GP 4. The book was twice as long as the original edition and had been extensively revised; it could not be printed until 1946 for lack of approval to supply the paper for it to be printed on.

[26] Jaspers (1950d).

[27] Jaspers (1953a).

[28] Cf. RAR.

[29] For biographical data on this figure consult Young-Bruehl (1982) and *Hannah* Arendt *– Karl Jaspers. Correspondence 1926-1969* (AJC).

philosophical terms, the chapter addresses once again and more extensively the question as to whether any 'authority' of scientific truth is conceivable under the conditions of modernity. This issue is introduced by turning to the discussion carried out in the corespondence between Jaspers and Carl Friedrich von Weizsäcker.[30] This chapter concludes with Jaspers' last critical remarks on psychoanalysis, which were made accessible to a wider public in 1964 within the context of televized lectures. At this time the publication of Mitscherlich's book *Society without a Father: A Contribution to Social Psychology* (*Auf dem Weg zur vaterlosen Gesellschaft*) resulted in widespread recognition of psychoanalysis as the leading theory of many intellectuals,[31] this being a development which Jaspers had endeavored to prevent since the 1950's. In 1968, Jürgen Habermas' socio-philosophical book *Knowledge and Human Interests* (*Erkenntnis und Interesse*), which was oriented in the same direction as Mitscherlich's works, succeeded in conveying, to the critical body of university students, an image of Freud's psychology as a mode of self-enlightenment.[32] In the conclusion to this study, the growing societal role of psychoanalysis will be illuminated from Jaspers' contrary perspective, namely his appeal to the intellectual elite to entertain a model of life conduct based on existence philosophy. In the 1970's and 1980's, the socio-psychological life orientation propagated by Mitscherlich, Habermas and others was quite successful, whereas Jaspers' model of life conduct based on existence philosophy was neglected in the intellectual as well as the public sphere, in theory as well as in practice.

In concluding I would like to point out that for pragmatic reasons the concepts 'existence philosophy' and 'existence-philosophical' will be used to denote the philosophy of Karl Jaspers. He himself came to view the term with growing skepticism, however, as he took offense at the ubiquitous, catchphrase use of the word after 1945.[33] For this reason he almost stopped using the term altogether.[34]

---

[30] For biographical data on von Weizsäcker cf. Wein (1988).

[31] Cf. Mitscherlich (1963). A few years later he coauthored a book with his wife Margarethe Mitscherlich-Nielsen entitled *The Inability to Mourn: Principles of Collective Behavior* (*Die Unfähigkeit zu trauern. Grundlagen kollektiven Verhaltens*), in which psychoanalysis is recommended as the basis for collective mourning. Cf. Mitscherlich/Mitscherlich-Nielsen (1967).

[32] Cf. Habermas (1968) and Wiggershaus (1986).

[33] Cf. Jaspers (1938), pg. 86f..

[34] Cf. *Von der Wahrheit* (*On Truth*), pp. 209f. and pp. 566ff..

CHAPTER 2

THE CRITIQUE OF PSYCHOANALYSIS 1913-1920

> Look, we have coarse senses. Know each other? We would
> have to break open our skulls and tear the thoughts out of the
> fibers of our brains.
>
> Georg Büchner [35]

After three years working as a psychiatrist "without very much clinical experience, but with a very sharpened clinical perspective",[36] Jaspers published his *General Psychopathology* [37] in 1913. Its methodological systematics brought remarkably early fame for the young psychiatrist. As a representative of the Heidelberg school of psychiatry, Werner Janzarik looks back and gives merit to the work for having established psychopathology as a "fundamental [psychiatric] discipline".[38]

Jaspers' article entitled "Causal and 'Understandable' Connections between Life Fate and Psychosis in Cases of Dementia Praecox" ("Kausale und 'verständliche' Zusammenhänge zwischen Schicksal und Psychose bei der Dementia praecox [Schizophrenie]"), which appeared shortly before the *General Psychopathology*, as well as the 1913 textbook itself already manifest a certain somewhat critical vein as regards psychoanalysis. The extensively revised edition of 1920[39] obviously intensifies what were originally mild reservations. This is largely attributable to Jaspers' increasingly philosophical perspective, which begins to express itself more clearly for the first time in his 1919 *Psychology of World Views*.[40] The third, further revised edition of the *General Psychopathology* from 1923 does not add any new aspects to Jaspers' critique of Freud's thought,[41] unlike the fourth and last revised edition from

---

[35] Georg Büchner, *Danton's Death,* 1835.

[36] Schneider (1938), pg. 16.

[37] Karl Jaspers, General Psychopathology. Guidelines for Students, Physicians and Psychologists, Berlin 1913 (AP 1).

[38] Janzarik (1976), pg. 73.

[39] Karl Jaspers, General Psychopathology. For Students, Physicians and Psychologists; second, revised edition, Berlin 1920 (AP 2).

[40] Cf. PWV, pp. IX-XII.

[41] Karl Jaspers, General Psychopathology. For Students, Physicians and Psychologists; third, expanded and revised edition, Berlin 1923 (GP 3).

1941/42, which shows itself most clearly to have been informed by the now mature existence philosophy of the author.[42]

This chapter will only address the early critique of psychoanalysis as it presents itself in the first three editions of the *General Psychopathology*. This cannot be done without elucidating to a certain extent the discussion on the formation of psychiatric theories which was being carried out during this time. For this reason an excursus on the history of psychiatry as it unfolds within the specific context of the field of psychopathology which had constituted itself in Heidelberg during these years will be necessary. The chapter concludes with elucidations on psychotherapy in practice which are formulated almost identically in all three editions of the *General Psychopathology* and a comparative analysis of Freud's self-conceptualization as a therapist.

THE 1913 *GENERAL PSYCHOPATHOLOGY*

Jaspers and Psychiatry in Heidelberg

The fact that Jaspers succeeded in writing the *General Psychopathology* in just three years is not attributable to his intellectual talent alone, but also to the favorable working conditions he found himself in. Due to a severe, chronic lung ailment the "scientific research apprentice" at the Psychiatric and Neurological Clinic of Heidelberg was relieved of his normal clinical duties and was thus in a position to spend much time studying psychiatric literature and tending to individual patients on an intensive basis. Jaspers found the scientific climate of the Heidelberg Clinic under the directorship of Franz Nissl critical and stimulating, a fact which must have promoted the unusual degree of productivity enormously.[43]

From the perspective of the history of psychiatry, Jaspers belonged to the 'older' circle of psychopathologists working in Heidelberg. The representatives of this circle who continue to be regarded as having been most influential were Hans W. Gruhle, Karl Wilmanns and Willi Mayer-Gross. To an even greater degree than Jaspers, they continued to adhere to Emil Kraepelin's concept of "original" nosology,[44] which was based on the idea of the "disease entity" ("Krankheitseinheit").[45] Jaspers himself describes the beginnings of psychopathology in Heidelberg as being critically oriented towards Kraepelin as one who looked beyond changes in

---

[42] Karl Jaspers, General Psychopathology (1946; fourth, completely revised edition), Berlin ⁹1973 (GP 4.).

[43] Cf. PAJK, pg. 12-15; cf. PhA, pg. 19.

[44] Emil Kraepelin (1856-1926) was instrumental in shaping the concept of psychiatric nosology in the various editons of his *Compendium* (*Kompendium*) and later his *Textbook of Psychiatry* (*Lehrbuch der Psychiatrie*) from 1883 on. Paul Hoff distinguises three phases of Kraepelinian nosology, with the "middle phase", which is relevant in this context, dating back to the period between 1891 and 1915. Cf. Hoff (1994), pg. 170-174.

[45] Janzarik (1976), p. 74.

clinical symptoms in the course of their manifestation, scientifically systematizing certain distinguishable "processes of illness". As Jaspers writes,

> Intellectualy speaking, the common property of the clinic was Kraepelinian psychiatry with modifications. [...] One held up the notion of a polarity between the two large areas of dementia praecox (later called schizophrenia) and manic-depressive disorders. The notion of the disease entity was elucidated, and observations were always made in reference to this idea but without really knowing what it was. Biographical processes, as part of the development of a personality which, understandably, underwent certain transformations in the course of a person's life phases, were distinguished from processes involving violent ruptures which caused human beings to change radically for reasons which one held to be organic without really understanding them.[46]

To understand the affinity to Kraepelin's position on the part of the Heidelberg School, it is necessary to outline the discussion on psychiatric doctrines of disease as it was conducted in the 19th century. As Jaspers showed in what is still considered a "brilliant" treatment of this discussion in the "historical chapter" of his *General Psychopathology*, the focus of scientific research began to shift beginning around 1860. Psychiatry relocated, moving from the mental asylums to the universities as they gained independent institutional status.[47] In 1864, Wilhelm Griesinger was awarded the first chair of psychiatiry, in Berlin. As a general rule, psychiatric training had previously been integrated into what is now called internal medicine. Griesinger was the one who, as early as 1845, with the publication of the first edition of his textbook entitled *Pathology and Therapy of Mental Diseases* (*Pathologie und Therapie der psychischen Krankheiten*), made constructive efforts to liberate the community of clinical psychiatrists from the notion that they had to align themselves into two strictly divided camps: the somaticists and the psychicists. Jaspers describes the situation as follows: "On the one side a purely medical perspective reined, and on the other a primarily psychological one."[48]

Jaspers evaluates the position of the so-called psychicists in a reductionist manner, claiming that their "philosophico-metaphysical and theological ties" had caused them to create "dogmatic constructions" like those to be found in Heinroth's "Doctrine of Mental Illness as a Result of 'Sin'" or Ideler's notion that mental illness was attributable to "usurious passions".[49] When defining the task of the somaticist, Jaspers also limits it to aetiology following Jacobi's notion that "brain processes which are perceivable by the senses" constitute the "essential" aspect of psychiatric illnesses and that these are what the symptoms ultimately result from.[50] Jaspers associates the

---

[46] PAKJ, pg. 15; cf. PhA, pg. 20.

[47] Cf. Ackerknecht (1985), p. 62.

[48] AP 1, pg. 330; cf. AP 4, S. 709 and GP 4, S. 850f.

[49] Cf. AP 1, pg. 330f.; cf. AP 4, S. 709 and GP 4, S. 850f. Cf. Heinroth, Christian August, *Textbook of Mental Diseases* (*Lehrbuch der Störungen des Seelenlebens*), Leipzig 1818 and *Psychology as a Doctrine of Self-Revelation* (*Die Psychologie als Selbsterkenntnislehre*), Leipzig 1827.

[50] AP 1, pg. 331. Jaspers cites Maximilian Jacobi (1775-1858) and his works *Observations on Pathology and Therapy of Diseases Connected with Madness* (*Beobachtungen über die Pathologie und Therapie der mit dem Irresein verbundenen Krankheiten*), Elberfeld 1830, and *The Main Forms of Mental Illness* (*Die Hauptformen der Seelenstörungen*), Leipzig 1844.

somaticists with the "phantastic construction" of Theodor Meynert, for example, and with what he terms pejoratively as the "constructive theories" of Carl Wernicke.[51] His critique is not aimed at the assumption that mental illness has a somatic basis, but rather at the apparent certainty with which a psychosomatic correlation is made.

Jaspers also viewed Wilhelm Griesinger as one of those working in the last third of the 19th century who had bridged somatically and scientifically oriented psychiatry. He sees Griesinger as a precursor of the school which defined the psychiatric perspective in purely somatological terms, thus drawing attention away from psychopathological and psychodynamic aspects. As Jaspers writes:

> Historically speaking, the dominion of the dogma which declares that mental illnesses are illnesses of the brain has had a beneficial and a detrimental effect. This view promoted brain research. [...] It had a negative effect on psychopathological research; involuntarily some psychiatrists were taken possession by the feeling that all they had to do was to find out exactly how the brain worked; then they would also know all about the psyche and its diseases.[52]

Jaspers opposes this view by formulating the goal of the Heidelberg School:

> For the psychiatrist who understands himself to be a psychopathologist, holding this position would constitute a betrayal of his genuine task. He does not want to examine brain processes, which is the task of neurologists and brain histologists, but rather psychic processes.[53]

And yet more recent studies concur in claiming that although Griesinger's work has a somatological orientation, he did in fact integrate psychodynamic and sociopsychiatric aspects into his psychiatric systematics.[54]

Michael Schmidt-Degenhard is also one to clearly assert that the "polarity of psychicists and somaticists" is not properly reflected in the "extreme somato- or psychogenesis" of severe mental illnesses. As regards the psychicists, Schmidt-Degenhard points out that their reception of Schelling's philosophy of nature led them to view psychophysical disease phenomena from an empirical perspective.[55] However one is inclined to evaluate the specifics of such assessments, the general view that Jaspers leveled a wholesale reproach at 19th-century psychicists on account of their speculative-moralizing tone seems to be in need of revision.

The somaticists, like Schmidt-Degenhard, ascribed to the human being what they deemed to be an extensively "invulnerable psychic substance" which was immune to somatic influence. This special, practically transcendental status of the psyche had

---

[51] AP 1, pg. 331; cf. AP 4, pg. 710 and GP 4, pg. 851.

[52] AP 1, pg. 194.

[53] AP 1, pg. 31.

[54] Ackerknecht (1985) provides an extensive and critical treatment of Griesinger's psychiatry which also foregrounds psychodynamics and ego psychology. Cf. Ackerknecht (1985), pg. 63-72. In regard to Griesinger, Heimann refers to the "relativity of possible theoretical positions" which preclude any kind of theoretical determinism. Cf. Heimann (1976), p. 30. In another study he inquires into the psychodynamic aspects of Griesinger's psychopathological approach. Cf. Heimann (1988), pg. 126.

[55] Schmidt-Degenhard (1983), pg. 22f..

the limitation of being unreachable, however, which meant that the somaticists had no "access to the inner life story" of a human being.[56] In his late works, Jaspers approaches this notion.[57]

In this context we should take another look at Emil Kraepelin's nosological systematics of psychiatry. As Hoff shows, Kraepelin's approach aims to integrate aspects of brain anatomy and experimental psychology as well as symptomatological observations on the development of disease, treating all as equally significant. Ideally the results were to complement each other.[58] Jaspers sums up this approach succinctly as follows:

> Disease patterns which have identical causes, identical basic psychological forms, identical development and progression and identical outcome and diagnostic brain findings, i.e. which manifest overall identical patterns, are genuine, natural disease entities.[59]

Jaspers does not follow Kraepelin in the conviction associated with him that "disease entities" can be definitively demarcated, however. The *Psychopathology* relativizes the "disease entity" as a regulative, pragmatically oriented "idea in the Kantian sense of the word".[60] Kraepelin's futile attempts to provide a psychological diagnosis of progressive paralysis which was as exact as that yieled by brain organic findings and could complement it is seized upon by Jaspers as an argument for limiting psychosomatic correlation in both directions to the status of a regulative idea. As he writes:

> Even a disease whose bodily manifestations were well-known could not be diagnosed psychologically with any certainty and this continues to be impossible; how should one then be able to find and define an unknown disease by psychological means?[61]

Unlike Kraepelin, Jaspers proves to be an epistemological skeptic who only acknowledges "types" of symptom complexes which overlap but never lead to diagnostically "demarcated diseases".[62]

And yet for reasons of orientation and in keeping with Kraepelin's approach, he himself distinguishes various "psychoses", which he mainly classifies according to two groups on the basis of the presumed cause, these being "exogenic" and "endogenic psychoses". He writes:

> From an aetiological perspective we distinguish (exogenic) psychoses, i.e. those essentially caused by tangible bodily processes or external effects, which are also referred to as organic or symptomatic psychoses, from functional or idiopathic psychoses, which are essentially caused by unknown or endogenic causes.[63]

---

[56] Schmidt-Degenhard (1983), pg. 21.

[57] Schmid-Degenhard (1983), pg. 21.

[58] Hoff (1985), pg. 51.

[59] AP 1, pg. 260.

[60] AP 1, pg. 263.

[61] AP 1, pg. 263. To be sure, Jaspers interprets the concept "disease entity" as it is used by Kraepelin too one-sidedly. After all, Kraepelin was only too willing to admit that many sets of symptoms could not be standardized and that these were in fact the most important sources of insight, as Heimann has shown. Cf. Heimann (1980), pg. 266.

[62] AP 1, pg. 262.

[63] AP 1, pg. 265.

The first group corresponds to the "symptomatic psychoses" described by Karl Bonhoeffer, in which diverse detectable noxa produce relatively similar symptom patterns.[64] The endogenic psychoses whose causes remained unexplainable were classified by Jaspers following Kraepelin and the psychopathologists in Heidelberg according to observations on disease progression into two groups: one was defined as the "process" of an incurable, progredient disease and the other as the "development of a personality". As such it was characterized by temporary disease phases which in their view were to be associated psychodynamically with the character and biography of the person in question.[65] For one, Jaspers classified forms of schizophrenia which were at that time still in part referred to as Dementia praecox and which had been described by Eugen Bleuler[66] as process psychoses, whereas manic-depressive disorders and abnormal experiential reactions, i.e. the neuroses, were viewed as typical representatives of developmental psychoses. As far as the history of such terminology goes, one might add that the term "psychosis" has been used since the beginning of the 20th century for mental diseases with somatic causes, whereas the term "neurosis" has primarily been used to denote experiential or environmentally determined disorders.[67]

Psychopathology at the Divide Between the Natural Sciences and the Humanities

Jaspers' *General Psychopathology* does not intend to subscribe to a purely scientific or psychodynamic conception of disease. Jaspers designated such one-sided aetiological schemata as "somatic and philosophical prejudices" which encumbered the process of psychopathological inquiry.[68] He saw the psychiatry of his age as having to navigate between the Skylla of scientific "brain mythology" and the Charybdis of hermeneutic "psychomythology". Jaspers associates the ideotype of strictly somatic pathogenesis with Carl Wernicke and opposes it to Freud's model of strictly psychical pathogenesis of psychiatric diseases in his chapter entitled "Theories" from the second edition of the *General Psychopathology* on.[69] Jaspers' "methodological dualism" gives pathogenetic primacy to scientific medicine when it comes to determining the ultimate cause of disease while delegating a supplementary, psychoplastic role to the psychodynamic approach, will be shown in the course of this study.[70]

---

[64] Cf. Bonhoeffer (1910).
[65] AP 1, pg. 265f.
[66] Cf. Bleuler (1911).
[67] Cf. Janzarik (1976), pg. 15.
[68] AP 1, pg. 10.
[69] Cf. AP 2, pp. 283-295. In the fourth edition of the textbook, Jaspers expands the chapter on theories, now with the new heading "Explanatory Theories – Their Meaning and Value". Cf. GP 4, pp. 530-552; AQP 4, pp. 444-463.
[70] The term "pathogenic" refers to factors which influence the development and progression of a disease considerably, whereas the term "pathoplastic" is used to designate factors which shape a pathological disorder in a certain way without having any significant effect on their genesis and development.

In this polarized climate, Jaspers considers the humanistic method to be considerably "more subtle, better developed and more transparent" than the scientific one. This conviction inspires him to proclaim: "We must learn from philologists."[71] In particular, he attempts to depict his version of Edmund Husserl's "phenomenology" in his article on method entitled "The Phenomenological Method in Psychopathology" ("Die phänomenologische Methode in der Psychopathologie") without adopting the ontological direction Husserl had begun to take. The approach which Jaspers investigates in 1913 designates Max Weber and Georg Simmel[72] as its warrantors, whereas his *General Psychopathology* concentrates on Weber along with Husserl. In his philosophical autobiography, Jaspers expresses a certain indebtedness to the "descriptive and analytical psychology" of Wilhelm Dilthey, which, as he says, helped him to develop his own "*verstehende Psychologie*".[73]

Following the methodological discussion which was being carried out in the humanties, Jaspers defines the scientific analysis of "objective causal connections" as "explaining" ("Erklären"), whereas he designates the "understanding of psychic events 'from within'" as "understanding" ("Verstehen").[74] For the most part he orients himself to Dilthey's dichomotomy, according to which natural events can only be explained externally with the help of logical regularities which have been arrived at using inductive reasoning, whereas inner meaning-making processes can only be grasped through individual empathy. To be sure, Jaspers modifies Dilthey's concepts to a certain extent. He writes:

> The fact that genetic understanding is also referred to as 'psychological explanation' is slightly misleading. I explain the action of a human being 'psychologically', i.e. I understand it, when I attribute it to its motivations, whereas I explain it causally if I deem it to be unexplainable and as a result the cause of verifiable brain processes.[75]

For Jaspers, scientific "explanation" entails making objectifiable ascriptions of regularities using empirico-inductive means. Ultimately, these are always based on biological foundations which are to be conceived of as highly complex structures manifesting themselves indirectly via psychic mechanisms. By entertaining this view, Jaspers shows himself to be firmly footed in the traditional, widely established understanding of science which asigns to the natural sciences as disciplines operating on inductive observation compelling general validity. In 1894, Wilhelm Windelband differentiates between the "ideographic" humanities and the "nomothetic" tradition of the natural sciences in this sense.[76]

What is truly innovative about Jaspers' psychiatric approach lies in the unusual reception of the humanities as a scholarly tradition and its application for his psychopathological method. Jaspers differentiates between "static", "rational" and

---

[71] PAKJ, pg. 17; cf. PhA, pg. 22.

[72] In his article on Dementia praecox from the year 1913, Jaspers only cites Simmel's *Problems Concerning the History of Philosophy* (*Probleme der Geschichtsphilosophie*), Chap. 1 and Weber's *Roscher and Knies* (*Roscher und Knies*). Cf. GSP, pg. 329, Simmel (1907) and Weber (1903/06).

[73] Cf. PAKJ, pg. 18 ; PhA, pg. 23.

[74] AP 1, pg. 14; cf. GP 4, pg. 28.

[75] AP 1, pg. 146.

[76] Cf. Windelband (1894), pg. 17-41, pg. 26.

"genetic" "understanding", conceiving of the first two forms as feeding the third during the hermeneutic process. Reference is often made to his "three-step" psychopathological method. The first step involves "rational" and "static" understanding of isolated psychic phenomena, the second constitutes "genetically" associative understanding and the third the classification of symptoms according to ideotypical disease entities.[77]

According to Jaspers, a "static understanding" of what the patients "really" experienced can be achieved in three ways: 1) through observation of externally perceivable behavior, facial expressions and gestures; 2) through direct exploration of the patient; and 3) through having the patient draw up written documentation, primarily in the form of biographic "self-description".[78] In light of Jaspers' demand for premise-free insight, his notion of "static understanding" would seem to approximate empirico-positivistically oriented realism. Jaspers writes:

> We must begin with a clear representation of what is actually going on in the patient, what he is really experiencing, how things arise in his consciousness, what are his own feelings, and so forth; and at this stage we must put aside altogether such considerations as the relationships between experiences, or their summation as a whole, and more especially must we avoid trying to supply any basic constructs or frames of reference.[79]

Jaspers speaks of the "unprejudiced, direct comprehension of psychic events" and the "irreducible quality of psychic phenomena".[80] He is very interested in investing his phenomenological method with the claim to objectivity made by the natural sciences. As he contends, by means of "comparison, repetition, verification of the results of empathy", the "direct comprehension of expression phenomena" could almost reach the empirico-objective status of "scientific results".[81]

This postulate of seemingly premise-free insight into facts which Jaspers derives from Husserl was called into question early on by Arthur Kronfeld, who argued that Jaspers unjustifiably aimed to endow his psychological understanding with "apriori features of absolute validity" and to establish the method of "indirect insight in the study of the psyche".[82] In a similar vein, Manfred Spitzer now speaks of the "logical inconsistency" connected with Jaspers' insistence that his method was free of premises and theories.[83]

In Jaspers' system, "rational understanding", which limits itself to the reconstruction of logico-rational connections of thought and is equally problematic in epistemological terms, constitutes the other pre-stage of "genetic understanding". According to Jaspers, if one wanted to interpret the clearly definable, static phenomena of consciousness and the rationally logical contents in terms of their psychodynamic connectedness, the only gauge which could be applied to such "genetic understanding" was so-called "evidential experience".[84] As Jaspers explains, the obtainable degree of

---

[77] Cf. Spitzer (1985), pg. 237.
[78] Jaspers (1968), pg. 1317; cf. Jaspers (1912a), pg. 320.
[79] Jaspers (1968), pg. 1316; cf. Jaspers (1912a), pg. 317.
[80] Jaspers (1968), pg. 1316; cf. Jaspers (1912a), pg. 318f..
[81] Jaspers (1968), pg. 1317; cf. Jaspers (1912a), pg. 319.
[82] Kronfeld (1920), pg. 445.
[83] Spitzer (1985), pg. 243.
[84] Jaspers (1913a), pg. 331.

evidence depends on the personality of the interpreting subject and the quality of the "objective" materials to be interpreted which are acquired in the process of static and rational understanding.[85]

According to this, psychology of understanding can only offer "ideotypical connections", making its findings only "inherently evident" or "more or less understandable", for which reason it could not compete with the explanatory disciplines which operated on the basis of "inductive" principles.[86] Jaspers adopts Weber's methodological concept of the "ideotype" but does not exhaust its epistemological substance; for Jaspers, the construct merely acts as a relative paradigm used to recognize and classify symptomatic and motivational connections in the case of mental disorders. Unlike Weber, Jaspers did not employ it to make any definitive statements on aetiological connections.[87] In the *Psychopathology* he clearly expresses his disinclination towards the nomothetic claims made in the field of psychological hermeneutics. As he writes,

> I hope that one notices the strong aversion against theories and constructs which expresses itself in this book, an aversion I am well aware of. [...] In the field of psychopathology, the real foundation of our research is psychic life as we are to envision it by understanding sensually perceived gestures and verbal expression.[88]

Thus Jaspers' methodological dualism strictly differentiates between causally compelling, generally valid "science" and the very subjective "adeptness and art" of understanding.[89] As he argues, the natural scientific connections of psychiatry can be theoreticized, whereas psychological moments of understanding defied "any consistent systematization" per se and were typically inclined to take on literary-essayistic forms of depiction.[90] According to this, the "instinctive adeptness" of the interpreter oriented towards the psychology of understanding constituted a vague tool of insight prone to error. For this reason, Jaspers always gave preference to objective science over the individual art of understanding insofar as the former succeeded in extending its limits to the art of interpretation.[91] Jaspers does not believe that his approach to understanding was capable of clarifying "extra-conscious foundations" in which the objectifiable psychic aspect swims like the "foam on the ocean as a thin superficial layer".[92] In his eye, psychological hermeneutics was only capable of rudimentarily sounding out and connecting unconscious motivations without ever reaching the unfathomable depths of the sea of the unconscious. For Jaspers what was truly "unconscious" was never fathomable. In contrast, he held the "unnoticed" to be capable of reaching consciousness. He writes:

> Under favorable conditions, we can become aware of unnoticed psychic events and confirm their existence; in principle, we can never become aware of extra-conscious events.

---

[85] Jaspers (1913b), pg. 332.
[86] Jaspers (1913b), pg. 332.
[87] AP 1, pg. 270.
[88] AP 1, pg. 11f..
[89] Cf. AP 1, pg. 2.
[90] Jaspers (1913b), pg. 336. Cf. Freud, Works II, pg. 160; Freud (1895), pg. 327.
[91] AP 1, pg. 2.
[92] Jaspers (1968), pg. 1323; cf. Jaspers (1912a). pg. 327.

The expansion of our knowledge beyond the wide range of unnoticed psychic life, the illumination of psychic life for consciousness is an important task of psychology.[93]

Thus for Jaspers psychological hermeneutics was primarily descriptive in nature and in some cases it was capable of indicating causes of described symptomatic complexes in terms of character and biography but it was incapable of explaining the deeper causes of pathogenesis like the natural scientific method sometimes could, for example in the case of progressive paralysis. Jaspers illustrates this notion himself using a model of disease in which the symptoms correspond to the "layers of an onion". The innermost layers of the onions, which stand for the causes of psychic disorder, are pathogenetically speaking the decisive ones, even if the disease phenomena can be influenced pathoplastically by biographic experience of the outer layers. Jaspers sketches the pathogenetic core as constituting "extra-conscious dispositions, predispositions, psychic constitutions and extra-conscious mechanisms"[94] which, as "extremely complicated biological processes", elude our knowledge "to an immeasurable degree", thus permitting no direct correlations between changes in brain activity and psychic disorders.[95]

In postulating an infinite horizon of causal connections, Jaspers contends that explaining "causality" principally forms the core of pathogenesis whereas the "understandable connections" merely constitute a peripheral "asset" with no decisive effect.[96] Thus Jaspers expressly relativizes the aetiological scope of psychological hermeneutics in relation to natural scientific analysis. He elucidates the notion of a last somatic cause of disease in 1913 using "reactive depression" as an example.[97] According to Jaspers, psychological hermeneutics only provided a limited degree of conclusiveness, and it could not lead to aetiologically univocal ascriptions.

We find this position expressed again in Jaspers' assessment of Ernst Kretschmer's study entitled *Sensitive Delusions of Reference* (*Der sensitive Beziehungswahn*) To be sure, he credits Kretschmer for having plausibly described this type of paranoia as constituting a mixture of "character, milieu and experience" in connection with "heredity and exhaustibility", but nevertheless Jaspers airs misgivings concerning such a definitive pathogenic reconstruction. "We must not lose sight of the fact that from a psychological perspective, the mechanism of paranoid conversion confronts us with something which is completely uncomprehensible. Understanding has many merits, but here it reaches its limits," he writes.[98]

On the other hand, Jaspers attempts to defend his methodology against the reproach that he denies all possibility of understandability when it comes to the psyche.[99] In responding to Eugen Bleuler in 1914, he champions his dictum of extra-conscious causalities which, as he contends, allows us to approximately envision what are incredibly complex connections.[100] Jaspers speaks of hypothetical

---

[93] AP 1, pg. 16; cf. AP 4, pg. 9f. and GP 4, pg. 10.
[94] AP 1, pg. 49.
[95] AP 1, pg. 192.
[96] AP 1, pg. 148.
[97] Cf. Jaspers (1913b), pg. 336 and pp. 338-345.
[98] Jaspers (1918), pg. 124.
[99] Cf. Jaspers (1915) and Bleuler (1914).
[100] Cf. Jaspers (1915).

"as-if-understanding". From the perspective of infinite causality, the lines between physical and psychic causes of diseases become blurred without Jaspers rejecting the hypothesis of the ultimate primacy of the somatic, however. In the sense of this "as-if-understanding", Jaspers acknowledges the psychoanalytically oriented schizophrenia research carried out by Eugen Bleuler. As he says, it had drawn "convincing, understandable connections between experiences and the nature of psychosis".[101]

If one attempts to locate Jaspers' place in respect to the two camps – the psychicists and the somaticists – the fact that for all the proclaimed complexity of cause and effect he assumes psychic disorders to be somatically determined places him more than marginally in the camp of the "somaticists".[102] His methodology does, to be sure, emphasize the "subjective side of experience", but it limits its importance to descriptive and pathoplastic elements of psychopathology.

THE 1913 CRITIQUE OF PSYCHOANALYSIS

In 1913 Jaspers shows himself favorably inclined toward psychoanalysis, and this is in no small part due to the research carried out on schizophrenia in Zurich by Eugen Bleuler and C.G. Jung. The only writings by Freud himself which impress Jaspers are the early *Studies on Hysteria*, a product of collaboration with Josef Breuer which was published in 1895.[103] Nevertheless, in 1913 he places Freud in the small circle of psychiatrists whom he views as the "outstanding understanding psychologists".[104] Similarly ambitendent is the way in which his *General Psychopathology* lauds psychoanalysis as a form related to the "psychology of understanding" while at the same time partially revoking his praise by speaking of "phantastic aspects" which only allow one to penetrate the Freudian hermeneutics to its "valuable core" against resistance.[105] He shows himself open to psychodynamic thought while at the same time distancing himself from approaches towards understanding which deem themselves capable of providing definitive explanations of pathogenesis.[106] In this vein he speaks of "occasional surprising insights" and "evident" descriptions of psychoanalysis but rejects its aetiological claims as a whole quite decidedly. In his view, psychoanalysis employed "constructions of extra-conscious events" which it was incapable of verifying.[107]

This is the only criticism of psychoanalysis put forth in the first edition of the *General Psychopathology*. The critical remarks which Jaspers had made previously in his article entitled "Causal and 'Understandable' Connections between Life Fate and Psychosis in Cases of Dementia praecox (Schizophrenia)"[108] do not enter into his *Psychopathology* until he publishes the second edition in 1920. His reservations

---

[101] Jaspers (1913b), pg. 344f.. Jaspers' references are to Bleuler 1911.
[102] Cf. Schmitt (1980), pg. 47.
[103] Cf. AP 1, pg. 176-178 and this monograph, pg. 31f..
[104] AP 1, pg. 150.
[105] AP 1, pg. 16.
[106] Cf. AP 1, pg. 15f..
[107] AP 1, pg. 150.
[108] Cf. GSP, pg. 329-412, pg. 337f..

towards psychodynamic theories of psychoanalysis occasion him to merely maintain that their claim of objectivity made them "defenseless in the light of all criticism".[109] By making this seemingly complaisant remark, Jaspers is alluding to two monographs which were published before his *Psychopathology*.

For one, he is referring to Arthur Kronfeld's 1912 study entitled *On Freud's Psychological Theories and Related Views: Systematics and Critical Commentary* (*Über die psychologischen Theorien Freuds und verwandte Anschauungen. Systematik und kritische Erörterung*).[110] Kronfeld was one of Jaspers' colleagues at the Heidelberg Clinic and furthermore, he belonged to the circle of neo-Kantian philosophers which gravitated around Leonard Nelson. Secondly, Jaspers mentions an investigation entitled *Freud's Psychoanalytic Method* (*Die psychoanalytische Methode Freuds*) which appeared in 1910[111] as a critique of psychoanalysis which he felt had to be taken seriously. It had been authored by the psychiatrist and Kraepelin disciple Max Isserlin from Munich, who had already caused a stir in emerging psychoanalytic circles in 1907 by a critique much less polemical in import than the 1910 publication.

Psychoanalysis as a 'Psychology of Understanding'

In comparison to the extensive critiques of psychoanalysis formulated by Kronfeld and Isserlin, Jaspers' article "Causal and 'Understandable' Connections between Life Fate and Psychosis in Cases of Dementia praecox (Schizophrenia)" elaborates on only a few critical key words. As it were, he appears to be taking a more or less benevolent side glance at the hermeneutic endeavors made by psychoanalysis from his own methodological vantage point.[112] He welcomes the "Freudian psychological doctrine" as a promising innovation in what he generally views as a discipline which has remained "impoverished", i.e. the psychology of understanding. Psychoanalysis impresses him by virtue of the "number of colleagues" and the "interesting subject matter".[113] Jaspers emphasizes quite credibly that unlike others, he had no intention to aggravate the polarization of "Freud followers and Freud spurners" but rather to help develop what made sense to him in a "positive" and "critical" manner. He holds up Zurich's psychiatric school and its research on schizophrenia as exemplary. The only express mention which Jaspers makes of Freud's works is to his *Studies on Hysteria*. He does cite further readings, including "the writings of some of his students", however.[114] Jaspers interprets psychoanalysis completely from the perspective of his own psychology of understanding and views

---

[109] AP 1, pg. 150.

[110] Kronfeld (1912), pg. 130-248.

[111] Isserlin (1910), pp. 53-80.

[112] Jaspers (1913b), pp. 329-412, pp. 337f..

[113] Jaspers (1913b), p. 337.

[114] Jaspers (1913b), pp. 337f. and AP 1, p. 173 and 178. In his *General Psychopathology*, Jaspers cites Jung's *Diagnostic Studies of Association* (*Diagnostische Assoziationsstudien*) and gives him credit for having coined the term "complex". He also cites Zurich studies published under the title *Dementia praecox*. Cf. Jung (1906), Jung (1907) and Bleuler (1911).

the objectivizing tendency as an unnecessary kind of self-misconception on the part of what he saw to be, on the whole, an impressive form of psychological hermeneutics. In his eye, Freud illuminated "convincing" individual connections, penetrated far into "unnoticed psychic life" and explicated "in part Nietzsche's doctrines in quite some detail".[115] Jaspers' judgment remains skeptical, but there is a noticeble apologetic tenor never to be found again in this form. The unbiased reader is to be brought to read Freud's work under the corrective perspective of Karl Jaspers.

By committing psychoanalysis to the descriptive and at best pathoplastic level of a philosophy of understanding, Jaspers refrains from applying a rigid notion of science as the yardstick for his assessment. To him this simply appears inappropriate. Metascientific skepsis prods him to point out that even in cases of maximum understandability, "personal dispositions of character" in their biological and biographical determinacy must be added to the equation as unclarifiable factors of disease. Thus for Jaspers, pathogenesis is ultimately subject to unrecognizable "extra-conscious mechanisms" which place unalterable limits on the pathoplastic approach of understanding and make the psychoanalytic "claim of unlimited understandability" seem absurd.[116]

Whether Jaspers' cursory critique affected Freud's scientific self-conceptualization in any tangible way is at least questionable, for as a neurologist rooted in the natural sciences, Freud did not forget to emphasize that neurotic disorders were caused by unelicitable biological and constitutional conditions as well as accidental experiences, particularly considering the fact that disorders manifested themselves somatically.[117] For one, this notion expresses itself in the term "overdetermination" ("Überdeterminierung") coined by Freud in 1895, which Jaspers makes positive reference to in the second edition of his *Psychopathology*, albeit without making clear whether or not he understands it in the sense of multi-factoral genesis, as Freud would seem to invite his readers to do. One gets the impression that Jaspers understands Freud's postulate to mean that "every aspect of psychic life is understandable (meaningfully determined)".[118]

Furthermore, Jaspers finds fault with the theoretical reductionism or – in his words – the "increasingly simplicistic vein" of psychoanalytical hermeneutics. As he contends, it sacrificed the "boundless diversity" of understandable connections. In particular he is disturbed by Freud's curbing of the aetiological discussion by attributing "practically every aspect of psychic life to sexuality". This critical impetus is directed not so much at Freud himself as at the simplifying writings of "some of his students", however.[119]

---

[115] Jaspers (1913b), pg. 337. Freud himself affirms a certain affinity of psychoanalysis to Nietzsche's thought. Cf. Freud, Works XX, pg. 60. Freud writes: "Nietsche, [...] whose guesses and intuitions often agree in the most astonishing way with the laborious findings of psychoanalysis, was for a long time avoided by me on that very account; I was less concerned with the question of priority than with keeping my mind unembarrassed." Cf. Freud (1925), pg. 86.

[116] Jaspers (1913b), pg. 337.

[117] Freud, Works IX, p. 279; cf. Freud (1906a), pg. 159.

[118] Jaspers (1913b), pg. 337.

[119] Jaspers (1913b), pg. 338.

And yet Jaspers cites two examples of what he thinks approaches a successful connection between elements of understanding and causality in psychopathology, this being a connection which psychoanalysis had done much to illuminate: the early investigations of hysteria, conducted by Freud in collaboration with the French researcher Pierre Janet, and psychodynamic research on schizophrenia like that which had been carried out by Bleuler and Jung in Zurich.[120] The possible correlation between understandable connections and causal conditions in cases of hysteria and schizophrenia is referred to by Jaspers in a positive sense as a kind of "as-if-understanding". As Jaspers indicates, this concept showed that it was important to always remain aware of the hypothetical, orientative character of aetiological ascriptions. Whether the tentative ascriptions made in the cases of hysteria and schizophrenia patients on the basis of such "as-if-understanding" actually elicited valid statements concerning the aetiology of neuroses and psychoses had to be left open, he says. This is the position taken by Jaspers in 1913. He undecisively remarks, "one would be well-advised to suspend definitive judgment. In any case, the Freudian researchers are very careful about making quick assumptions.[121]

In Jaspers' *General Psychopathology*, which appears later, the open 'wait-and-see' attitude has been replaced by noticeable skepsis concerning the expansion of the hermeneutical claim hailed by psychoanalysis. The Zurich School, which Jaspers had held up as an paragon of psychoanalysis, is now subjected to more acerbic criticism for not having stayed with "tangible, evident subject matter". Instead, by applying Freud's "unbridled method", this school erroneously believed to have "'understood' almost all aspects of psychosis", "rediscovering the meaning in madness" in the process, says Jaspers. As he critically remarks, their findings were not "ripe" for "objective formulation".[122] Only the *Studies on Hysteria*, the product of Freud's collaboration with Breuer, continued to be mentioned commendatorily, with Jaspers expanding on earlier assessments by remarking that "Freud's later development [had] led him far away from these developments".[123] One should add here that previous to the publication of Freud's and Breuer's work on hysteria, research like that conducted by the Frenchman Pierre Janet published in his study entitled *The Mental State of the Hysterical* (*Geisteszustand des Hysterischen*) was esteemed by Jaspers.[124] Janet had documented the findings of his research on hysteria shortly before Freud and had carried out a private feud over who had the right to claim the discovery. He later criticized the psychoanalytic theory of neurosis in a vein similar to that of Jaspers. Just how well Jaspers knew Janet's work is not known; it is only possible to approximately reconstruct the evidence of Jaspers' engagement with Janet's research. In any case Jaspers preferenced Janet over Freud as a source of reliable scientific knowledge concerning psychodynamic thought. As Jaspers writes, "recent French

---

[120] Jaspers (1913b), pg. 337.
[121] Jaspers (1913b), pg. 338.
[122] AP 1, pg. 178. Among other works, Jaspers cites Jung (1907), Bleuler (1911) and Maeder (1910).
[123] AP 1, pg. 176.
[124] Cf. Janet (1894). As Jaspers' library in Basle shows, the book was copiously studied throughout.

psychiatry laid the broad foundation for psychopathology of the neuroses (hysteria, psychasthenia, neurasthenia). Its most brilliant promoter is Janet."[125]

Historically speaking, the time during which Janet and Freud described the 'talking cure' as a method for treating hysteria is looked upon as a period of transition in which the first phase of "dynamic psychiatry" was coming to an end.[126] As far as methods of treatment were concerned, the historian of psychiatry Henri F. Ellenberger identifies as the typical feature of this phase the fact that hypnosis was used as the 'via regia' to the unconscious and that this method was used in combination with suggestion and interlocutionary rapport in exchanges between the patient and the physician.[127] According to Ellenberger, the second phase of "dynamic psychiatry" was characterized by a differentiated but at the same time controversial form of psychoanalytic interlocution which Freud developed after a transitional phase during which he experimented with treating hysteria using catharsis.[128] Borrowing the distinctions made by Ellenberger, one can maintain that Jaspers only acknowledged the merit of psychoanalysis until the time when it entered the second phase of "dynamic psychiatry" and that this was a position which he would never revise.

THE 1920 CRITIQUE OF PSYCHOANALYSIS

What Remains? Pierre Janet and Freud's 'Studies on Hysteria'

His critical as well as apologetic sketch of psychoanalysis as a psychology of understanding as formulated in the article from 1913 was not incorporated into the *General Psychopathology* until he published the second edition in 1920. By way of an explanation he writes, "the critical stance towards Freud's teachings can be expressed in the following theses, which I formulated in an earlier piece of work."[129] What is new is a critical review which primarily concentrates on the early *Studies on Hysteria* from 1895 as well as on two "summarizing" overviews published by Freud, the lectures delivered in America entitled *On Psychoanalysis. Five Lectures* (*Über Psychoanalyse. Fünf Vorlesungen*) and the *Introductory Lectures on Psychoanalysis* (*Vorlesungen zur Einführung in die Psychoanalyse*), held in 1916/1917 in Vienna.[130] Jaspers also briefly mentions the *Interpretation of Dreams* (*Die Traumdeutung*) from 1900 as the most important theoretical work of Sigmund Freud.[131]

---

[125] AP 1, pg. 332. Jaspers makes this statement in the context of his short history of psychiatry. In Jaspers (1913), pg. 336 we read: "Within the realm of psychiatry the psychology of understanding has been active at all times. [...] Janet is our most excellent present-day researcher in this discipline."

[126] Cf. Ellenberger (1970), pg. 174.

[127] Cf. Ellenberger (1970), pg. 111.

[128] Cf. Ellenberger (1970), pp. 171-174.

[129] Cf. Jaspers (1913b), pg. 337-338 and AP 2, pg. 294.

[130] Cf. Freud (1895), Freud (1910) and Freud (1917).

[131] Cf. Freud (1900).

These works are to be found in Jaspers' private library today. The *Introductory Lectures on Psychoanalysis* in particular have many markings, whereas the American series of lectures and the *Interpretation of Dreams* only seem to have been studied sporadically or selectively.[132] In his copy of *Studies on Hysteria,* which Jaspers deemed to be the "most fruitful part of Freud's doctrine", traces of his readings are found almost exclusively in the parts co-authored by Freud and Breuer.[133] Moreover, the library copy makes it evident that Jaspers' affinity to the early writings of Freud contrasts markedly with his retrospective derogation.[134] For we find a conspicuous exclamation mark in the margin at the place where Freud debases his early method of treatment: "psychoanalysis in the true sense of the word began when hypnosis was dispensed with as an aid."[135]

The fact that Jaspers valued the contemporaneous research on hysteria conducted by Pierre Janet over that of Freud's is made clear by his copy of Freud's *Lectures*, as he comments on the passage in which Freud writes disparagingly of Janet's work[136] quite critically: "Polemics! Janet is worth more than Freud!" Jaspers' remarks

---

[132] The private library of Karl Jaspers is to be found all in one place in Basle, with Dr. Hans Saner as its literary executor. It contains the following works of Sigmund Freud: *Studien über Hysterie (Studies on Hysteria*; second edition, Leipzig 1909; in particular the introduction, which Freud and Breuer collaborated on, is marked, as is the case study of Anna O.); *Die Traumdeutung (The Interpretation of Dreams*; third edition, Leipzig 1911) (without markings); *Der Witz und seine Beziehung zum Unbewußten (Jokes and Their Relation to the Unconscious*; second edition, Leipzig 1912, very few markings; cf. Freud [1905b]); *Drei Abhandlungen zur Sexualtheorie (Three Essays on the Theory of Sexuality*; second edition, Leipzig 1910; no markings; cf. Freud [1905c]); *Der Wahn und die Träume in W. Jensens 'Gradiva' (Delusions and Dreams in Jensen's 'Gradiva'*; second edition, Leipzig 1912, no markings; cf. Freud [1907]); *Sammlung kleiner Schriften zur Neurosenlehre 1893-1906 (Collection of Short Writings on the Theory of Neuroses*; second edition, Leipzig 1911, no markings; cf. Freud [1906b]); *Sammlung kleiner Schriften zur Neurosenlehre – Zweite Folge (Second Collection of Short Writings on the Theory of Neuroses*; Leipzig 1909, only *Bruchstücke einer Hysterieanalyse* [Fragment of an Analysis of a Case of Hysteria] is marked; cf. Freud 1905a); *Über Psychoanalyse. Fünf Vorlesungen (Five Lectures on Psychoanalysis*; second edition, Leipzig 1912, only lectures 3-5 are marked sporadically; vgl. Freud [1910b]); *Eine Kindheitserinnerung des Leonardo da Vinci (Leonardo da Vinci and a Memory of his Childhood*; Leipzig 1910, marked all the way through; cf. Freud [1910a]) and *Vorlesungen zur Einführung in die Psychoanalyse (Introductory Lectures on Psychoanalysis*; second edition, Leipzig 1918, marked all the way through with some marginal notes; cf. Freud [1917]). Saner points out that during his move to Basle in 1948, Jaspers had to leave many volumes of his library behind in Heidelberg so that it is questionable whether the private library is in fact complete. What must also be taken into consideration of course is the fact that Jaspers also had the opportunity to make extensive use of the university library.

[133] Cf. AP 2, pg. 291.

[134] AP 2, pg. 291.

[135] Cf. Freud (1895), pg. 332.

[136] Cf. Freud, Works XVI, pg. 289: "But since then he has expressed himself with exaggerated reserve, as if he wanted to admit that the unconscious had been nothing more to him than a form of words, a makeshift, *une façon de parler* – that he had meant nothing real by it. Since then I have ceased to understand Janet's writings: but I think he has unnecessarily forfeited much credit." Cf. Freud (1917), pg. 289.

concerning psychoanalytic practice also give striking testimony to this tendency, as will be seen in the course of this chapter.

In general one can contend that as far as Jaspers' critique of psychoanalysis in the second edition of his *General Psychopathology* is concerned, it bears more clearly the signature of the future philosopher, who held an official position as a psychologist in the Philosophical Faculty until 1920, but who quite intentionally transgressed these boundaries. The expression of this change of perspective was Jaspers' *Psychology of World Views*, whose aim was to exert a diagnostically illuminating effect on "questions which were increasingly concerned with world views" but which for Jaspers became "unconsciously my path to philosophy".[137] The pronounced philosophical strain of Jaspers' critique of psychoanalysis also lies in the fact that in his reading of Freud, Jaspers was confronted with quite a pointed cultural-critical position, which he found articulated in the copiously studied *Introductory Lectures to Psychoanalysis*. "One can apply [psychoanalysis] to cultural history, the study of religion and mythology as well as to the doctrine of neuroses without violating its nature."[138]

Theory of Neurosis as Cultural Criticism

Whereas in the year 1913 Freud was hailed by Jaspers as one of the "most outstanding understanding psychologists", the second edition of the *Psychopathology* published in 1920 takes the opposite stance, namely that "Freud demonstrated a peculiar lack of intellect in his understanding ascriptions". Jaspers now considers psychoanalytic interpretations to be for the most part coarse and trivializing.[139] The fourth edition of his textbook published two decades later refers to the "methodical comprehension of something which had always been present, but which was fading out of existence and which appeared in striking reverse [...] in Freud's psychoanalysis";[140] psychoanalysis is no longer credited with any merit for the development of a psychology of understanding around the turn of the century at all.[141]

The reason for such polemic derogation lies primarily in the theory of neurosis with its focus on "sexuality", a theory which was also attacked by Janet and Jung in different ways.[142] Jaspers compares psychoanalysis with the demand for philosophical probity. He writes: "Freud often sees what happens when sexuality is repressed extraordinarily aptly. But not once does he ask what happens when the intellect is repressed."[143] Jaspers is probably referring directly to Freud's *Introductory Lectures*, which claim that psychoanalysis had promoted the "education for truthfulness towards [ourselves]", this being a statement which occasioned the future existence

---

[137] PAKJ, pg. 25; cf. PhA, pg. 32.
[138] Jaspers marks this sentence in his copies of the *Introductory Lectures on Psychoanalysis* with an exclamation mark and underlinings. Cf. Freud, Works XVI, pg. 389; Freud (1917), pg. 404.
[139] AP 2, pg. 292f.
[140] GP 4, pg. 302 (cf. AP 4, pg. 251).
[141] AP 4, pg. 251.
[142] AP 2, pg. 292.
[143] AP 2, pg. 292.

philosopher to underline large portions of the text. What he found particularly note-worthy was the fact that Freud viewed such "education for truthfulnes" as a means of emancipating oneself as an individual from society's "morality".[144] Thus it is not surprising that Jaspers revokes his praise of Freud as an Enlightenist who partially perpetuated the tradition of understanding established by Nietzsche, now speaking of Freud, in contrary, as a psychologist who did not measure up to the "great self-confessors" Nietzsche and Kierkegaard. Jaspers had studied both these figures previous vious to his work on the *Psychology of World Views* as representatives of a psychology of understanding and had adopted them as models for his philosophy. In his eye they had made "a clear view of every corner of the human psyche communicable".[145]

Essentially, Jaspers does not go beyond his critique of psychoanalysis from the year 1913 by putting forth any substantial new arguments. He contends that it is not necessary to deal in any depth with psychoanalysis by claiming in a cavalier fashion that its theoretical foundation was constantly changing. Jaspers briefly treats the "topical model" of Freud's neurosis theory, which does not yet differentiate between the Ego, the I and the Superego. His discussion of the connections between the "unconscious", preconscious censorship and the encoded dreams which resulted from the interaction of these instances, slips of the tonque and symptoms of neurotic disorders lead over to a critique of Freud's thesis that the sexual content of the unconscious was primarily responsible for the establishment of these three types of encoding. Jaspers introduces the position of C.G. Jung, who had developed the "libido" concept as a means of desexualizing psychoanalysis.[146] Jaspers' review of Jung's book entitled *Transformations and Symbols of Libido* (*Wandlungen und Symbole der Libido*), which contained a new interpretation of the concept of libido, was positive. Jaspers welcomes the fact that Jung's "fundamentally new" theory of neurosis looked upon "libido" as the expression of a "system of all drives", of which the sexual drive was only the most prominent one.[147] From Freuds 1916/1917 *Lectures* Jaspers inferred that Jung's relativization of the sexual aspect was not received positively. Thus Jaspers counters the psychoanalytic theory of neurosis with the critique of the apostate and former Freud student C.G. Jung.[148] As early as 1913, Jung's *Attempt to Depict a Psychoanalytic Theory* (*Versuch einer Darstellung der psychoanalytischen Theorie*) with its "substantial modifications of Freud's notions in an applaudable direction" had drawn Jaspers' attention.[149] At this time C.G. Jung had definitively divorced himself from Freud's concept of psychoanalysis.[150] Jaspers quotes a rhetorical question raised by Jung which expresses his renunciation of the theory of childhood sexuality as the cause of neurosis, writing: "We don't ask any

---

[144] In Jaspers' copy of the *Introductory Lectures on Psychoanalysis*, these passages have thick underlinings. Cf. Freud, Works XVI, pg. 434; Freud (1917), pg. 450f.
[145] PW, pg. X.
[146] Cf. AP 2, pg. 292.
[147] Jaspers (1913c), pg. 549. For all this praise, Jaspers does not forget to criticize the "speculative" and "vague" character of Jung's work, which "desired to be empirical".
[148] Cf. GP 4, pg. 210.
[149] Cf. Jaspers (1914).
[150] Gay (1988), pg. 236.

more whether the patient has a father or a mother complex or whether he has binding unconscious phantasies of incest. [...] Instead we ask 'Which task is the patient reluctant to fulfill?' 'Which difficulties of life is he attempting to evade?'"[151] Jaspers prizes the fact that Jung locates the main sources of neurosis in "current conflicts" rather than in "long-past dreams", not allowing the patient to escape from reality by dealing exclusively with the envisioned past. As Jaspers maintains, Jung had the "merit" of having diminished the "overestimation of past psychic traumas".[152]

And yet Jaspers comes close to Freud's position of the aetiology of neurosis insofar as he quotes his early "concept of 'overdetermination'" affirmatively.[153] The concept, which Freud had developed at the time he was writing his *Studies on Hysteria*, meant that the network of traumatizing conditions must be accompanied by a specific "constitution" in order to produce a neurosis.[154] In Jaspers' approach, the term "overdetermination" stands for the psychopathological fact that an "experience with little meaning" could trigger a disorder because the "soil" had already been tilled by "other experiences".[155]

Pierre Janet's theory of neurosis evidences clear parallels to that of Jaspers, who esteems his French colleague like no other author in this transitional period. Like Freud he bases his theory on psychodynamic experiences, so-called "fixed ideas", but he correlates them with an organic substrate without which, as Janet contends, the symptoms would not emerge. Using a model similar to Jaspers' layered onion paradigm, Janet depicts a case of paranoia in an article written in 1906 which was illuminated by biographical events but was also accompanied by progressive paralysis. As Janet posits, in his paralytic delusion the patient "fell in the direction in which he had already been leaning before".[156]

Unquestionably, Jaspers has an appreciation for the early Freud and his *Studies on Hysteria*. This has to do in no small part with the fact that Freud did not come to foreground sexuality so conspicuously as the motor of pathological psychodynamics until later – most prominently in *Three Essays on the Theory of Sexuality* (*Drei Abhandlungen zur Sexualtheorie*) of 1905.[157] In his article "My Views on the Part Played by Sexuality in the Aetiology of the Neuroses" ("Ansichten über die Rolle der Sexualität in der Ätiologie der Neurosen"), Freud expressly distances himself from the "purely psychological theory" of his early phase, in which "the sexual factor" had been "regarded as no more significant than any other emotional source of feeling".[158] For Freud it is clear that his "insistence on the importance of sexuality in all human achievements" and the "[attempt to enlarge] the concept of sexuality" had always generated the most resistance against psychoanalysis.[159] As far as Jaspers is concerned, this explanation is in part quite apt, even though his motives for

---

[151] Jaspers (1914).
[152] AP 2, pg. 210.
[153] Cf. AP 2, pg. 212f.; Laplanche/Pontalis, pg. 252f.
[154] Freud, Works II, pg. 263; Freud (1895), pg. 261.
[155] AP 2, pg. 213.
[156] Janet (1906), pp. 329-332.
[157] Freud (1905c).
[158] Freud, Works VII, pg. 272; cf. Freud (1906a), pg. 158f.
[159] Freud, Works VII, pg. 134; cf. Freud (1905c), pg. 32.

criticizing psychoanalysis by no means exhaust themselves in bourgeois resentment but rather extend far beyond such factors in philosophical terms, as will be shown later on.

In keeping with such reservations, Jaspers challenges the psychoanalytic critique of bourgeois sexual morality in 1920. He reproaches Freud in a cultural-critical vein for affirming the "large measure of human beings" – those who are merely "sensual", the "city-dwellers with a chaotic psychic life" – in their life conduct by formulating a theory which appealed to "vitality and the sexual aspect" instead of provoking "the spiritual and intellectual aspect" in man. Remarks made by Freud in his *Introductory Lectures*, which Jaspers highlights with exclamation marks and underlinings, hail psychoanalysis as a critical corrective for "conventional sexual morality" and as such invest it with the status of a cultural-critical instrument which far exceeds its clinical purpose, – one which shows the patient that societal "morality" is neither "wise" nor "truthful".

At this time, Jaspers still attempts to distinguish between Freud's theories themselves and the reception of his "elegant, sometimes fascinating" writings.[160] Irrespective of Freud, he paints his own picture of a decadent European Bohemian *fin-de-siècle* culture.

> Freedom from fetters without the bathos of new fetters, indulgence, self-abandonment, skepsis and resignation – this is the world view for some nervous types, for aesthetic *bon vivants*, for the literary set.[161]

Not so much the Vienna of Sigmund Freud served Jaspers as the epitome of the *fin-de-siècle* era but rather Munich as he knew it from his years of study there at the turn of the last century.[162] The equally pessimistic and elegant cultural elite was susceptible to literary-religious mysticism and cultivated a cult of eroticism,[163] misinterpreting the Enlightenment as the liberation from all established norms. This was the view put forth by Jaspers in 1931 in the cultural-critical work entitled *Man in the Modern Age* (*Die geistige Situation der Zeit*). This work will be examined in the following chapter in the context of psychoanalysis.

PRACTICAL CRITIQUE OF PSYCHOANALYSIS IN THE YEARS 1913-1920

As concerned methods of treatment, Jaspers did not follow Freud's lead after his *Studies on Hysteria* any more either. In 1906 Freud expressly revoked his concept on how hysteria resulted and was to be treated, a concept mainly associated with the

---

[160] AP 2, pg. 293.

[161] AP 2, pg. 293.

[162] Jaspers studied law in Munich in the summer of 1902, moved in literary circles in Schwabing and took private graphological instruction from Ludwig Klages. Max Weber, who cultivated relationships to members of Schwabing's *bohème* during these years which were mediated by Otto Gross and Else Jaffé-Richthofen, will have told Jaspers about this colony of artists as well. Weber's assessment of Gross and the "Erotic Movement" in a letter which Jaspers found cited in Marianne Weber's Weber biography helped to cement Jaspers' view of *fin-de-siècle bohème* life in Munich. Cf. Jaspers (1996), Green (1974), pg. 126-131 and this monograph, pp. 77-79.

[163] Cf. Ellenberger (1970), pp. 278-284.

term "abreaction".[164] This very concept, which had been coined in collaboration with Breuer, is foregreounded in Jaspers' draft of a concept of psychotherapeutic practice.

Jaspers divides up "therapeutic tasks" into somatic and psychotherapeutic possibilities for treatment. In light of the great lack of effective options available during his time, Jaspers assessed perspectives for somatic treatment as "previously sparse", notwithstanding emerging possibilities for treating paralysis. He speaks out in favor of humane support of the afflicted patients in the sense of "custodial psychiatry".[165]

In addition, Jaspers cited quieting and ergotherapeutic measures as further possibilities for treatment depending on how acute or chronic the condition in question was.[166] The phase of effective somatotherapy began in the 1930's, after malaria treatment of progressive paralysis proved to be successful in 1917. It was during this phase that controversial shock methods (insuline, cardiazol and electroshock) and questionable brain surgery were introduced. From 1952 on, somatic therapies were improved considerably by the introduction of highly-effective psychopharmaceuticals.

Suggestion and Psychoanalytic 'Confession'

Jaspers defines the "individual psychic influencing of patients" in keeping with terminological conventions which had emerged during his time as "psychotherapy", dividing it into three areas: purely suggestive treatment, psychoanalytically oriented "abreaction" and rank "educational therapy".[167]

Jaspers describes suggestion in part as a kind of value and judgment formation which occurs through the "special psychic influence" of a third person without oneself or any "generally understandable motivations" being involved.[168] In other words, for Jaspers the main feature of suggestion is that it causes acts of volition to occur heteronomically, whether intentionally or not, thus limiting a personality's self-determination and causing it to suffer. As he elucidates, in psychotherapy, suggestive-manipulative methods are employed systematically for certain indications. But the more store a person lays by independent decision-making, the more the use of suggestive therapy must be viewed as intractable, he contends. For this reason, Jaspers distinguished between suggestive and cathartive methods of psychotherapy on the one hand and the "educational" method, which was intended to be relatively free of suggestive influencing, on the other. What he aims at is a less authoritative form of psychotherapy for "educated patients" whose freedom was not to be impaired by suggestive-hypnotic or cathartic procedures.

Jaspers counts psychoanalysis as one of these "educational" types of psychotherapy and is on the whole quite reserved in his assessment of its chances of success. His criticism of psychoanalysis is apparently quite moderate, as he explains its lack

---

[164] Freud, Works VII, pg. 272; cf. Freud (1906a), pg. 151.
[165] PhA, pg. 21.
[166] AP 1, pg. 321. Cf. Ackerknecht (1985), pg. 101f..
[167] Cf. AP 1, pg. 322.
[168] AP 1, pg. 165.

of therapeutic success in general by claiming that such a method was applied "schematically to all human beings".[169] As he argues, what is decisive for all forms of psychotherapy is the inner correspondence between the type of therapy which is offered and the needs of the patient in question. "One type is suitable for this patient, the other for the next." This pragmatic, sober stance appears at first sight to be quite neutral, but the critical voice asserts itself when Jaspers adds: "Whatever is successful at a certain time is characteristic of the human beings who inhabit it."[170] In light of his derogatory remarks concerning *fin-de-siècle bohème* culture, this statement harbors acerbic criticism of the psychoanalytic culture of psychotherapy.

Thus Jaspers' aim is to reduce psychoanalytic therapy to the unspecific form of treatment which had been practiced by Freud, but also by Janet, during the phase of transition from suggestive hypnosis treatment to cathartic "abreaction" as described in *Studies on Hysteria* around 1890. His focus is on the early "principle" that the patient should be able to "express himself" without being subjected to moral evaluation. Jaspers strips psychoanalysis of certain salient features it came to develop – like interpretations based on transferral and resistance –, presenting the psychoanalytical process as one form of "confession" among others whose common denominator was often the "relieving effect" of verbalizing something. When he interprets psychoanalysis as a kind of "confession", Jaspers invokes the early Freud, who, in his *Studies on Hysteria*, likened psychoanalytic catharsis to the relieving effect of a religious "confession".[171]

Freud's *Studies on Hysteria* adds associative "remembering" to "abreaction" as another therapeutic option accompanied by interpretations on the part of the physician.[172] This aspect is not taken into consideration by Jaspers. His psychotherapeutic concept contents itself with the method of pure cathartic "abreaction", citing, as an additional source, Ludwig Frank's study entitled *Affect Disorders (Affektstörungen)*.[173] Frank, who worked as a psychiatrist in Zurich without being associated with any school, was well-known for his development and modification of cathartic psychotherapy as it had been devised by Breuer and Freud. Understandably, Jaspers was attracted to his approach, particularly considering the fact that Frank had distanced himself from the "current *Ordensschule*".[174] Jaspers' *General Psychopathology* aligned itself with Frank as well as Freud's "original views" as formulated in his *Studies of Hysteria*,[175] whereas the author of this work distanced himself from Frank and Jaspers because in their works, as he writes, the "part played by psychosexual factors and infantilism, the importance of dreams and of unconscious symbolism"[176] was only found in its germ stage.

As regards the less demanding cathartic method of treatment, for which Jaspers turns to early psychoanalysis as his taskmaster, Freud's later understanding of

---

[169] Cf. AP 1, pg. 323.
[170] AP 1, p. 325.
[171] Freud, Works II, pg. 8; cf. Freud (1895), p. 87.
[172] Freud, Works II, pg. 9; cf. Freud (1895), p. 87f..
[173] AP 1, pg. 323; cf. Frank (1913).
[174] Cf. Jaspers (1913c), pg. 89.
[175] AP 1, pg. 176.
[176] Cf. Freud, Works II, pg. xxxi; cf. Freud (1895), pg. 79

himself did not seem suitable for providing impetus for an educatively demanding form of psychotherapy. According to Jaspers, this depended completely upon the "art of the psychiatric personality". For, as he contends, pedagogically ambitious psychotherapy is based on a relationship of correspondence between the personal life philosophy of the physician and the expectations of the patient, which always "unnoticeably" exerted pressure.[177] According to this view, scientific criteria defining what is appropriate did not decide the success or failure of psychotherapy. Instead, it depended on the ability of the psychotherapist to impress his or her patients personally as a "priest and philosopher" and to thus influence them emotionally.[178] Jaspers looks to history for instances of successful cognitive-affective training of the will, citing the "exercitia spiritualia" carried out by Ignatius of Loyola and personality building efforts as recommended by Stoic philosophy and in particular Nietzsche with his demand for "uncompromising probity" as a means of life conduct.[179]

In terms of the history of psychiatry, this interpretation of psychotherapy as a philosophico-religious form of life conduct can be traced back to the tradition of religiously and philosophically inspired "medical men and priests".[180] If one agrees with Henri F. Ellenberger's assessment, only institutionally established "schools" or "sects" had the capacity to pass on sophisticated theories of life conduct in Greek and Roman antiquity with any long-term success. Ellenberger makes pronounced forms of psychic training, suggestive persuasion and training of the will responsible for such intensive socialization efforts as they had become typical for Pythagoreans, Stoics and in modern times the Jesuits. One could in fact speak in terms of "philo-sophical psychotherapy", he maintains.[181] As regards the history of philosophy, Pierre Hadot emphasizes that during antiquity, philosophical discourse was often preceded by an "existential decision" which entailed a "complete change in the way of life" effected in no small part by the shaping influence deriving from membership in a philosophical school.[182]

The sociological parallel drawn between modern psychotherapy and philoso-phico-religious practices is also underscored by Jaspers. Every psychology of under-standing is based on the cultural imprint of its interpreter, he contends.[183] For this reason, Jaspers also speaks of the "battle of understanding insights" and the "battle of personalities" which desired to "understand each other" by "simultaneously" grasping and disposing of the other side in accordance with each side's own patterns of interpretation. In this context Jaspers cites a passage from Freud's works which used the theoreme of resistance as a means of discrediting opinions as putatively

---

[177] AP 1, pg. 325.

[178] AP 1, pg. 324.

[179] AP 1, pg. 324f.

[180] Cf. Ellenberger (1970), pg. 40.

[181] Ellenberger (1970), pp. 40-45. More recently, various philosophical inquiries have called attention to this *Philosophy of the Art of Life*. Cf. Schmid (1998).

[182] Cf. Hadot (2002), pg. 2f. Hadot focuses his inquiry on Plato's Academy, the School of Aristoteles, cynicism, stoicism, Plotin and Neo-platonism as ancient examples for such a comprehensive model of philosophy.

[183] AP 2, pg. 293.

pathological.[184] According to this approach, the hermeneutics which is relevant from the perspective of psychotherapy is always determined by the perspectivizing premise of the special interpreter. Karl Popper succeeded Jaspers in aptly remarking:

> It is characteristic of all these dogmatic systems and especially of the esoteric systems that their admirers assert of all critics that 'they do not understand'; but these admirers forget that understanding must lead to agreement only in the case of sentences with a trivial content. In all other cases, one can understand *and* disagree.[185]

This view contradicts Jaspers' methodological assumption that the psychology of understanding is to be kept free of normative premises.[186] Decades later, Jaspers reflects upon this self-contradiction, namely that his philosophy of understanding had not intended to "be a philosophy",[187] but rather a "view of naked reality".[188] In retrospect he confesses that his approach towards understanding had been "identical" with the tradition of "philosophical understanding".[189] In response to the "objectionable" basic position of Freud, it had been important to develop a way of thinking which derived from "other origins", this having made Freud an "enemy" of his "youth".[190] In other words, with his demanding, educative version of psychotherapy, Jaspers endeavors to establish a philosophical school of life which looked upon psychoanalytic methods as a source of competition in the realm of psychic guidance.

One element of this philosophical culture was certainly to be found in Jaspers' notion of truthfulness, a quality he felt the psychoanalytic method as well as other schools of psychotherapy were incapable of cultivating. In this vein, he inserts a cynical and disillusioned understanding of the physician's identity in his *General Psychopathology* which reads: "I ensure that his life lie is maintained." In Jaspers' view, the literary figure from Ibsen's play *The Wild Duck* unmasks the often propagated "cult of rectitude" subscribed to by the therapist. As the Ibsenian sentiment goes: "Deprive the average human being of his life lie, and you rob him of his happiness."[191] But Jaspers calls into question not only the will of the patient to be truthful, but also that of the physician, referring to many colleagues in the profession as "devout flatheads" and "swindlers" whose suggestive and manipulative behavior, he claims, only bolstered the questionable expectations of the patients.[192]

In opposition to this situation, Jaspers orients his ideal conception of a psychiatrist capable of performing acceptable psychotherapy on the basis of three criteria. He had to have "character", he had to subscribe to an acceptable world view and he had to radiate the "humanity" of a physician. For him, none of these characteristics are inherent in the nature of a specialized form of medicine; they belong to the realm of a morally convincing form of life shaped by philosophical reflection. Thus

---

[184] AP 2, pg. 293.
[185] Popper (1966), pg. 299; cf. Popper (1992), pg. 358.
[186] AP 2, pg. 15.
[187] PWV, pg. XI.
[188] PWV, pg. X.
[189] Cf. PWV, pg. IX.
[190] PW, p. IXf..
[191] AP 1, pg. 324.
[192] AP 1, p. 325.

Jaspers' main concern is apparently the ethos of unembellished probity demonstrated by a personality steeped in reflection, – reflection intended to protect the person from acting suggestively or manupulatively when aiming to promote the self-education of the patient through psychotherapeutic means. This ideal already points to the idea, articulated in his later philosophy, of a communicative process whose goal was to promote individual self-reflection free of all compulsion.

'Existential Communication' or 'Dealing with Resistance'

Jaspers does not comment extensively on his ideas about this philosophical form of communication in the first three editions of the *General Psychopathology*. Some remarks are to be found in the manuscript for a lecture entitled "Solitude" ("Einsamkeit") from the year 1915/16 which was never published during Jaspers' lifetime.[193] This lecture documents an important step on the way to the concept of "existential communication" which Jaspers places in the center of his 1932 *Philosophy*.[194] What he means by this is a completely open, critical and fair exchange between independent persons on an equal level, which he also sees as the prerequisite and medium for "enlightenment of existence".[195] Jaspers does not want his kind of existential communication to be confused with a harmonious idyll and for this reason he designates it using the concept "loving struggle".[196] These existence-philosophical concepts cannot be grasped without taking into consideration the real-life situation of Jaspers' marriage with Gertrud Mayer, whom he wedded in 1910. The bride came from an old Jewish family from Prenzlau near Berlin. When Jaspers met her, she was in the process of preparing for her *Abitur* after having worked for some years as a psychiatric nurse. Her goal was to study philosophy. In 1967 Jaspers writes, "I am convinced that if my philosophy has any depth, I never would have achieved it without Gertrud."[197]

The communicative confrontation which Jaspers has in mind is to take on the form of a Socratic dialogue in which each partner in communication is challenged to gain insight into his or her truth, but without "the least exertion of force", "intellectual superiority or suggestive influencing".[198] The fact that the partners in dialogue are to recognize their own individual "solitude" as the point of departure and point of destination for the communicative process is the basic tenet which Jaspers foregrounds in the title of his article.

Jaspers measures the mode of communication used in the psychiatrist-patient relationship using the demanding notion of what the communicative relationship between partners in love should look like as his gauge.[199] Accordingly, he contrasts the ideal of co-equality in partnership, i.e. mutual self-disclosure, with the relationship

---

[193] The manuscript exists in a handwritten and a typed copy with the heading "Vortrag 1915" and "Vortrag 1916". Cf. Leonhard (1983), pp. 70-73 and Jaspers (1983).
[194] Cf. PhA 2, pp. 50-117.
[195] Ph 2, pg. 60; cf. Salamun (1985), pp. 72-88.
[196] Ph 2, pg. 242.
[197] Cf. Jaspers (1967b), pg. 32.
[198] Ph 2, pg. 243.
[199] Ph 2, pg. 243.

of power which characterizes psychotherapeutic practice. He comes to the conclusion, affirmed by many medico-ethical studies, that the communicative relationship between physician and patient is a-symmetrical because due to his neediness,
only the patient has the compulsion to speak of his personal emotional problems.
According to Jaspers, what results is an imbalance of power. Because the psychiatrist cannot disclose himself, he is tempted to succumb to the "instinct of relishing
power", i.e. he tolerates the one-sided submissiveness of the patient while adopting
the manner of an actor to produce a therapeutic effect.[200] At the time Jaspers formulated this critique, the figure of Jesus served as an example for this negative ideotype.
In this form of overcoming solitude, the individuality of a person was neglected more
than it was promoted, so Jaspers maintained.

In contrast, the Socratic type of psychiatrist is held up by Jaspers as a positive, if
rare alternative. As he contends, this type of psychiatrist attempts to establish a
symmetrical relationship with the patient in order to employ the "maieutic method of
awakening" and thus to help him adopt the "full responsibility of individuality".[201]
The goal of such self-responsible individuality transcended the purely medical task,
which consisted in eliminating the emotional limitations on the patient's freedom
induced by the disease. Jaspers' educative psychotherapeutic goal was to achieve the
highest possible degree of independence in the shaping of an individual's life. He
formulates the philosophical ideal of complete self-determination with his sights set
on this goal.

The ideal of communication as free mutual interchange without relinquishment
of individuality on the part of the partners in dialogue seemed practically impossible
to fulfill when such communication involved patient and physician for, as he
remarked, "good psychiatrists" in the sense of the ideal described above and, as it
were, equally "good" patients rarely came together.[202] This assessment seems to
have been made in part on the basis of Jaspers' own sobering and confusing experiences as a psychotherapist at the Heidelberg Clinic between the years 1909 and
1913, which showed him just what dangers lied in dealing with patients in an unreflected manner. In a letter to the Swiss psychoanalyst Oskar Pfister, Jaspers confesses in retrospect:

> I was reluctant concerning psychotherapy for the following reasons: as long as I treated
> patients I was so deeply affected by their fates that I was incapable of doing any other
> work. Furthermore, after having had such good experiences, as all those who take
> their work seriously, I usually had the awkward feeling that I really didn't know how I
> had done it.[203]

In his *Psychopathology* from the year 1941/42, Jaspers also rejects transference
as a methodological element of psychotherapy even though he is thoroughly aware
of its psychodynamic potential. He writes:

> One of the relationships between individuals which is of importance for the psychiatrist
> is that which Freud describes as a *'transference'* of admiring, loving and also hostile

---

[200] WF, pg. 22.
[201] WF, p. 23f..
[202] AP 1, pg. 326.
[203] Letter from Karl Jaspers to Oskar Pfister from September 20, 1952, JLE-GLA.

feelings onto the doctor. This transference is unavoidable in psychotherapy and it can be a dangerous reef on which to break if we do not recognise it and deal with it.[204]

In contrast, Freud developed the suggestive-cathartic method described in the *Studies on Hysteria,* transforming it into the actual psychoanalytic transference therapy. He summed up his new insights in his *Introductory Lectures on Psychoanalysis* from 1917. From the instability of many therapeutic successes, he concluded that the "affective relationship was more powerful than all the cathartic work" and that the personal influence of the physician in the therapeutic process actually played a more crucial role than "abreaction" or "confession". Freud wanted to make use of this circumstance but he soon realized that this affective aspect of the patient-physician relationship was often uncontrollable and led to erotically awkward situations.[205]

Whereas Freud wanted to take advantage of the element of affective attachment, which was hard to control, by devising the psychoanalytical technique of transference analysis, Jaspers rejected this form of verbal interaction. Freud looked upon the affects which developed in the course of psychoanalytic treatment as a positive phenomenon covered by his theoreme of 'transference love'. This theoreme posited that the affects directed at the analyst during the therapeutic procedure – which could range from feelings of love to those of hate – did not genuinely apply to him or her; instead they expressed "attitudes, wishes and feelings towards father, mother and other persons".[206] The patient 'projected' – this is the psychoanalytical term coined by Freud – affects onto the analyst which he had developed previously in regard to early relationships. They had been harbored and allowed to ferment more or less unconsciously ever since. The new couch treatment was designed to promote a regression of the patient which would enable him to remember traumata from early childhood more easily. During the transference process which took place between patient and analyst, the early affects of the patient were consciously awakened and connected with the psychoanalyst so that they could be worked through during transference analysis.[207] The basis for this process was the asymmetrically fixated structure of treatment primarily characterized by the "free associations" of the patient and the "evenly-suspended attention" of the therapist.[208] The affects which occur in the

---

[204] GP 4, pg. 805.

[205] Cf. Freud, Works XX, pg. 27; Cf. Freud (1925), pg. 52.

[206] Peters (2000), pg. 581.

[207] The term 'transference' denotes the process by which unconscious feelings are connected with certain persons in a current relationship although they actually developed in early relationship constellations. According to psychoanalytic theory, this process occurs "to an extreme degree within the framework of the analytic relationship", constituting a "repetition of infantile models". Cf. Laplanche/Pontalis (1973), pg. 43ff.

[208] 'Free associations' were developed as a psychoanalytic method in the work which led to the *Studies on Hysteria*. They consist of saying everything "which comes to mind without leaving anything out, whether it derives from a given element (a word, number, dream image or any kind of association) or spontaneously". Freud elucidates the concept of "evenly-suspended attention" in his *Recommendations to Physicians Practising Psycho-Analysis (Ratschläge für den Arzt bei der psychoanalytischen Behandlung)*. Cf. Freud, Works, XXII, pg. 111; Freud (1912), pg. 377. The analyst should listen to the analysand in such a way that "no element of what is said" is given preference "a priori", which requires that he allow his "own unconscious activity to

relationship – in particular originating from early childhood – provided primary interpretative material. The interpretation of such affects in the course of the analytic process – giving and receiving interpretations – by the analyst and the patient was intended to make the neurotic conflicts and structures so transparent that the gained insight resulted in an improved capacity to manage conflicts or to allow the personality to mature. Freud writes:

> In psychoanalysis we act upon the transference itself, resolve what opposes it, adjust the instrument with which we wish to make our impact. Thus it becomes possible for us to derive an entirely fresh advantage from the power of suggestion; we get it into our hands. The patient does not suggest to himself whatever he pleases: we guide his suggestion so far as he is in any way accessible to its influence.[209]

Freud attempts to allay the suspicion that suggestive "influencing of the patient [made] the objective reliability of our findings dubious" by claiming that the success of the therapy was the ultimate criteria for its validation. This showed that one had intuitively given the patient "anticipatory ideas" which corresponded to the "reality in him". Freud solves the problem of unfounded interpretations by pointing out their obvious ineffectivity. "Whatever in the doctor's conjectures is inaccurate drops out in the course of the analysis; it has to be withdrawn and replaced by something more correct.[210] Freud, like Jaspers, sees the "[a]buse of analysis" in the relationship between analyst and analysand as a real possibility since, as he confesses, transference is a "dangerous instrument in the hands of an unconscientious doctor". But Freud sees the dangers of the transference relationship as an unavoidable risk, which he defends by using a medical metaphor. "[I]f a knife does not cut, it cannot be used for healing either."[211]

In his early writings on psychoanalysis, Jaspers already advocates a high degree of autonomy for the patient, arguing that suggestive influencing by the physician was only justified in the case of clearly limited medical indications. For Jaspers, such indications also legitimized the use of suggestive elements by those applying the pedagogical form of psychotherapy whose goal was self-education. Jaspers opposed Freud's view that such suggestive techniques could only have any long-term effect if the psychodynamic constellation had been aptly interpreted, with the therapeutic success – like the results of a successful experiment – serving as scientific validation of the 'hypothesis'. For Jaspers, the success of the treatment or the lack thereof depended on the degree to which the verbal and non-verbal patterns of interpretation offered by the analyst – his meaning-oriented aura – struck a chord in the analysand. As Jaspers contends, this law of correspondence or affinity was valid for the "good psychiatrist" in particular, albeit one who was only "good for a certain circle of individuals" with whom he was compatible.[212]

function as freely as possible" and that he interrupt "motivations" which "usually [guide] his attention". Cf. Laplanche/Pontalis, pg. 177 and pg. 169.
[209] Freud, Works XVI, pg. 451f.; cf. Freud (1917), pg. 469f..
[210] Freud, Works XVI, pg. 452; cf. Freud (1917), pg. 470.
[211] Freud, Works XVI, pg. 463; cf. Freud (1917), pg. 482.
[212] AP 1, pg. 326.

Jaspers assesses the affective dynamics in the treatment relationship using his ideal of philosophical communication as his yardstick, this communication process being intended as symmetrical and free of suggestive elements so as to allow for self-realization without heteronomous influence. In taking this position, Jaspers presumably draws on his own clinic experience with psychotherapy. Without saying as much, he writes:

> The desire of many [...] doctors to dismiss all these transferences, submissions and dependencies, these one-sided erotic relationships, in order to create the one desired relationship of understanding communication founders on the elementary needs of the patients who simply want someone they can dearly love and who will save them.[213]

Jaspers saw the gulf between "the one who wants to understand and the one who is to be understood"[214] as constitutive. A method of psychiatric communication whose purpose was to clarify the mutual occurrence of affect in the therapeutic process was not his concern. He merely conceded that some patients demanded a matter-of-fact, philosophical discussion between equals. From a less immediate perspective, the danger that suggestion might effect a blurring of insight seemed to be averted, and with the methodological tool of the humanities, maximum insight still seemed obtainable. Accordingly, his phenomenological method for comprehending "what patients really experience" involved no interactive modalities. The assessment of external behavior such as facial expressions and gestures as well as directive exploration of the patients and the interpretation of their self-exploratory writings ("self-descriptions") constituted what was essentially a one-sided process similar to that entailing the discovery and interpretation of sources in the humanities.[215]

---

[213] GP 4, pg. 805
[214] Cf. AP 4, pg. 674
[215] Jaspers (1912a), pg. 320.

CHAPTER 3

LIFE CONDUCT IN MODERN TIMES

> For he had been asked with a kind of appalled air how he could have engaged with another person so totally without keeping part of his own person in a hiding place, with him replying by 'admitting' out of prudence that his idea of love without reservation had indeed failed.
>
> Uwe Johnson[216]

MAX WEBER AS 'CRISIS'-INDICATOR

The term 'crisis' was a "frequently used catchword" in circulation since World War I. It attests to the ubiquitous lack of orientation in modern societies. Diverse "theories of crisis" attempted to diagnose the causes of the loss of coherent value systems as well as to make prognoses about the future. [217] The "erosion of previous certainties" was identified as the "core of the crisis"; traditional orientation systems – "ideologies of political integration, philosphical world views and last but not least, the religion of the Christian churches" – had lost their authority due to internal and external disintegration.[218]

According to this diagnosis, the crisis of modern times consisted in the lack of a coherent and integrative culture of orientation which presupposed the following understanding of culture: culture, of whatever origin, presents itself to the individual as a

> suprapersonal system of interpretations, values, forms of expression [and...] certain patterns of interpretation and schemes of meaning vis-a-vis the world and the individual's own existential orientation in it, conveying to him at the same time modes of orientation and prioritized rules which he can utilize in communicative and decision-making situations.[219]

And yet the crisis of modern times as it is understood in this way is not equatable with a complete desintegration of various subjective and collective cultural certainties; it only implies that the heterogenic cultures of interpretation appear from the outside as a "pluralism of life philosophies". Within such a pluralistic, "fragmented

---

[216] Johnson (1981), pg. 70f.
[217] Koselleck (1976), col. 1239.
[218] Drehsen/Sparn (1996), pg. 15.
[219] Grimm (1987), pg. 119; cf. Drehsen/Sparn (1996), pg. 20.

society" they compete with each other in terms of the interpretations they offer. So the diagnosis goes.[220]

The sciences contributed in no small measure to the erosion of traditional systems of orientation, creating their own new value patterns and also making it in part their task to systematize the newly generated, diverse value canons and to evaluate them in their normative frames of reference. Thus one speaks retrospectively of the "genesis of the social sciences from the spirit of a perception of crisis", these new disciplines having been etablished around 1900 as an "instance of societal self-reflection".[221]

Max Weber was one of the most important founders of German sociology, which came into being around 1900.[222] Due to his analysis of modern societies and modern science, which we find formulated in condensed form in his lecture entitled "Science as a Vocation" ("Wissenschaft als Beruf"),[223] he was viewed by critical intellectuals as a "fundamental skepticist" who diagnosed the disease of the times and traced it back to its metaphysical roots, but who also rejected many of the scientifically designed "paths to presumable salvation".[224] Having heard the lecture delivered at the end of 1918, the philosopher Karl Löwith maintained that Weber, in the condition of "a general desintegration of all internal and external holdings" which prevailed after World War I, had torn "the veil of all desirabilities".[225]

Apart from crisis, what one called 'Weltanschauung' had shaped intellectual discourse to a considerable degree since the turn of the century. One thing it expressed was the desire for a coherent, cohesive interpretation of individual and collective spheres of life. The meaning of the concept 'Weltanschauung', which reflected the manifestations of deteriorating value patterns, was directed towards a "totalizing knowledge or view of the world". In the increasingly value-fragmented climate of modern times, 'Weltanschauungen' endeavored to orient the individual's subjective relationship to the world by providing "norms of thought, action and configuration" which were designed to afford "social generalization".[226] The persistent use of the term 'Weltanschauung' can be read as an indication that in modern times, coherent interpretations of the world had come into a crisis which provoked ongoing discussion.

In this climate, Jaspers' 1919 book *Psychology of World Views* aimed to provide clarifying orientation for intellectuals. He told his publisher that "questions concerning world views" were surfacing "all over" and that "none of [his] books would attract more interest" than this one".[227] In the style of Max Weber's sociological analysis of modern times, the book attempted to conduct an unbiased investigation of various philosophical, religious and cultural value systems. In his *Psychology of*

---

[220] Drehsen/Sparn (1996), pg. 19.

[221] Drehsen/Sparn (1996), pg. 21.

[222] Cf. Mommsen (1988), pp. 11-38.

[223] Weber (1989), pp. 3-31; cf. Weber (1919), pp. 582-613.

[224] Kracauer (1922), pg. 165.

[225] Löwith (1994), pg. 17; cf. Löwith (1986), pg. 16f.

[226] Cf. Mies (1999).

[227] Letter from Karl Jaspers to Julius Springer from April 30, 1918, in Sarkowski (1982), pg. 32.

World Views Jaspers remarked, however, that his psychology of understanding contained normative premises which his *Philosophy* had developed further.[228] In this way he retrospectively affirms the judgment issued by Siegfried Kracauer concerning his putatively value-free analysis of world views, namely that he had been, as it were, "ambushed by values from behind".[229] After 1945, Hannah Arendt called his book "without a doubt the first book of the new 'school'" of "existence philosophy".[230] By virtue of its implicit claim to philosophical truth, Jaspers' *Psychology of World Views* held a great fascination for her and other young intellectuals, especially considering the fact that Jaspers simultaneously promised to supply an antiideological analysis of the age. Arendt writes:

> What I have learned from you and what has helped me, in the following years, to come to terms with reality without making a pact with it like people used to make pacts with the devil, is that all that counts is truth and not world views, – that it is necessary to live and think in the outdoors and not in any 'housing', no matter how beautifully it is furnished.[231]

Not until the publication of *Man in the Modern Age* in 1931, a time when the Weimar Republic had come into crisis, does Jaspers openly present an existence-philosophically accentuated diagnosis of modernity. Jaspers seized upon the catchword 'crisis' – as a word to be found in every newspaper[232] – and diagnosed as its core a public "lack of confidence"[233] which he judged to be the result of unsuccessful secularization. The book contains the essence, formulated programmatically, of the three-volume *Philosophy* which was soon to appear, placing it expressly within the framework of socio-political and cultural conditions. The diagnosis of modern times put forth in *Man in the Modern Age*, whose symbolic meaning as volume 1000 of the *Sammlung Göschen* was quickly affirmed by the great interest it awakened, culminates in an "active forecast"[234]. Jaspers offers individuals in mass society a therapeutic remedy – existence-philosophical life conduct – as the only means of escaping the crisis.

Jaspers sharpened his focus on the topic of 'life conduct' in modern times by turning to Max Weber, the perspective of whose epoch-making sociological investigations of religion was oriented to the question of rationally systematized life conduct. Thus it is certainly not surprising that from 1920 on, Jaspers no longer made reference to Weber's methodology alone,[235] but also characterized him as an "existential philosopher".[236] He was the "heart of the times", holding up the mirror to it

---

[228] Cf. PW, pg. X and this study, pg. 30.
[229] Kracauer (1924), pg. 260.
[230] Arendt (1948), pg. 74.
[231] Arendt (1948), pg. 8 and later Arendt (1976), pg. 7.
[232] MMA, pg. 80; cf. GS, pg. 76.
[233] MMA, pg. 80; cf. GS, pg. 76.
[234] MMA, pg. 196; cf. GS, pg. 201.
[235] Cf. AP 1, pg. 7. Jaspers cites the early methodological articles "Roscher and Knies and the Logical Problems of Historical National Economy" ("Roscher und Knies und die logischen Probleme der historischen Nationalökonomie") and "'Objectivity' in Social Science and Social Policy" ("Die 'Objektivität' sozialwissenschaftlicher und sozialpolitischer Erkenntnis"). Cf. Weber (1903/06) and Weber (1949b); Weber (1904).
[236] Jaspers (1921), pg. 36.

and shaping it "spiritually", says Jaspers in praise of him.[237] From the vantage point of the 1950's Jaspers writes, "Among my contemporaries I only knew one whom I deemed to be a truly great philosopher, and that was Max Weber."[238] In 1932 Jaspers ascribes a cryptic aura to the figure of Max Weber by referring to him as a "visible secret" capable of giving existence-philosophical self-reflection decisive orientation.[239] Jaspers' *Man in the Modern Age* had already borne witness to the important role Weber played for existence philosophy, stylizing him as a mysterious, publicly anonymous prophet while not mentioning him by name in terms of his programmatic importance. Jaspers writes:

> The man who, in search of independence, gives expression to true being is radically different from the prophets of an earlier day. [...] His essence is an obvious mystery. [...] This inviolable anonymity is his sign.[240]

And yet at the end of his life, Jaspers must revoke his monopolizing interpretation of Weber because biographical details are made known to him which no longer allow him to view Weber without reservation as an inspiring prophet of his existence philosophy.[241] To his versant student Hannah Arendt, Jaspers relates that his understanding of Weber has become "better and deeper". For him Weber is the epitome of "modern man", as he who had been subjected to the "absolute disruption" of the age, had lived "passionately" and had struggled with himself "without direction". What now impresses Jaspers as Weber's monumental accomplishment is the fact that he had endured the metaphysical emptiness of modernity with intellectual probity and had not filled the void with surrogate meaning.[242] This sober reflection on Max Weber as it correlates a personal philosophy of values with life conduct has been investigated more carefully by Dieter Henrich.[243] Other studies do no more than to provide superficial biographical analyses[244] or limit themselves in completely other ways to metascientific aspects of Weber's reception.[245]

The concept of existence-philosophical life conduct in modern times as it presents itself in *Man in the Modern Age* forms the focus of this chapter. In light of the eminent role which Jaspers ascribes to Weber, the interpretation will make extensive reference to Weber concerning his understanding of modernity and his concept of life conduct. Since for Jaspers, Weber's own life conduct is of crucial significance for his role as the 'prophet' of existence philosophy, the chapter will

---

[237] Jaspers (1921), pp. 32-36.
[238] Jaspers writes this in a letter written on the occasion of Martin Heidegger's birthday but never sent, in which he adds, "When I look beyond him I see no one among my 'colleagues' who would have moved me, except through utilizable accomplishments, other than himself as a philosopher, except for you." Cf. Jaspers (1978), pg. 169.
[239] Jaspers (1932a), pg. 114.
[240] MMA, pg. 172f.
[241] Cf. this study, pp. 124-131.
[242] Cf. letter from Karl Jaspers to Hannah Arendt from April 29, 1966, in AJC, pg. 671.
[243] Henrich presented the results of his investigation, formulated in his book entitled *Denken im Blick auf Max Weber*, at a symposium held in Heidelberg on the occasion of Jaspers' 100th birthday in 1983. Cf. Henrich (1986).
[244] Cf. Green (1974), pp. 336-347.
[245] Most noteworthy are Frommer/Frommer (1990) and Frommer (1990).

close with a look at some biographical circumstances which Jaspers could not reconcile with reality as he conceived of it. Just what connection is to be drawn between the interpretation of *Man in the Modern Age* as it presents itself from a Weberian perspective and Jaspers' critique of psychoanalysis can only be indicated cursorily at this stage of the investigation.

'DISENCHANTMENT OF THE WORLD' AND INTELLECTUAL LIFE CONDUCT

With his thesis of the "disenchantment of the world", Weber views the orientation crisis of modern times as the result of the accelerated "intellectualization and *rationalization* " of life circumstances. Enormous scientific progress had promoted a specific kind of "cognition" or "belief" that the exact "knowledge of life circumstances" could be preserved as long as intellectual attempts were made to do so. Thus there were "no fundamentally mysterious, uncalculable powers" any more which one had to imagine as forces hidden behind unexplainable connections. Instead, "one could in principle master everything through *calculation*". Thus, in order to control our world we no longer needed to resort to any magical-religious practices in order to influence unknown forces in a positive way.[246] And yet Weber's thesis by no means develops a perspective informed by an optimistic view of progress, for, as Weber sees it, the rational transparency of the world ultimately makes unresolvable contradictions concerning the design of the world all the more pronounced. As Weber writes:

> The tension between religion and intellectual knowledge definitely comes to the fore wherever rational, empirical knowledge has consistently worked through to the disenchantment of the world and its transformation into a causal mechanism. For then science encounters the claims of the ethical postulate that the world is a God-ordained, and hence somehow *meaningfully* and ethically oriented, cosmos.[247]

In light of such irresolvable aporias Weber speaks ironically of the fact that "the calculation of consistent rationalism has not easily come out even, with nothing left over".[248]

Weber repeatedly points to the problematics of the theodicy which had accompanied the history of religion, namely the fact that the "need for an ethical interpretation of the 'meaning' of the distribution of fortunes among men" had been confronted time and again with the experience of "undeserved suffering" so that all attempts to formulate harmoniously coherent theologies had reached certain limits.[249] Arguing in this vein, Weber associates the "experience of the irrationality of the world" with the concept of the theodicy, which he understands to be the historico-philosophical result of "world history" through the ages until modern times,[250] rejecting all interpretations of history based on an optimistic view of progress or inherent

---

[246] Weber (1989), pg. 13f.; cf. Weber (1919b), pg. 494.
[247] Weber (1991), pg. 350f.; cf. Weber (1920a), pg. 564.
[248] Weber (1991), pg. 281; cf. Weber (1920a), pg. 253.
[249] Weber (1991), pg. 275; cf. Weber (1020a), pg. 247.
[250] Weber (1991), pg. 122f.; cf. Weber (1919a), pg. 741.

meaning. At the very latest, the European catastrophe constituted by World War I bore testimony only too clearly to the relativity of all previous authorities and traditions and made attempts to assign this period of history some kind of "pervasive meaning"[251] appear as irrefutably dubious undertakings. And yet the very fact that the notion of purpose had been so conspicuously abandonned or at least recognized as full of contradictions prompted new efforts on the part of intellectuals to provide compensatory systems.

According to Weber, the sciences radically negated religion's capacity to provide meaning in a disenchanted world but could guarantee no new, meaningfully coherent world view themselves. As he contends, their task was instead to illustrate the limits of meaningful and comprehensible connections in an intellectually searching manner; they were not capable themselves of supplying any truly comprehensive goals for individual and collection life systems. Weber comes to the sobering conclusion that the "ultimate, most sublime values" were no longer part of a generally shared world view and that they only gained authority within "the smallest groups, between individuals", in which "something pulsates *in pianissimo*".[252] Weber describes modern times in religious terms, calling them a "godless, prophetless age" in which the religious world view no longer held any validity and scientifically legitimized, generally valid ascriptions of meaning and value concerning questions of life conduct were impossible to make.[253]

In other words, Weber posits that patterns for investing reality with meaning in the scientific age of modernity had to be inescapably subjectivized. In accordance with this view, recent secularization theories have described modernity as "having only a minimal societal framework".[254] As they contend, subjectivized systems of meaning only have "absolute validity" for the individual. In extreme cases, the "radical subjectivization of self-understanding and the radical objectifization of the disenchanted world" creates a deep chasm between the public perception of life as devoid of meaning and private perceptions of life as meaningful, Luckmann observes.[255] In principle this concept of secularization entertains the notion that in modern times, systems of meaning which aim for ultimate validity had abandoned the public sphere and entered private, very individualized realms of life. As Kippenberg argues, "[t]he more the 'meaning' of the world appears problematical, the more 'meaning' becomes a category of life conduct".[256] One could argue that intellectual probity must be compromised if one is to achieve a harmonization of a subjective world view with objectively ascertainable limits of knowledge and the aporias which accompany them.[257]

---

[251] Weber (1968), pg. 506; cf. Weber (1922b), pg. 301.
[252] Weber (1989), pg. 30; cf. Weber (1919b), pg. 612.
[253] Weber (1989), pg. 28; cf. Weber (1919b), pg. 609f..
[254] Luckmann (1980), pg. 188.
[255] Luckmann (1980), pg. 195.
[256] Kippenberg (1989), pg. 195.
[257] The irresolvable tension between objectifiable "descriptions of the world" and subjective "notions of reality" are subjected to systematic analysis in Thomas Nagel's book entitled *Der Blick von nirgendwo*. Cf. Nagel (1992).

According to Weber, this subjectivization of patterns of life conduct primarily concerned critical intellectuals whose specific tendency to engage in self- and world-reflection quickly led them to recognize ruptures and contradictions in obsolete world views and the constructs of meaning and values which these had created. Weber defined the intellectuals belonging to various religions as well as those intellectual representatives of modernity who were critical of religion as being characterized by the "inner compulsion" to comprehend "the world as a meaningful cosmos".[258] According to this view, intellectuals have the deeply felt need to see that the "world order in its totality is, could, and somehow should be a meaningful 'cosmos'".[259] The longing of the intellectual for salvaton is thus to be understood as "deliverance from 'inner necessitation'". As Weber posits, intellectuals searched for more abstract, rationally more systematized ways of finding salvation than did the non-intellectuals, the latter primarily striving for "salvation from external distress" in concrete ways.[260] In the Weimar years, Siegfried Kracauer paints an apt portrait of the modern, bourgeois searchers of meaning with education but "no ties to any kind of faith" who found themselves in the "loneliness of the large cities" working as "scholars, merchants, physicians, lawyers, students and intellectuals of all kinds", befallen with a kind of "deep sadness" which was attributable to "the metaphysical affliction which stemmed from a lack of high meaning in the world".[261]

Viewing the intellectual as a person searching for meaning corresponds to Weber's definition of 'life conduct' as an intensification of the characteristic meaningfulness of social action.[262] According to this view, 'life conduct' constitutes regulated, rationalized and accustomed social action whose character manifests itself all the more clearly the more the "ultimate values" of actions are carried out within a framework of meaningfulness which is not tied to particular situations.[263] In allusion to the Judeo-Christian and ancient-Greek traditions, Weber demonstrates the cultural striving to overcome natural inertia. This involved the expectation that daily action be informed by individual decisions on values, but these were what enabled one to adopt a specific kind of life conduct in the first place. As he writes:

> The fruit of the tree of knowledge, which is distasteful to the complacent but which is, nonetheless, inescapable, consists in the insight that every single important activity and ultimately life as a whole, if it is not to be permitted to run on as an event in nature but is instead to be consciously guided, is a series of ultimate decisions through which the soul – as in Plato – chooses its own fate, i.e., the meaning of its activity and existence.[264]

Through externally prescribed values, social action becomes relatively independent of the contingent conditions which determine individual situations because its motivational power has a stronger influence than do such conditions; as such, it has the capacity to reduce the impact of distracting motives. Weber's study *Protestant*

---

[258] Weber (1922b), pg. 304.
[259] Weber (1991), pg. 281; cf. Weber (1920a), pg. 253.
[260] Weber (1968), pg. 506; cf. Weber (1922b), pg. 307.
[261] Kracauer (1922), pg. 160.
[262] Cf. Weber (1968), pg. 334; Weber (1922b), pg. 324.
[263] Weber (1991), pg. 287; cf. Weber (1920a), pg. 259.
[264] Cf. Weber (1949), pg. 18; Weber (1917), pg. 507f..

Ethics and the Spirit of Capitalism (*Die protestantische Ethik und der 'Geist' des Kapitalismus*) illustrates exemplarily that the cultivation of a specific form of life conduct rests in no small measure on the affirmation of meaningfulness which transcends the immediate success of actions by way of acting in the face of inescapable deficits of meaningfulness.[265] In this way various philosophical, social, political and medical patterns of meaning – as external norm prescriptions – can elicit specific patterns for life conduct from social action (depending on their motivational intensity) which guarantee a certain degree of consistency and independence from the situational circumstances which accompany social action.

To be sure, Weber's concept of life conduct can only be meaningfully applied in areas where a certain "individual realm of freedom" is given in research fields of sociological interest, a realm of freedom which enables the subject to make action-guiding normative decisions independent of certain situations in the first place. Wherever functional connections have been completely de-emotionalized in the interests of goal-oriented rationality, thus leaving no room for individual impulses to take action, Weber's ideal of individually normed life conduct can do no more than to drive home the contrast to the reality at hand as the object of investigation. As Wilhelm Hennis points out, the increasingly de-emotionalized life orders of the modern world make the "old European", liberal perspective of individual life conduct appear more and more antiquated.[266] But the very normative dependency of the concept of life conduct on individualistic ideas makes it an excellently suited instrument for sociological investigation designed to historically reconstruct the societal implications of Jaspers' existence philosophy.

And yet in Jaspers' approach, the central philosophical term 'existence', which motivates the transformation of social life in the direction of life conduct to a decisive degree, eludes in a certain sense purely rational understanding. For as Weber contends, the more radically "ends" and "values" deviate from one's own "ultimate values", the harder it would be for us "to understand them emphatically". As he argues, this might force one to satisfy oneself with purely descriptive interpretations.[267] In the course of this examination of Jaspers' concept of existence-philosophical life conduct, this will prove to be the case. Of course it must be admitted that even terms which are used descriptively are inevitably normative. The concern of value freedom well applied is to identify these premises and avoid succumbing to the belief that any of us has an objective instrumentarium at our disposal.[268]

---

[265] Cf. Weber (1904/05).
[266] Cf. Hennis (1987), pg. 110.
[267] Weber (1968), pg. 5f.; cf. Weber (1922b), pg. 5.
[268] The next chapter will address the special issue of scientific value freedom. Cf. this study, pp. 64-66.

MAN IN THE MODERN AGE (1931)

Diagnosis of Modernity Between Hybris and Modesty

Like Weber's works, *Man in the Modern Age* views modern secularization as a sociological phenomenon. There are no longer any pan-societal moral and normative codexes and the frameworks of meaningfulness which inform life conduct hardly transcend the sphere of individual existence. In the public and political sphere Jaspers now sees a dominance of pragmatic, goal-oriented and conventional forms of interaction divorced of transcendental beliefs. As he posits, these had led to a blatant "lack of trust" in society. When looked at from our present-day vantage point, this diagnosis of modernity can be evaluated as the typical judgment of a critic of modern "instrumental society" who ascertains the existence of an "instrumental stance" and laments the loss of "deeper meanings".[269]

In accordance with the sociological theory of secularization, the trust which Jaspers finds lacking in modern times is only found "in the smallest circles" of transcendentally rooted individual life conduct, but no longer in the form of pan-societal "confidence" which "extends to the totaliy".[270] Jaspers gives concrete descriptions of such isolated spheres where life conduct is practiced within the tide of mass society, spheres which are partly institutionalized such as life in marriage, family, friendship and the academic community. For him it is conceivable that impulses could emerge from such realms which might improve the situation of society as a whole.

The concern about preserving a transcendentally oriented form of "close kinship"[271] is paramount for Jaspers. Given such "close kinship", modern times appear as "the world's turn". Jaspers' depiction likens that of a medical metaphor for crisis which, according to Koselleck, alludes to the "brief turn in which life or death is decided".[272] Thus in Jaspers' eye, the situation of modernity can either reveal itself as "unsurpassably great in spiritual terms" or ultimately turn out to be the "most impoverished time of failing mankind".[273] Karl Löwith characterizes the missionary aspect of Jaspers' diagnosis of modernity precisely when he contends that Jaspers attempts "to open up new possibilities for 'metaphysics' by establishing an existential relationship between a modern existence devoid of faith and a 'hidden' but not 'vanished' transcendence".[274]

In contrast to Weber, Jaspers interprets the erosion of Christian and metaphysical patterns of meaning, which he refers to as the "loss of the sense of a divine presence in the world",[275] as the unavoidable consequence of modernity's faith in reason and technology. Unlike Weber, his theory of secularization views the modern age exclusively as the negative result of faith in progress and the intellectual 'hybris' of

---

[269] Taylor (1989), pg. 500.
[270] MMA, pg. 80; Cf. GS, p. 76.
[271] MMA, pg. 23; Cf. GS, p. 17.
[272] Koselleck (1976), col. 1235.
[273] MMA, pg. 21.
[274] Löwith (1933), pg. 20f..
[275] MMA, pg. 25; cf. GS, pg. 19.

civilized man who defines his world-immanent rationality in quasi absolute terms. According to Jaspers, modern man is led by "pride" to overestimate his rational capacity and thinks that he, as "master of the world", can "mould it to his liking".[276] As Jaspers' diagnosis goes, secularized man lacks the "religious conviction that man was as naught in the face of Transcendence", this being something which had been taken for granted in the previous world in which "[c]hanges were the outcome of God's will".[277] From the perspective of a history of ideas, Jaspers correlates rational self-confidence in the sense of common misconceptions with the French Revolution; had it not attempted to replace the teleology of salvific history which had prevailed during earlier times with "civilization" in perfected form?[278] In the course of this evaluation, Jaspers emphasizes the important role which the American Revolution – motivated by Protestant ideas – had played before 1789, having established modern individualism in the Constitution of 1776 as an example for all times to come.[279]

Jaspers places Protestantism alongside this epochal consciousness of general progress[280] which had renewed Christianity through a "return to its fundamentals"[281] without secularizing it, conceptualizing it more rigidly and absolutely in opposition to the secularization of the church".[282] In contrast to some other thinkers living in Weimarian Germany, Jaspers does not strive for a restoration of the Catholic Middle Ages in the sense of a celestial framework of values which encompassed all of society.[283] Siegfried Kracauer evokes the longing – widely felt by critical intellectuals of the time – for a world as "ordered cosmos", as a "homogenous whole penetrated by godly substance in which human beings and things harmoniously incorporated themselves".[284] Jaspers foregrounds the individualistic trait of reformed Christianity as the only modus with transcendental connectedness. *Man in the Modern Age* devaluates the French Revolution as a form of self-elevating belief in reason alongside traditional Catholicism as an external collective value canon.[285]

Unlike Weber, Jaspers exonerates Protestantism from the accusation that it had promoted a disenchantment of the world as a rational consequence of the process of the "European conquest of the world"[286] and scientific progress. He makes Enlightenist hybris solely responsible for the heuristic misjudgment which maintained that objective claims to knowledge had been extended to metaphysical questions and had eliminated "God the Creator" once and for all. Jaspers diagnoses the immanentistic strain of secularization as the result of the intellectual hybris generated by success in the sciences, a consequence which, he feels, would not have been compelling if a more modest attitude had been taken.[287]

---

[276] MMA, p. 11; cf. GS, pg. 7.
[277] MMA, p. 11; cf. GS, pg. 6f..
[278] MMA, pg. 13; cf. GS, pg. 8.
[279] MMA, pg. 14; cf. GS, pg. 9.
[280] Cf. MMA 12 and GS, pg. 8.
[281] MMA, pg. 14; cf. GS; pg. 9.
[282] MMA, pg. 14; cf. GS, pg. 9.
[283] Cf. Kracauer (1920), pg. 118.
[284] Cf. Kracauer (1920), pg. 118.
[285] Cf. MMA, pg. 17.
[286] MMA, pg. 23; cf. GS, pg. 17.
[287] Cf. MMA, pg. 20.

This judgment corresponds with Jaspers' metascientific position which maintains that one must draw a strict distinction between scientific and "philosophical", i.e. metaphysical truth in the traditional sense of the word. Due to the hypothetical conditions under which they gain insights, the sciences do not have the capacity to make ultimate statements about meaning, he posits.[288] On the other hand, "philosophical" insight lacks the ability to stake claims to objectifiable truth beyond the sphere of the individual, says Jaspers. In contending this, he thoroughly presupposes that a transcendent entity exists but that it can never be clearly verified and can only be expressed by the various religions, philosophies and arts indirectly via "ciphers".[289] The decisive criteria for measuring the quality of awestruck "metaphysical content" lies for Jaspers in the perceptible degree of existential seriousness of the human being, in his inner "sincerity".[290]

For Jaspers, the nature of the transcendental, which eludes all objectifization, has a parallel in Christian notions of the *deus absconditus*, a notion which Jaspers finds in Kant's writings and is attracted to. As he says, Kant "finally takes seriously the fact that God is concealed" and that the "only claim that God makes of man" consists in his "being free". This Kantian consciousness of freedom decidedly separates Jaspers from the epistemological 'hybris' which he so sweepingly ascribes to the Enlightenist spirit of the French Revolution. And yet he does not bring Kant's belief in a concealed existence of God in connection with the "miserable humility" which he identifies as a tendency of Catholic Christianity. In Jaspers' eye, Kant's epistemological skepsis, which manifests itself in condensed form in his notion of the *deus absconditus*, destroys all self-assured 'ontology', leaving 'the transcendental' as a mere "relative certainty". Thus the individual's belief in transcendence maintains a scientifically legitimated space free of intellectual conflict where it can unfold on completely individual terms.[291]

Thus the postulate of a concealed god constitutes an ideal surface for projecting transcendental notions of meaningfulness because it remains free of implications which require objectifization. The "ciphers of transcendence" as they were developed in the metaphysical tradition make no ontological claim to gnosis but merely prompt the individual to engage in an inward process of appropriation. The philosopher and Jaspers student Gerhard Krüger reveals this tenet of existence philosophy when he writes:

> But all aspects of God which become tangible are only 'ciphers' of transcendence, which are true only in the moment of the surge of faith. Whoever wants to hold onto such ciphers and claim lasting insight makes them into objects, and as objects, science cannot grant them any validity.[292]

---

[288] Jaspers makes no explicit mention of the "modern humanities" in this pronounced polarization. As he contends, they must be distinguished from the natural sciences due to the greater degree to which they are dependent on hypotheses, but due to their intersubjective, conventional nature, they do not extend into the sphere of "existential truth" as he specifically defines it.

[289] W, pg. 177.

[290] MMA, pg. 162; cf. GS, pg. 164.

[291] Jaspers/Heidegger (2003), pg. 88f.; cf. Jaspers/Heidegger (1990), pg. 89.

[292] Cf. Krüger (1958b), pg. 229.

If one follows Weber's sociology of religion, Jaspers' concept of existence-philosophical faith can be understood as a type of mystical salvific religion in which, in light of the postulate of distinct spheres of insight, the "tension between religion and intellectual cognition" need not ever even arise. In a very Kantian vein, Weber describes salvific insight as a "last response to the world" which goes back to a "subjective and direct perception of the meaning of the world" and which must be distinguished from intellectually conveyed knowledge about connections in the world.[293] As Weber argues, the more the intellectual disintegration and disenchantment of the real world progresses, the more "other-worldly, [the] more alienated from all structured forms of life" must the "need for 'salvation'" present itself, restricting its scope to the "specific religious essence" in order to avoid becoming entangled in blatant contradictions with growing *rationalization*.[294] Weber himself never believed an intellectually honest form of salvific faith was possible. Jaspers registered this with extreme dismay. In Weber's *Intermediate Reflection* (*Zwischenbetrachtung*) we read:

> There is absolutely no 'unbroken' religion working as a vital force which is not compelled at *some* point to demand the *credo non quod, sed quia absurdum* – the 'sacrifice of the intellect'.[295]

In his copy of Weber's book, Jaspers writes a remark in the margin, which reads: "This is the great, terrifying question."[296]

Existence-philosophical faith dispenses not only with objectifiable correlates of a conceptual nature; it also refrains from making any clear conventional connections in organizational and institutional terms. Thus it remains within the sociological framework of the secularization model favored by Weber which allows the public sphere to be shaped by relatively objectifiable scientific knowledge, relegating all ultimate questions of meaningfulness into the realm of private existence. Jaspers' model of existence philosophy transforms the modern necessity which stems from a collective loss of *Weltanschauung* into the virtue of a primarily inward, individual cosmos invested with meaningfulness which is independent of society and can never take on clear contours in the public sphere.

'Philosophical' Life Conduct in the Protestant 'Spirit'

Existence-philosophical faith does not express itself in clear confessions of faith; the inward, philosophical life which motivates action can only be divined indirectly by inferring it from actions. This special feature of existence-philosophical life conduct is structurally equivalent to the ideotypical pattern of ascetic Protestantism as

---

[293] This form of mystic salvific religion presupposes the "charisma of illumination", however, which makes the central "mystical experience" possible. Cf. Weber (1991), pg. 352; Weber (1920a), pg. 566.
[294] Weber (1991), pg. 357; cf. Weber (1920a), pg. 571.
[295] Cf. Weber (1991), pg. 352; Weber (1920a), pg. 566.
[296] Cf. Jaspers' library, Dr. Hans Saner, Basle.

described by Weber.[297] Being informed by the "predestination decree of the deus absconditus", Calvinistic Protestantism offered only one option, namely to assure oneself of the concealed existence of God through life conduct; this preserved one's membership, predestined by God, in the Circle of the Chosen. 'This-worldly' existence was viewed as a mere "passing through", but one upon which "an enormous emphasis" was laid, namely to fulfill "one' own appointment with salvation". The transcendentally rooted and in immanent terms highly rationalized life conduct which resulted from this notion demanded that the "irrational drives" be constantly overcome by means of ethically justified "actions".[298] The attempt to maintain uncertain faith in this indirect way was referred to as "sanctification".[299] The "religious virtuoso" could only "prove himself before God [...] through the ethical quality of his conduct in this world".[300] The primarily worldless inwardness of faith in the concealed God led to a world-dominating habitus as an indirect sign of grace. In the realm of religion, systematic secularization was responded to by a specific "ethicization" of faith.[301]

Sociologically speaking, existence-philosophical life conduct also constitutes a special mixture of escapism and world dominion. "Selfhood or self-existence first arises out of his being against the world in the world."[302] The orientation towards concealed transcendence does, to be sure, liberate the individual from conventional worldly authorities, but in turn it demands all the more urgently an ethically consistent life which must attest to its reality indirectly. As Jaspers writes:

> Every search for the unconditioned makes man, so to say, unnatural in his severity towards himself; for the genuineness of a being that is historically irreplaceable is associated with an immense exercise of self-restraint, with a vigorous control of the will. He only who uses an unbending force of self-discipline, sustained by an urgent feeling for the possibility of true fulfilment, walks along the road proper to man as man – a road primarily entered upon under the coercion of objective authority, but now deliberately and freely chosen by the self become aware of its own responsibility.[303]

In light of such internalized transcendence, individual self-examination is rigid and persistent, not unlike the kind found in Protestantism. As Jaspers writes, "[n]o man can contemplate his image in the mirror without some perplexity or dismay; and the more vigorously he aspires, the more sensitive will he be to the presence of other than aspiring elements in himself."[304]

Weber ascertains that the religious conscientiousness of the Protestants not only promoted their professional effectivity directly, but also indirectly insofar as their

---

[297] Cf. Habermas (1995). In regard to Jaspers' "philosophical faith", Habermas speaks of the "Reformist tradition" which he had philosophically appropriated, – a tradition which manifested a more than formal ethics. Cf. Habermas (1995).
[298] Weber (1904/05), pg. 118.
[299] Weber (1991), pg. 312; cf. Weber (1920a), pg. 526.
[300] Weber (1991), pg. 290f.; cf. Weber (1920a), pg. 262f..
[301] Cf. Kippenberg (1989), pg. 196.
[302] MMA, pg. 177; cf. GS, pg. 181.
[303] MMA, pg. 186; cf. GS, pg. 110.
[304] MMA, pg. 192, cf. GS, pg. 197.

personal trustworthiness increased their business reputation.[305] In analogy to the effects of Protestantism, Jaspers postulates a correlation between a conscientious relationship of transcendence and social trustworthiness with existence-philosophical tendencies. According to *Man in the Modern Age*, it is possible to counteract the primary symptom of modern society, i.e. the postulated "lack of trust", in this way. Of the moral elite in society Jaspers says that they "hold together with a loyalty which is stronger than any formal agreement could give"[306] and which was not covered by external codexes and principles of behavior. Instead, "solidarity" was called for, which relied on the voluntary responsibility of the individual whose inner conscientiousness produced a greater "intimacy of [...] communication"[307] and a "personal trustworthiness even so far as the unobjectified and unobjectifiable minutiæ of behavior are concerned [...]".[308]

Ultimately, social action serves this existence-philosophical elite as a realm in which to put existential truth to the test: Having no direct sign of a concealed godliness, transcendence could at least be experienced indirectly by attesting to one's convictions through action, Jaspers argues. Thus *Man in the Modern Age* accepts politically successful action only as a welcome possibility; the concern for individual and existential convictions are what stand in the center of Jaspers' concerns. The existence-philosophical cipher of "failure" did not classify the worldly success of actions as being decisive because it was more important to remain true to one's convictions than to act in a certain opportune way in a specific situation. "I must myself will what is going to happen, even though the end of all things be at hand," Jaspers writes.[309] For him, the "basic problem of our time"[310] is not how to establish a new ethics to improve the conditions of society, but rather whether and in what way a transcendental relationship can be achieved for the individual in the modern age. For Jaspers it boils down to "whether an independent human being in his self-comprehended destiny is still possible".[311] Thus Max Weber's dictum on religious ethics of conviction, whose "kingdom was 'not of this world'" and whose ideal convictions often failed in the face of political realities,[312] takes on special contours when reformulated by Jaspers.

One might suggest that *Man in the Modern Age* attempts to realize the hope which Weber briefly expresses at the end of his study on Protestantism, namely that only a "newly prophecy" or the "great rebirth of old ideas and ideals" could demolate the modern dwelling of the "specialist without spirit" and the "hedonist without heart" and illuminate the path in a new direction.[313]

---

[305] According to Weber, Protestant "sectarian membership – as opposed to membership in a 'church' into which one is 'born' and which lets its grace shine on the just and the unjust alike – [constitutes] an ethical, in particular business-ethical attestation of quality for the personality." Cf. Weber (1991), pg. 305; (Weber (1906a), pg. 211.
[306] MMA, pg. 189f.; cf. GS, pg. 194.
[307] MMA, pg. 190; cf. GS, pg. 195.
[308] MMA, pg. 190; cf. GS, pg. 195.
[309] MMA, pg. 201f.; cf. GS, pg. 207.
[310] MMA, pg. 203; cf. GS, pg. 209.
[311] MMA, pg. 203; cf. GS, pg. 209.
[312] Weber (1991), pg. 126; cf. Weber (1919a), pg. 246.
[313] Weber (1976), pg. 182; cf. Weber (1904/05), pg. 204.

The existence-philosophical life conduct recommended by Jaspers can be viewed as a modern version of the Protestant ideal, whose wordly success did not yet lead away from the search for the concealed deity. This presupposes that Jaspers eliminated the "secularizing influence"[314] which world-dominating action can possess for inwardness from his model. He did not believe that the self-generated dynamic of successful action necessarily led individuals commited to existence philosophy away from their actual motivation for taking action, namely to stand up to the test in light of the transcendental; such individuals could prevent professional success from becoming a purpose in and of itself.[315]

In light of the political realities of National Socialism, Karl Löwith criticizes the main apolitical tenet of Jaspers' *Man in the Modern Age* in 1940 when he writes

> All existing realities are 'transcended' by his 'existence' in order to arrive at a 'philo-sophical life' which is nowhere and everywhere. His thought 'encompasses' everything and grasps nothing. – In reality Hitler determined the conditions of the age with less spirit and the 'individuals' withdrew into the private sphere.[316]

Löwith's ironic tenor shows his critical acumen, sharpened by political reality, who in the light of his own experiences with National Socialism reproaches the existence-philosophical approach for its privatizing tendencies, seeing these as a weakness.[317]

After 1945, the "prophetic strain" in Jaspers' philosophy is interpreted by Reinhart Koselleck in a completely different way. Koselleck maintains that after his experiences with dictatorship, Jaspers attributed a greater inherent value to political reality. The "Suprapolitical" which expressed itself in an existence oriented toward a concealed deity becomes a "[non-]derivable element of the Political";[318] here Jaspers appears as a "potentially political philosopher" even though his "indirect political stance" remains a defining feature of his philosophy, Koselleck argues.[319]

Quite in the vein of Weber's demand for new prophets in modern times, Jaspers' *Man in the Modern Age* now sketches a concrete prophetic figure which expressed "true existence" for the moral elite and which differed radically from "earlier prophets" by virtue of its unliftable anonymity.[320] As Jaspers adds, the public anonymous prophet is "visible" only to "independent individuals" who, as the moral aristocracy of society, remain equally anonymous in public. Without a doubt Jaspers envisions Weber himself in the role of the prophet of existence-philosophical life conduct. In his monograph entitled *Max Weber – A German in Political Thought, Research and Philosophizing* Jaspers writes unequivocally:

> Max Weber did not conceptualize a philosophical system. It would be impossible to depict his philosophy as a doctrine. He rejected being referred to as a philosopher. And

---

[314] Weber (1976), pg. 174; cf. Weber (1904/05), pg. 196.
[315] Cf. Weber (1976), pg. 181; cf. Weber (1904/05), pg. 203.
[316] Löwith (1994), pg. 75; cf. Löwith (1986), pg. 71f..
[317] Löwith admits that he himself had been "politically [...] naive" and "indifferent" himself during the years before his compulsory emigration in 1936. Cf. Löwith (1994), pg. 69; Löwith (1986), pg. 66.
[318] Koselleck (1986), pg. 299.
[319] Koselleck (1986), pg. 296.
[320] MMA, pg. 175f., cf GS, pg. 179.

> yet for us he is the true philosopher of the times in which he lived. Because philosophy is not a progressive science which is cognizant of timeless truth, it must, being an historical existence which emerges from the absolute in light of transcendence, become a reality time and again. Max Weber did not teach a philosophy; he was a philosophy.[321]

The monography clearly stylizes Weber, the existence-philosophical figurehead, as an "obvious mystery",[322] thus returning to the characterization made in *Man in the Modern Age* which also attributed to the prophet the feature of anonymity, calling him an "obvious mystery" as well.[323] The fact that Weber's name is not even mentioned in *Man in the Modern Age* is consistent, for only in this way can the reader discern whether he himself is a member of the moral elite which is capable of recognizing the prophet despite its publicly "unliftable anonymity". In contrast, the *Philosophy* expressly invests Weber with a representative role for modernity, for as we read, he like no other "looks the destitution of our times in the eye", recognizing it with "comprehensive knowledge" and "exercising self-reliance in a decaying world".[324]

In keeping with Jaspers' model, the members of the moral elite stay "concealed" and are, like the prophet, only recognizable by other believers in existence philosophy.[325] Jaspers consciously demarcates their reality from the medial public sphere by accentuating their concealment as a contrast to the garish glint of mass society. As he writes:

> We doubt whether this reality has a public existence as that which every one knows and can know, that which from day to day the newspapers print and interpret. For it may exist in that which goes on behind the surface of things; in that which lies beyond the reach of all but the few; and in that to which still fewer have access in their activites. It may perhaps be a life of which no one thinks because no one is really conscious of it.[326]

Jaspers emphasizes that existence-philosophical life conduct can only be recognized indirectly on the basis of exceptional moral action. As he emphasizes, no sociological markings exist which refer directly to the individuals belonging to the group which would release them from their social anonymity. As Jaspers elucidates:

> Since there is no objective criterion of trustworthy self-hood, this could not be directly assembled to form influential groups. As has been well said: 'There is no trust (no organised association) of the persons who are the salt of the earth.' That is their weakness, inasmuch as their strength can only inhere in their insonspicuousness. There is among them a tie which does not take the form of any formal contract, but is stronger than any national, political, partisan, or social community, and stronger than the bonds of race. Never direct and immediate, it first becomes manifest in its consequences. [...] True nobility is not found in an isolated being. It exists in the interlinkage of independent human beings.[327]

---

[321] Cf. Jaspers (1932a), pg. 94.
[322] MMA, pg. 173; cf. GS, pg. 176.
[323] MMA, pg. 173 (GS, pg. 177) and Jaspers (1932a) pg. 114.
[324] Jaspers Ph 1, pg. IX.
[325] MMA, pg. 171; cf. GS, pg. 175.
[326] MMA, pg. 169; cf. GS, pg.172.
[327] MMA, pg. 189; cf. GS, pg. 193f..

This idealized societal elite of those who believe in existence philosophy is referred to by Jaspers as an "Invisible Church of a *corpus mysticum* in the anonymous
chain of the friends".[328] He claims to be able to shape this elite through his existence-philosophical ideas of socialization despite, or rather under the conditions of
societal anonymity. For him, individuals who were summoned in this way constituted "the origin of the loftiest soaring movement" which is "as yet possible in the
world". "They alone constitute true human beings."[329] And yet *Man in the Modern
Age* also interprets the social anonymity of this leading class as an age-unspecific
characteristic of intellectual-moral elites, and in doing so he directs his attention to
the pre-modern tradition. He writes: "Unknown to the masses, spiritual movements
may at all times have been going on in an invisible realm of the mind."[330]

Thus Jaspers does not aim to solve the normative crisis in the secularized public
sphere by setting up new ideal values which are clearly articulated and collectively
binding. For the most part, the public realm remains under the dominion of purely
instrumental frame of reference. As he sees it, this factual anonymity of values can
be overcome, however, if one is capable of recognizing the similarly anonymous
prophet as the central normative figure of personal life conduct. Whoever is up to
the challenge of reading the indirect signs may consider himself a member of the
moral elite which is responsible for assuring that, through its actions, the public
sphere gradually begins to take on meaningful contours again, but without adopting
collectively binding norms. Even after 1945, the notion of a small circle of trustworthy persons who constituted an intellectual elite retained its crucial significance
for Jaspers, even though he no longer emphasized the notion of public anonymity in
an affirmative manner.[331]

Charismatic Traditions – the University and 'Life of the Home'

According to Jaspers, existence-philosophical life conduct, which was to stop the
imminent "decay of mankind",[332] requires favorable socialization conditions in order
to convey to the future elite the "profoundest content of what has been handed down
to him".[333] *Man in the Modern Age* aptly sketches what existence-philosophical
socialization of the elite is intended to look like, and in addition, it dismisses two
alternative attempts to effect socialization which also hoped to deliver the Modern
Age from its crisis. For one, Jaspers rejects an educative model aimed at passing
down cultural traditions and secondly, he challenges a form of conveying purely
pragmatic, technical skills. As he writes:

> [A] man will look backwards, and will have his children taught as absolute that which
> he himself no longer regards as such. Another will reject this historical tradition, and

---

[328] MMA, pg. 190; cf. GS, pg. 195.

[329] MMA, pg. 191; cf. GS, pg. 195.

[330] MMA, pg. 169; cf. GS, pg. 172.

[331] A letter written by Jaspers to his friend Hannah Arendt from January 8, 1947
illustrates this. Cf. AJC, p. 107f..

[332] MMA, pg. 104; cf. GS, pg. 101.

[333] MMA, pg. 86; cf. GS, pg. 81.

will have education carried on as if it had no relationship with time at all, and consisted only of training for technical skill, the acquisition of realist knowledge, and information that will enable a child to take up a position towards the contemporary world.[334]

The first socialization model which attempts to convey traditional value patterns without believing in their authority can be described in Weber's sense as a pedagogical ideal aimed at cultivating values. The goal of this pedagogical model is to educate, "depending on the cultural ideals of the controlling class, different kinds of 'cultured individuals', i.e. human beings with a certain kind of internal and external life conduct".[335] The second type of socialization model can be described in Weber's terms as a specialized type which is oriented solely to technical, goal-oriented rational knowledge and educates its "pupils to demonstrate practical servicability for administrative purposes – in public agencies, offices, workshops, scientific and industrial laboratories, disciplined armies".[336] *Man in the Modern Age* sets the existence-philosophical type of socialization against a model for cultivating tradition which Jaspers sees as already eroded, and it also contrasts it with technical specialization, which Jaspers finds lacking in meaning. The existence-philosophical paradigm can be classified in accordance with a third "educative purpose" in Weber's sense of the word: the "awakening of charisma".[337] According to Weber, charismatic education is characterized by the very fact that it does not attempt to convey any doctrine but rather aims to potentiate an inward process of transformation which creates a new, completely changed identity. This "regeneration" entails the "development of the charismatic quality, and the testing, confirmation and selection of the qualified person".[338] Conceptually speaking and in accordance with this, the existence-philosophical utopia demands that education convey itself "indirectly" and without supplying a "recipe" to an "elite" which is characterized by its rigid commitment to "doctrine and discipline". In postulating a further aspect of his conception, Jaspers also follows Weber's model of charismatic socialization, namely when he speaks of a quasi-religious inner process – self-election through "inner being"[339] – whose aim was the "rebirth of human existence by means of which the past is transformed".[340] The goal of existence-philosophical socialization consists in an individual appropriation of the spiritual tradition and its personality ideals which Jaspers traces back to "the Jewish prophets and the Greek philosophers".[341] Thus the charismatic model of socialization conceptualized in *Man in the Modern Age* does not intend to effect an accumulation of cultural knowledge, but rather promotes individual and independent appropriation of philosophico-religious tradition as "remembered past".[342] What Jaspers does not desire is that an

---

[334] MMA, pg. 104; cf. GS, pg. 101f..
[335] Weber (1991), pg. 427; cf. Weber (1920a), pg. 409.
[336] Weber (1991), pg. 426; cf. Weber (1920a), pg. 408.
[337] Weber (1991), pg. 426; cf. Weber (1920a), pg. 408.
[338] Weber (1968), pg. 1143; cf. Weber (1922b), pg. 677.
[339] Cf. MMA, pg. 109; cf. GS, pg. 106.
[340] MMA, pg. 122; cf. pg. 121.
[341] MMA, pg. 188; cf. GS, pg. 193.
[342] MMA, pg. 195; cf. GS, pg. 201.

externally identical "philosophical life" as an ideal "type" emerge which could promote the formation of a school and do away with public anonymity.[343]

Despite the will to dispense with clear mediating processes, charismatic socialization possesses an identifiable affinity to several institutional realms which in Jaspers' view have the potential to promote its realization. In mass society the university, the family, marriage, and – as the least institutionalized realm – personal friendship have the capacity to promote the development of existence-philosophical life conduct to a decisive degree, Jaspers argues. For him the common denominator of such realms is the fact that they still offer "confidence", albeit "within very narrow circles".[344] By ascribing such features to these realms, Jaspers adheres strictly to the secularization thesis he shares with Weber which postulates a withdrawal of last value patterns from the public sphere and their relocation in the area of private life conduct. As Jaspers contends, those aspects of the university, marriage, family and friendship as institutions which can be shaped individually still allow to a larger extent for subjectively informed investments with meaning and corresponding life conduct, these having the capacity to create subtly discerned intersubjective commitments.

For Jaspers the university is a consciously elite institution, an "aristocratic affair of those who select themselves for its pursuit".[345] The self-selection demanded by Jaspers is not to be understood as a pedagogical program designed to produce and cultivate an educated class, nor is its task to create a cadre of specialists. Instead, the institution's primary function should be to open up stimulating space for individual self-education by means of charismatically socializing an elected elite of scientists and scholars; conveying the necessary scholarly, cultural and specialized knowledge is of secondary importance. In modern times the primary notion of a university has been almost completely abandoned for the benefit of pursuing secondary goals, so Jaspers contends. He writes:

> An enforced curriculum relieves the individual from the risks attendant upon seeking a path for himself. But without the hazards of liberty, there can be no possibility of independent thought. The final result is the skill of the specialised technician, and perhaps comprehensive knowledge[.][346]

Ideally, the university should, on an elementary level, impart scholarly, cultural and specialized "knowledge" and in addition promote charismatic socialization with the aim of generating "actual faith". Thus for Jaspers, socialization at the university constitutes a hybrid type of education combining all three types of education which Weber describes, but with the pedagogico-cultivative and the technico-pragmatic types being subordinated to the charismatic element. As Jaspers argues, the former have to do with objectifiable knowledge which can at best exhibit an awareness of their limits, assuming an optimal degree of scientific probity is given. "Genuine science is a knowledge that is accompanied by knowledge of the methods and limits

---

[343] MMA, pg. 198; cf. GS, pg. 203.
[344] MMA, pg. 80; cf. GS, pg. 76.
[345] MMA, pg. 137; cf. GS, pg. 137.
[346] MMA, pg. 137; cf. GS, pg. 137.

of knowledge."[347] Scientific awareness of the limits of objectifiable knowledge should awaken an interest in the vague knowledge of concealed transcendence lying beyond it, Jaspers says. Ideally, the separated spheres of knowledge and the accompanying modi of socialization can – from an existence-philosophical perspective – challenge and complement each other in terms of their differing cognitive perspectives.

Furthermore, the private aspects of the institutions of marriage and family are idealized by Jaspers in his notion of the "life of the home". He paints a picture of a miniscule, trustworthy and tradition-bound cosmos within mass society which plays a crucial role in promoting existence-philosophical life conduct. Jaspers writes:

> The home, the family community, is an outgrowth of the affection whereby the individual is bound to other members of that community in ties of life-long fidelity. Its aim is to bring up children in such a way as to incorporate them into the traditional substance of the society to which they belong, thus facilitating the perpetual intercommunication which only amid the difficulties of daily life can achieve unrestrained realisation.[348]

According to Jaspers' theory of secularization, the "life of the home" is, as a private refuge, one of the last "islands" in the "stream of the universal life order".[349] Jaspers sees marriage, like the university, as threatened by a public desintegration of values down to its very foundations, citing erotic liberality as a particularly large danger. As he contends, it causes a "chaos of wildness and bewilderment" which makes human beings lose their footing. Marriage is often now reduced to the status of a "contract", and as such it lacks all mutual trust and responsibility, he laments.[350]

Although less institutionalized than the university, marriage and the family, but legitimized through a bourgeois tradition, friendship takes on eminent significance for Jaspers' model designed to rekindle meaning-making in modern times. Friendship offers its own extremely rare and unprotected refuge where individuals can engage in open and trusting communication, inspiring each other in their endeavors to advance philosophical self-education and to preserve themselves in an ethically founded "solidarity of the self-existing".

Jaspers' selection of institutional realms is in no small measure influenced by his own biographical perspective. Apart from the fact that, as Jaspers says, the marriage with Gertrud Mayer invested existence philosophy with "depth" in the first place,[351] the biographical reference evidences itself in *Man in the Modern Age* exemplarily insofar as the work alludes to his own only friendship, the one with his brother-in-law Ernst Mayer. As Jaspers writes: "The others, those of the mass-categories, have dozens of men as friends who are not really friends; but a member of the élite is lucky if he has but one friend."[352] Jaspers' criticism of erotic liberality as a particular

---

[347] MMA, pg. 138; cf. GS, pg. 138.

[348] MMA, pg. 58; cf. GS, pg. 53.

[349] MMA, pg. 60; cf. GS, pg. 54.

[350] MMA, pg. 53; cf. GS, pg. 47.

[351] Cf. Jaspers (1967b) and this study, pg. 31.

[352] MMA, pg. 190; cf. GS, pg. 195. Jaspers got to know Ernst Mayer (1883-1952) during the time when they both studied medicine in Heidelberg. From this time on they were very close friends and when Jaspers married Mayer's sister Gertrud, family ties were established as well. Cf. PAKJ, pp. 40-45; PhA, pp. 47-53. For information on Ernst Mayer cf. Jaspers (1952a) and Raaflaub (1986).

threat to marriage which reduced its status to that of a "contract" and made it more difficult to cultivate mutual trust and honesty, becomes more understandable in the light of Jaspers' concrete look at the life conduct of Max Weber. This will be the focus of the next section.[353]

MAX WEBER AND LIFE CONDUCT

For Jaspers there exists only one, completely polarized, alternative between ethical non-committalism – a condition of "Nothingness"[354] – and the morally consistent decision of the individual to commit himself completely and uncomprisingly to life conduct in the sense of existence philosophy, which Jaspers calls the "absolute historicity of one's foundation".[355] According to Jaspers, its strict reference to transcendence excludes the "accomodation to various philosophies, as if there were various philosophies among which it was necessary to choose".[356] In other words, Jaspers does not propagate a pluralism of possible values, but rather a monism with individual existence as its frame of reference. This presupposes the reality of concealed transcendence as something which relativizes all other possible value systems.

In contrast, Max Weber sketches what he views as the mark of modernity, namely a new form of "polytheism" which replaced "[t]he lofty rationalism of an ethical-methodical conduct of life, which flows out of every religious prophecy", this having itself dethroned the polytheism of ancient times.[357] One main feature of this "polytheism of values" diagnosed by Weber is their mutual exclusivity; in the process of searching for values, no "gradual preferencing" occurs, but rather affirmation of one value means the negation of another, or at least strained coexistence insofar as mutually exclusive values are held by one and the same individual.[358]

Jaspers rejects such conflicting value pluralism categorically, but on the other hand he views Weber as a veritable guarantor for his existence-philosophical conception. He can only sustain this view by interpreting Weber in such a way as to avoid viewing the conflict-laden notion of value pluralism as Weber's 'last word'. Where Weber elucidates "ultimate conflicts most extensively", the "whole issue is relativized, becoming a mere possibility", says Jaspers. To illustrate this, Jaspers quotes Weber in claiming that "mentally constructed types of conflicts concerning life orders" were merely an expression of the recognition that "at this point, inner conflicts are possible and adequate", but not that "there is no perspective from which

---

[353] MMA, pg. 53; cf. GS, pg. 47.
[354] MMA, pg. 145; cf. GS, pg. 146.
[355] MMA, pg. 145f.; cf. GS, pg. 146f..
[356] MMA, pg. 145; cf. GS, pg. 146.
[357] Weber (1919b), pg. 605.
[358] Cf. Schluchter (1996), pg. 224f. and Weber (1949), pg. 14f. and 17f.; cf. Weber (1917), pg. 503f. and 507.

these could be viewed as resolved".[359] In other words, Jaspers attempts to take the
bite out of Weber's value pluralism by evaluating in particular those value conflicts
which are irresolvable from a moral-philosophical perspective in terms of purely
scientific, value-neutral, "sociological" analysis. And yet Jaspers does not irrevoca-
bly ascribe to Weber a philosophical confession which leans in either the direction
of value monism or value pluralism but rather remains extremely vague, maintaining
that Weber, in his sociological diagnosis of value pluralism, had merely limited it by
making a few marginal remarks.[360]

Towards the end of his life, Jaspers was forced to change his opinion on Weber's
value theory and most of all, he felt it necessary to revoke his idealization of Weber
as a prophetic figure in regard to existence-philosophical life conduct. The reason
for this lay in biographical disclosures which compelled Jaspers to reread Weber's
work. As Dieter Heinrich reports, in the 1960's Jaspers found himself confronted
with "love letters" written by Weber to his close friend Else Jaffé-Richthofen which
clearly documented Weber's attempts to keep his wife Marianne from discovering
"the kind of relationship he had entered into" and to conceal the fact that he had
"indeed used various tricks to hide it".[361] As a result, Jaspers had begun to "persistently rethink his view of Weber" because "the testimony of his work had formerly
presented an image" which, he claims, had divorced itself from "essential traits". As
Henrich tells us, Jaspers' Weber dossier contained notes written with "great anger".
They read: "Max Weber has committed betrayal. He has betrayed Marianne, himself, and all of those who saw his image."[362] Henrich's interpretation aptly avoids
the simplifying notion that "Jaspers' connection to Max Weber" was based on petty
prudery which did not extend beyond "trivial sociological knowledge about universities in small towns".[363] Henrich is right in seeing the wrathful disillusionment
experienced by Jaspers as founded not in any kind of antiquated bourgeois moralism, but rather in the sense of his philosophy; Jaspers' faith in Weber's "truthfulness", this expressing, for Jaspers, the man's "nature most clearly and prominently",
had been disappointed. As Henrich argues, Jaspers must have believed that "anyone
who looks the world in the face with such truthfulness" gained the "power to do so
from an intact foundation of human existence", i.e. possessed an integrative power
of a comprehensive, ethical nature which was to be found in what Jaspers called
"'communication'".[364] In his eye, Weber had profoundly failed to live up to the
expectation of reliability and trustworthiness in the intimate refuge of marriage, the

---

[359] Jaspers (1932a), pg. 97. Jaspers is refering to Weber, *Sociology of Religion* 1, pg.
537: "The constructed scheme, of course, only serves the purpose of offering an ideal
typical means of orientation. It does not teach a philosophy of its own. The theoretically
constructed types of conflicting 'life orders' are merely intended to show that at certain
points such and such internal conflicts are possible and 'adequate'. They are not
intended to show that there is no standpoint from which the conflicts could not be held
to be resolved in a higher synthesis." Weber (1991), pg. 323; cf. RS 1, pg. 537.
[360] Jaspers (1932a), pg. 97.
[361] Henrich (1986), pg. 24.
[362] Henrich (1986), pg. 26.
[363] Henrich (1986), pg. 26.
[364] Henrich (1986), pg. 25.

very institution built so profoundly on trust. Thus the position which Jaspers had held, namely that Weber did not teach a philosophy of truthfulness but rather embodied it, was clearly refuted as far as the center of existence-philosophical life conduct – the private sphere – was concerned.

In this time of personal disillusionment, Jaspers reread Weber's *Intermediate Reflection*.[365] Here the erotic is prized – probably not without autobiographical references – as an inner-wordly value which potentially collides with transcendentally oriented frameworks of values.[366] The intensive study of those passages in Weber's *Intermediate Reflection* devoted to the topic of erotic deliverance, traces of which are to be found in Jaspers' copy of Weber's *Sociology of Religion*, indicate the direction his new study of Weber's text had taken. Here Weber describes erotic, "marriage-free sexual life" as "innerworldly deliverance from the rational". This realm is placed in opposition to a "supraworldly ethic of deliverance", which is to say the "religious ethic of brotherhood" with its demand for interpersonal truthfulness.[367] Weber gave equal priority to immanent erotic deliverance from the yoke of intellectualism as well as transcendentally motivated "ethical responsibility for one another" so that – in case an individual recognized the legitimacy of both spheres of values – an irresolvable conflict of values could possibly arise.[368] Thus modern value pluralism or "polytheism" constituted a potential problem which, for Weber, was characteristically intrasubjective, – a problem which could not be resolved by a subordinated instance in one direction or the other. Thus Jaspers was forced to recognize that his earlier line of argumentation had been disillusionary. He had aimed to interpret Weber in the sense of transcendental value monism, opining that value conflicts did not constitute the final state of affairs, but were ultimately relativized by a transcendental dimension.

To be sure, what turned out to be a misinterpretation found affirmation in Weber's early writings. In regard to the psychoanalytically based notion of a life of erotic liberality, Weber had asserted a "heroic ethics" explicitly informed by Kantian-idealistic and Christian ideas against an "average ethics" which raised the human being's "everyday nature" to a normative standard. Else Jaffé-Richthofen, the later inamorate of Max Weber, was involved in a passionate relationship with Otto Gross at the time the controversy broke out and in 1907, Weber took a skeptical look at the psychoanalytically tinged "erotic movement" of the bourgeois *bohème*. Its notions of erotic deliverance took an intentionally antagonistic stance towards marriage as a civil institution. As Gross writes:

> The times of crisis experienced by high cultures have always followed laments about the relaxation of the marital institution and family ties. Marriage is essentially a peasant institution – as yet no one has identified this 'tendency towards immorality' as the life-affirming ethical cry for deliverance of humanity.[369]

Jaspers was cognizant of the critique of "average ethics" expressed in Weber's letter to Else Jaffé-Richthofen concerning the psychoanalytically based idea of erotic

---

[365] Cf. Weber (1991), pp. 523-559; Weber (1920a), pp. 536-573.
[366] Henrich (1986), pg. 26.
[367] Weber (1991), pg. 348; cf. Weber (1920a), pg. 561.
[368] Weber (1991), pg. 350; cf. Weber (1920a), pg. 563.
[369] Gross (1913), pg. 15f..

liberation because Marianne Weber included it in her 1926 Weber biography, to be sure quoting Otto Gross anonymously as "Dr. X".[370] Jaspers seems to have read Weber's later valorization of eroticism as innerwordly deliverance in the form articulated in his *Intermediate Reflection* as a purely sociological description of one conceivable intrasubjective value without connecting it to Weber as an individual until the biographical disclosures concerning Weber's relationship to Else Jaffé-Richthofen reached Jaspers' ears. Until this time, Jaspers held the view that Weber would solve any potential conflicts between the notion of erotic deliverance and responsible marriage exemplarily in the sense of interpersonal truthfulness.

As the notes in his Weber dossier evidence, the late disillusionment about Weber's pluralistic value theory made Jaspers keenly aware of the differences between Weber and himself. As Jaspers writes:

> [Weber's] rational stature shows [...] the battles, but not the unity [...]. In Weber's case, I have taken the latter to be self-evident for a long time. This assumption is clearly not correct. – The irresolvable question remains as to how far it would have been possible [...] to engage with Max Weber and communicate with him about that which cannot be grasped and articulated as a position, – that which extents beyond the rational discussion about interpretations of values, approaching [...] questions concerning the disclosure of existence. – I never realized any of this during Max Weber's lifetime – living, for my part, on the basis of something which Max Weber perhaps would not have been able to affirm, but might have tolerated had it been reshaped into a 'standpoint'.[371]

From the perspective of a history of ideas one can, in focusing one's attention on those passages in *Intermediate Reflection* which recognize responsible ethics as a possible standpoint, discern certain ideas which Jaspers shares with Weber. The former speaks of the "heterogenous" category of "ethical responsibility for one another" in marriage as opposed to "the purely erotic sphere" and describes the "feeling of a love which is conscious of responsibility throughout all the nuances of the organic life process 'up to the pianissimo of old age'". Weber values the notion of marriage which is rooted in complete truthfulness as something "unique and supreme".[372] As his copy of *Sociology of Religion* shows, Jaspers interprets these lines of Weber biographically as a confirmation of his responsible marriage to Marianne Weber; his marginal note refers to the "dedication"[373] of the book, which reads "Marianne Weber. 1893 'up to the pianissimo of old age'".[374] That Weber does not estimate the ethos of truthfulness which lies behind this concept of marriage as an elementary ideal in the sense of virtue ethics but rather makes his existence dependent upon a transcendental, inaccessible source is shown by his further formulations. He writes: "Rarely does life grant such value in pure form. He to whom it is given may speak of fate's fortune and grace – not of his own 'merit'."[375]

---

[370] Cf. Marianne Weber (1926), pp. 378-384.
[371] Henrich (1986), pg. 29.
[372] Weber (1991), pg. 350; cf. Weber (1920a), pg. 563.
[373] Cf. Jaspers' marginal note in his copy of Weber's *Religionssoziologie*, Vol. 1 (Weber 1922b), which is to be found in Jaspers' library entrusted to Dr. Hans Saner in Basle.
[374] Weber (1920b), dedication page without pagination.
[375] Weber (1991), pg. 350; cf. Weber (1920a), pg. 563.

In his *Philosophy* Jaspers makes reference to the transcendental source of marital love relationships as well. What Weber calls "grace of fate" Jaspers calls the "enounter of those who recognize that they have always belonged to each other",[376] and Weber's "fortune" corresponds to Jaspers' historical fortuitousness as "luck" which "the eternal dimension of time" is subject to.[377] In Jaspers' case this "metaphysical love"[378] also conflicts with erotic love, which, as he writes, only knows "the phantastic consciousness of eternity produced by intoxication".[379] Jaspers does not remain entangled in an ambivalence towards values like the later Weber in his *Intermediate Reflection*. Instead, he speaks unequivocally in favor of truthful marriage as a "miracle of history" which is capable of regulating "wild sexuality" and had founded the tradition rooted in commitment which prevails "between the spouses and towards the children".[380]

The interpretation of Jaspers' disillusionment over Weber shows that the martial ideal of truthfulness plays a central role in existence-philosophical life conduct and that Jaspers prizes the institution of marriage as a special realm in which existential interaction is put to the test. For Jaspers, private institutions in particular function as refuges and open realms in which to realize existence-philosophical life conduct in a secularized mass society. They demand and potentiate communication which is both truthworthy and deeply commited to unwavering responsibility and which can, as such, express and confirm Jaspers' inner existential faith. As Jaspers writes:

> But what is requisite is that a man, in conjunction with other men, should merge himself in the world as a historically concrete entity, so that, amid the universal homelessness, he may win for himself a new home. His remoteness from the world sets him free to immerse his being.[381]

For Jaspers, a veritably truthful and responsible life is basically only possible in private realms of life. As he contends, time cannot create any "genuine relationships"; these had to be "freely engendered by the individual in community life" as an "exclusive unconditioned" without returning to "authoritative forms" of institutional frameworks.[382] Thus existence-philosophical life conduct apparently realizes itself in the "personal destiny of the individual"; in further social action, i.e. in the "destiny of the contemporary titanic apparatus" it only expresses itself indirectly, so Jaspers' conceptualization.[383] In entertaining such ideas, Jaspers follows Weber and his concept of life conduct, which considers personal space in rationalized modernity to be the prerequisite for individual decisions on which actions to take. Existence philosophy also returns to the normative premise of Weber's sociology and systematizes it, making a philosophical norm out of it which is brought into play as a means of countering the factual rationalization tendencies of the modern age.

---

[376] KSP, pg. 149.
[377] KSP, pg. 151.
[378] KSP, pg. 149.
[379] KSP, pg. 150.
[380] KSP, pg. 148.
[381] MMA, pg. 184; cf. GS, pg. 188.
[382] MMA, pg. 183; cf. GS, pg. 187.
[383] MMA, pg. 170; cf. GS, pg. 174.

Looking back at the chapter as a whole one can say that *Man in the Modern Age* constitutes the sober description of an epoch no longer invested with the capacity to offer collective, all-encompassing patterns of meaning and culture, – an epoch which demanded of the individual that he ultimately choose his own patterns of life conduct. As far as this is concerned, Jaspers deems it possible and necessary for the individual to tap into the metaphysical tradition. In Jaspers' case, such a move resulted in the formulation of an ideal of existence-philosophical life conduct which, sociologically speaking, manifests a great affinity to the Protestant salvific type of life conduct championed by Weber. In this sense, Jaspers also shows a preference for relatively private institutional patterns which accommodate individualistic desires for freedom in terms of commitments to values and ascriptions of responsibility and are not de-emotionalized in the sense of goal-oriented rationality. From this perspective, the ethicization of philosophical religiosity expresses itself primarily in private institutions, with a tendency towards entering the public sphere. And yet for Jaspers, successful action indicated no more than an individual's inner viewpoint and was not seen as a goal in itself.

It is in terms of its transcendentally founded claim to truth that existence-philosophical life conduct shows itself to be incompatible with the pluralization of value patterns in modern times, as Jaspers' reading of Weber's *Intermediate Reflection* illustrates. Ultimately Jaspers was forced to vouch alone for that which he thought he had recognized as an indication of something sublime in Max Weber's private life conduct. As he writes,

> if that which extends beyond the intimacy of fortunate hours with those whom one is closest to, that which extends beyond reliable faithfulness fails in the ultimate, inner sense of the human being, then Max Weber is like the appearance of the origin in eternal presence, like perfection in the smallest dimension, for here all potential lies.[384]

---

[384] Jaspers (1932a), pg. 112.

CHAPTER 4

CRITIQUE OF PSYCHOANALYSIS IN 1931

> The root of all evil. Being one is godly and good; whence
> comes the pressing desire/among humans that there be but
> one and one be all?
>
> Hölderlin[385]

As the last chapter already indicated, the high expectations which modernity put on progress in the sciences are criticized in *Man in the Modern Age*, which puts forth arguments similar to those formulated by Max Weber. Jaspers challenges an optimistic view of progress which believes it can offer long-term solutions to human problems through scientific thought. He speaks of an overestimation of what the sciences are capable of doing which he characterizes acerbically as follows:

> a utopian knowledge concerning all that can further production, and the technical mas-
> tery of every difficulty in this field; welfare as the possibility of the life of the commu-
> nity at large, [...] and, in general, a faith in the data of the understanding regarded as
> dogmas unquestionably valid.[386]

Man in the Modern Age designates the disciplines of sociology, biological anthropology and psychology as the most questionable representatives of such methodologically uncritical science informed by an optimistic view of progress, and in doing so he refers specifically to Marxism, the "race theory" and psychoanalysis as especially dubious.[387] According to Jaspers, these three sciences, as "substitutes" for philosophy "devoid of hope", endeavored to gain insight into "man's being as a whole".[388] What Jaspers meant was that these sciences authoritatively construed their limited and often questionable insights as generalized value patterns of modern life conduct, thus exercising a form of ideological patronization.

Jaspers' assessment is based on Weber not only insofar as the latter had formulated a fundamental analysis of the sciences' belief in progress and self-authorization; Weber had also made some critical remarks about Marxism, race hygiene and

---

[385] Hölderlin (1969), pg. 36.
[386] MMA, pg. 138; cf. GS, pg. 138.
[387] MMA, pg. 157; cf. GS, pg. 159.
[388] MMA, pg. 148; Cf. GS, pg. 150.

psychoanalysis which Jaspers in part took note of.[389] Despite the many similar thoughts on these issues, a comparison between Weber and Jaspers also reveals illuminating differences, however. For this reason, this chapter will begin with presenting Weber's fundamental position of scientific value freedom and his specific critique of science before Jaspers' critique as formulated in *Man in the Modern Age* is discussed at length and compared to Weber's position. This will be followed by an excursus on Freud's own opinion concerning scientific value freedom as it is expressed in a work entitled *Concerning a World View (Über eine Weltanschauung).*[390]

MAX WEBER'S 'DOCTRINE OF SCIENCE'

'Value-Free' Science in Modern Times

According to Weber, the scientist, in particular the sociologist, is relatively free to let his special research interests guide his perspective within the complex network of factors which determine any given event. For Weber, this act of asserting a theoretical value judgment which determines the way in which reality is interpreted constitutes an act of heuristic creativity. As Weber writes,

> [...] without the investigator's evaluative ideas, there would be no principle of selection of subject-matter and no meaningful knowledge of the concrete reality. Just as without the investigator's conviction regarding the significance of particular cultural facts, every attempt to analyze concrete reality is absolutely meaningless, so the direction of his personal belief, the refraction of values in the prism of his mind, gives direction to his work.[391]

And yet, despite the complexity of reality and its connections, the range of adequate theoretical perspectives on value judgments made on any object of study is of course naturally limited and cannot be arbitrarily chosen. In a climate of accelerated cultural change, questions of study soon become obsolete and lose their power to provide insights so that in the new, normative constellation, the search for fresh,

---

[389] Jaspers was familiar with Weber's biting criticism of Otto Gross' psychoanalytic ideas, for it had been treated in Marianne Weber's biography from 1926; to be sure, Gross was referred to here anonymously as "Dr. X". Jaspers' private copy of the biography shows numerous pencil markings. Cf. Marianne Weber (1926), pp. 378-384. Concerning Weber's critique of marxism, which Jaspers had read in the *Doctrine of Science*, Jaspers interprets him in 1932 as follows: "Thus he pounced on the Marxist constructions by rejecting their absolutization and the totalizaiton of a world view." Cf. Jaspers (1932a), pg. 89. Jaspers might have read the printed form of Weber's extensive dispute with Alfred Ploetz at the Sociologists' Conference in 1910. Considering how relevant the topic was for the psychiatric discussion in Heidelberg, there were surely forums for taking up discussion with Weber. This holds true for other topics as well. To be sure, the pages on which the dispute between Weber and Ploetz is documented were not cut open in Jaspers' copy of the proceedings from the Sociologists' Conference.
[390] Cf. Freud, Works XXII, pp. 158-182; cf. Freud (1933), pp. 170-197.
[391] Cf. Weber (1949), pg. 82; Weber (1904), pg. 182.

fruitful perspectives is necessary if the sociologist wants to adequately grasp the specific nature of his age. As Weber writes,

> [t]he cultural problems which move men form themselves ever new and in different colors, and the boundaries of that area in the infinite stream of concrete events which acquires meaning and significance for us [...] are constantly subject to change.[392]

In Weber's eye, the "points of departure of the cultural sciences" must therefore be "changeable" if one does not want to risk "Chinese ossification of intellectual life".[393] By calling for variability in terms of the premises of sociological research as the seasonable condition for possible "objectivity", Weber acts to a high degree in accordance with the modern consciousness of crisis. In this situation, the theoretical value judgments which a researcher makes can have a considerable cultural influence on the society which they address. As Weber remarks, "the values to which the scientific genius relates the object of his inquiry may determine, i.e., decide the 'conception' of a whole epoch".[394] For any limited research perspective constitutes *nolens volens* a certain evaluation, as one draws attention away from analyses of reality which operate from a different vantage point. As Weber writes, "the more 'general' the problem involved, i.e., [...] the broader its cultural *significance*, the less subject it is to a single unambiguous answer on the basis of the data of empirical sciences and the greater the role played by value-ideas [...]".[395] The task of the humanities and the social sciences, namely to give orientation, is thus in no way neutral. The cultural-anthropological premise of Weber's sociology, which accentuates an individual concept of value- and purpose-oriented action, is a striking example of this. Weber writes:

> The transcendental presupposition of every *cultural science* lies not in our finding a certain culture of any 'culture' in general to be *valuable* but rather in the fact that we are *cultural beings*, endowed with the capacity and the will to take a deliberate attitude towards the world and to lend it *significance*. Whatever this significance may be, it will lead us to judge certain phenomena of human existence in its light and to respond to them as being (positively or negatively) meaningful.[396]

In regard to society's public sphere, the postulate of value freedom demands that theoretical value judgments be cleary indicated as normative scientific premises.

On the basis of these theoretical value judgments, scientific "objectivity" as a concept can only be used in quotation marks, Weber emphasizes. The same holds for the concept of "science 'without preconceptions'".[397] Often these statements concerning Weber's "postulate of value freedom" are interpreted erroneously. Weber defines "value freedom" as a "trivial" demand, this being

> that the investigator and teacher should keep unconditionally separate the establishment of empirical facts (including the 'value-oriented' conduct of the empirical individual whom he is investigating) and *his* own practical evaluations, i.e., his evaluation of these

---

[392] Cf. Weber (1949), pg. 84; Weber (1904), pg. 184.
[393] Cf. Weber (1949), pg. 84; Weber (1904), pg. 184.
[394] Cf. Weber (1949), pg. 82; Weber (1904), pg.182.
[395] Cf. Weber (1949), pg. 56; Weber (1904), pg. 153.
[396] Weber (1949), pg. 81; cf. Weber (1904), pg. 180.
[397] Cf. Weber (1989), pg. 18; cf. Weber (1919h), pg. 598.

facts as satisfactory or unsatisfactory (including among these facts evaluations made by
the empirical persons who are the objects of investigation). [398]

When Weber demands that facts and value judgments be distinguished from one
another, this does not mean that he is championing a positivistic perspective on
science. For Weber, scientific fact-finding is not merely the result of a logico-
rational procedure. It requires theoretical value judgments which determine, to a
decisive degree, the selection of the objects to be investigated, the questions to be
raised and the mode of the interpretation to be performed.

When value judgments are also used for practical purposes in order to change
expected, dreaded or inconclusive investigative results, Weber clearly speaks out
against etiquetting them as part of the scientific process. In this sense the postulate
of value freedom means that scientific interpretations must not be influenced by
practical, result-oriented value preferences beyond normative specifications. Scientific impartiality as a virtue entails the capacity to refrain from shunning potentially
undesirable insights by misinterpreting them despite strong self-interests which
prompt one to do so. In other words, "intellectual probity" demands that the scientist
recognize in particular "personally uncomfortable" facts.[399] He must "subordinate
himself to his task and [...] repress the impulse to exhibit his personal tastes or other
sentiments unnecessarily".[400]

Not until heuristically necessary theoretical value judgments are distinguished
from unreflected praxis-oriented ones can possible misunderstandings be reduced,
Weber maintains. When he cites "factual truth", he is not using this as an argument
in favor of scientific positivism.[401] On the contrary, in the interest of "intellectual
probity", Weber rejects the tacet legitimization of value judgments on the basis of
scientific authority, with scientists claiming that facts 'speak for themselves' without
having called attention to implicit theoretical value judgments beforehand. As
Weber sees it, scientific "objectivities" appear suggestive in the context of the modern orientation crisis in particular. Their unavoidable relativity, which, as he says,
results from the theoretical value judgments they are based on, is often not perceived
as such, and what appears to be their compelling generalizability is postulated on the
basis of the logico-rational procedure by which they are yielded.

Moreover, practical value judgments are not identified as such due to what appears to be a pure claim to objectivity. For this reason, the lectern as the symbol of
the uncontrollable power of the professor is in danger of being abused for political
and cultural value judgments, Weber cautions. Such practical judgments belong in
"newspapers, assemblies [...] and essays", he says; one must not proclaim
"evaluations on ultimate questions 'in the name of science' in governmentally
privileged lecture halls in which they are neither controlled, checked by discussion,
nor subject to contradiction".[402]

---

[398] Cf. Weber (1949), pg. 11; cf. Weber (1917), pg. 500.
[399] Cf. Weber (1949), pg. 5; Weber (1917), pg. 493.
[400] Cf. Weber (1949), pg. 54f.; cf. Weber (1904), pg. 151.
[401] Weber (1949), pg. 58; cf. Weber (1904), pg. 155.
[402] Cf. Weber (1949), pg. 4; cf. Weber (1917), p. 492.

Monocausal Research and Philosophy of History

The theoretical value judgments of every empirically oriented social science are of necessity accompanied by perspective reductionism. This Weber prizes as a truly creative aspect of every scientific inquiry. The motivational dynamics of his interest in investigating Protestantism, which looks into the influence of the Protestant ethic on the development of capitalism, can be cited as a striking example of how to limit one's perspective of multi-factoral economic life to good purpose. Following this argument, it would have been possible for Weber to make geographic, social or political determinants of the economic system the central perspective of his socio-logy rather than opting for its "religious determination". The attempt to take all such perspectives into consideration would be equivalent to "navigating the boundless", says Weber.[403] The aim to exact a totality of vision by claiming that a research per-spective which is of necessity reductive is able to gain insights into reality as a whole is rejected by Weber, because for him, such an attempt merely constitutes an "abstraction of the 'total context'".[404] In other words, the monocausal analysis of history must not be transformed into a monocausal philosophy of history via a gen-eralizing superelevation of its constitutive value judgment because as a mere heuris-tic instrument, it can only be used to any good purpose if employed within a limited framework. If one aims to provide the decisive factor for describing a complex event, this puts excessive demands on the heuristically, necessarily reductive value judgment in question.

In various places, Weber particularly criticizes the "materialistic concept of his-tory", anthropology based on race hygiene and certain types of psychoanalytic thought as more or less monocausally oriented philosophies of history. According to his assessment, all three disciplines succumb to the temptation – so prevalent in modern times – to normatively derive from specialized scientific knowledge an ideological philosophy of history.

In view of the critique of psychoanalysis articulated in *Man in the Modern Age,* Weber's consideration of Freud disciple Otto Gross' idiosyncratic approach to psychoanalysis is meaningful. The latter's psychoanalytic theory about the patho-genic effect of repressed sexuality aims to reform bourgeois life conduct by radically liberalizing eroticism. Most of all, Weber took offense at the fact that this psycho-analytic theorist set an erotic ideal of life conduct against the bourgeois ideal and claimed his ideal could be scientifically legitimized by virtue of its psychological truth. Weber speaks of a "psychiatric ethics" which champions utilitaristic cost-benefit rationality based on the hypothesis of emotional well-being which used the "psychiatrist as an authority". Weber clearly subjects Gross' psychoanalytic ap-proach to the limits of the postulate of value freedom when he writes that "no science and so scientific insight, as important as it may be, – and I count Freud's discoveries, should they turn out to be valid in the long run, as certainly belonging to

---

[403] Cf. Weber (1991), pg. 268; Weber (1920a), pp. 238-239.
[404] Weber (1907), pg. 316.

the most important ones –, supplies a 'world view'".[405] To Gross's credit, Weber recognizes that any fresh enthusiasm for new insights – and he speaks here of "apparently unavoidable childhood stage" of the discipline – typically brings with itself an overestimation of its import so that one could easily be led to believe oneself a "discoverer of new values, called to reform 'ethics'".[406]

In another work Weber addresses the dogmatic, hermetic group formation of psychoanalysts without referring to them by name when he writes:

> You must realize that certain theories of a medical nature, certain psychiatric theories, are quite evidently on the way to forming a sect, i.e. that a theory formulated by a famous Viennese psychiatrist has led to the formation of a sect which has already reached the point of barring those who do not belong to them from any participation in their meetings and being secretive.[407]

In expressing this sentiment he points out that psychoanalytic ideas exert a strong influence on the entire life conduct of those who propagate them due to the intense reception of such ideas in a confessionally defined, closed community. As a practical example, Weber cites Otto Gross and the way he experienced him in Heidelberg. He writes:

> The 'complex-free' human being as the ideal and a form of life conduct which promises to create and maintain such a 'complex-free' human being is the object of this sectarian enterprise. The most diverse branches of life are regulated on the basis of these ideals – this being a fact which no one who looks at these theories as psychiatric in nature and intended for scientific purposes, could conclude.[408]

In the 20th century, the danger that scientifically based philosophies of history might monopolize individual and collective life conduct has become horrific reality in many respects. Karl Dietrich Bracher speaks of this development in his book entitled *Era of Ideologies* (*Zeit der Ideologien*).[409] And today probably no one would disagree that in addition to National Socialism, the Soviet brand of Marxism, as another political ideology, made it almost impossible for inhabitants of many Eastern European countries to exercise the relatively high degree of freedom in regard to life conduct which had increasingly asserted itself in Western culture during the Modern Age. In another arena, the notion of race hygiene argued by such theorists as Alfred Ploetz became an ideological instrument used by the National Socialists. In the course of cooperation with political powers, the uncorroborated findings of scientists working in this area gained more scientific recognition after research funding was granted by the State. In turn, the State's new interests received medical legitimization. Only recently, Detlev Peukert took Weber's critical remarks on Alfred Ploetz and the theory of race hygiene which is associated with him one step further, interpretating them even more drastically in the context of the social

---

[405] Letter from Max Weber to Else Jaffé-Richthofen from September 13, 1907, in Weber (1990), pg. 403.
[406] Letter from Max Weber to Else Jaffé-Richthofen from September 13, 1907, in Weber (1990), pg. 396.
[407] Weber (1910), pg. 446.
[408] Weber (1910), pg. 446.
[409] Cf. Bracher (1984).

sciences and the humanities in light of developments which occured during the National Socialist years. As Peukert contends, since the beginning of society's orientation crisis at the turn of the century – during the Weimar years in particular – , various humanities had abused their increasing authority as disciplines by abetting "the empowerment of the totalitarian system in its public treatment of human beings" in the course of "socio-cultural ideologization processes". Peukert argues that in times of historic crisis, the "aim to better", usually put forth without any criminal intentions, often turns into "normation and registering strategies which lead to the exclusion of all who do not comply with the norm, ultimately resulting in the stigmatization of such persons as 'inferior' or even 'unworthy of living'". Peukert sees this as a phenomenon to be found not only during the years of Nazi dictatorship.[410]

With its cultural-critical approach, psychoanalysis primarily targeted the personality and life conduct of individuals, and as compared to marxism and race hygiene, it had fewer pan-societial implications, Bracher observes. In this respect its impact was similar to that of artistic and literary circles during the Weimar years, which was also limited to the private sphere, he contends, writing:

> Whoever could read, write, paint or compose wanted to proclaim a new 'movement'. This was certainly to the benefit of literature and art. It flourished, experimented, took completely new, unknown paths which the collapse of previous authorities had opened up.[411]

In contrast to the relatively small impact of private innovations, Bracher emphasizes the consequences of politically prescribed reformations, which had great repercussions for the private sphere. He writes:

> As opposed to art, political thought was thrown into a state of confusion by the fragmentation of the ideational framework, which opened up inauspicious possibilities when experimentation and a cult of intuition lessened society's sense of responsibility and its awareness of the consequences.[412]

When Weber expresses his disdain for the historico-philosophical goals of Marxism and race hygiene more clearly than he had articulated his rejection of the psychoanalytically informed cultural ideals of Otto Gross, he is passing judgment as a pluralistic, liberal sociologist who holds the freedom of the individual to shape his own existence in high esteem as a value premise. Therefore he only exercised fierce criticism when efforts were being made to scientifically legitimize a type of life conduct which was implemented in the sense of a political program against the will of the individuals who were affected.

For Jaspers, the much less pronounced role which psychoanalysis played as a politico-societal instrument of power during the years of the Weimar Republic gave him no cause to attack it less vehemently than the philosophy of history formulated by Marxism or proponents of race hygiene. On the contrary, the liberal culture of life conduct which he associated with it was precisely what caused psychoanalysis to

---

[410] Cf. Peukert (1989), pp. 55-121, pg. 67f..

[411] Bracher (1984), pg. 50f..

[412] Bracher (1984), pg. 50f..

provoke him so much, for it competed with what he was attempting to convey in existence-philosophical terms. Otto Gross' "erotic movement" in particular was taken by Jaspers as condensed evidence of his diffuse apprehensiveness.[413] At the end of this chapter these connections will be elucidated more extensively.

KARL JASPERS AND THE 'HUMAN SCIENCES'

Critique of Ideologies: Marxism, Race Hygiene and Psychoanalysis

Weber's liberal stance, which held that the individual should not be unjustifiably limited in his capacity to make his own decisions by scientific "objectivities", echos in Jaspers' writings, for example in the following passage.

> What the individual can be transformed into sociologically or psychologically or anthropologically, is not accepted by him as cogent without qualification. By comprehending cognisable reality as something particular and relative, he emancipates himself from that which the sciences would like definitively to make of him.[414]

In another passage we find thoughts in a similar vein which correspond with Weber's critique of scientific philosophies of history, reading:

> The cognitions of human existence which are to be grasped in particular trends have become, as sociology, psychology, and anthropology, the typical modern sciences, which, when they put forward a claim to absolute validity and pretend themselves to be capable of cognising man's being as a whole, must be rejected as utterly inadequate substitutes for philosophy.[415]

Time and again Jaspers emphasizes that even human self-recognition is subject to clear this-worldly limitations. "All cognition in the world, human cognition included, is a particular perspective [...]."[416] Thus *Man in the Modern Age* foregrounds this argument steeped in epistemological skepticism in order to constrict the practical claim made by three "typically modern sciences". Jaspers writes:

> No sociology can tell me what I will as destiny; no psychology can make it clear to me what I really am; the true being of man cannot be bred as a race. In all directions we reach the limit of what can be planned and made.[417]

In particular, Jaspers dismisses the belief in progress which informed the psychologically, sociologically and biologico-anthropologically oriented sciences, writing:

> The idea of mere life as completed in a condition wherein there are no tensions is, in this mode of cognition, involuntarily regarded as attainable. There is deemed possible a sociological order wherein all will enter into their rights; a mind wherein the uncon-

---

[413] Jaspers was familiar with Weber's criticism of Gross as it was articulated in 1907; Marianne Weber had cited it in her 1926 biography of her husband. Cf. this study, pg. 59f.

[414] MMA, pg. 158f.; cf. GS, pg. 160f..

[415] MMA, pg. 148; cf. GS, pg. 150.

[416] MMA, pg. 148; cf. GS, pg. 149.

[417] MMA, pg. 157; Cf. GS, pg. 158f..

scious and the conscious will be amicable companions as soon as the former has been
purged of all its complexes; a racial vitality which, after an efficient process of artificial
selection has done its work, will lead to the universalisation of a healthy mind and body
so that all will be satisfied in a perfected life.[418]

As Jaspers emphasizes, these sciences cannot do away with the question of theodicy. He contends – not unlike Weber – that mankind and the world he lives in
evidence a residual sum of imperfection which always provokes new philosphico-
metaphysical attempts at compensating for this fact. As Jaspers sees it, the three
sciences which subscribe to the faith in progress have the tendency to usurp control.
The critic has a point when he reproaches them for fostering a real aggression
against metaphysical attempts to address the question of theodicy. As Jaspers maintains, Marxism desires to reveal "spiritual life" as "a superstructure erected upon
material foundations", psychoanalysis disdains "culture" for enacting the "sublima-
tion of repressed impulses" and "obsessional neurosis" and race theory develops a
purely biological philosophy of history. Jaspers sums up his diagnosis by saying that
for these respective reasons, all three disciplines had effected the "ruin of true human existence" and had furthermore attempted to destroy "philosophical faith".[419]

For Jaspers this existence-philosophical faith is contingent on the fact that humankind is not completely defined, in other words, that metaphysically speaking,
human beings remain lacking in something. Expressed positively, one could say that
man is "incomplete and insusceptible of completion", that he "in all his cognitions,
still does not discover himself to be thoroughly known", and is "delivered over to
something other than himself".[420] This existence-philosophical anthropology is characterized by the relatively open attitude it adopts in terms of potential types of individual self-definition. As Jaspers writes:

> Man is always something more than what he knows of himself. He is not what he is
> simply once for all, but is a process; he is not merely an extant life, but is, within that
> life, endowed with possibilities through the freedom he possesses to make himself what
> he will by the activities on which he decides.[421]

To be sure, Jaspers' existence philosophy does not tolerate all forms of self-
definition; these must at least evidence a pre-modern perspective of transcendance
which *Man in the Modern Age* perceives as being attacked by the three disciplines it
criticizes.

The reproach that these three disciplines exceed the "limits of the cognisable"[422]
corresponds – so to say, as a counter-measure – to a rigid interpretation of the postulate of value-freedom. Thus *Man in the Modern Age* subsumes the empirical sciences under the term "specific expert knowledge", which is intended to signalize
their value neutrality. For Jaspers, such scientific "expert knowledge" possesses no
normativity of its own but rather this is supplied by the specific contexts of application. "The best laws, the most admirable institutions, the most trustworthy acquire-
ments of knowledge, the most effective technique, can be used in conflicting

---

[418] MMA, pg. 147; cf. GS, pg. 148.
[419] MMA, pg. 157; cf. GS, pg. 159.
[420] MMA, pg. 148; cf. GS, pg. 149.
[421] MMA, pg. 146; cf. GS, pg. 147.
[422] MMA, pg. 159; cf. GS, pg. 161.

ways,"[423] Jaspers writes. He prescribes "substantial" normation processes as necessary supplements to the purely instrumental, goal-oriented rationality of the sciences, – processes which he thinks are crucial for the intended purposes. From his
perspective the best we can expect is that use – oriented to the tenets of existence
philosophy – is made of the as yet purpose-free instrumental possibilities. "Exis-
tence-philosophy is the way of thought by means of which man seeks to become
himself; it makes use of expert knowledge while at the same time going beyond
it."[424]. Therefore in Jaspers' eye what is crucial when evaluating expert knowledge
is primarily the personal ethos of the scientist, "man's being" and his "inward attitude".[425] Thus this notion of science as pure "expert knowledge" identifies in an
almost positivistic way the epistemological sphere of science with compelling, generally valid objectivity and couples it secondarily with the necessary supplement of
individually defined purposes of application. The suggestive concept of "expert
knowledge" would seem to want to deny that, as Weber posits, the empirically oriented human and social sciences can never be free of theoretical value judgments.

   In other places Jaspers allows that Weber's postulate of value freedom is right in
maintaining that theoretical value judgments are responsible for the selection of the
material, i.e. that the decision in favor of a certain kind of critical inquiry rests on a
subjective decision about values.[426] The scientific investigation itself, as an "act of
insight", is considered by Jaspers to be free of the investigator's own "desires and
sympathies", which were merely capable of "providing fruitful impulses" and "rendering a clear-sighted perspective".[427] Apparently even the less rigid notion of scientific value freedom which Jaspers at times entertains does not correspond to
Weber's understanding of the term, however. For Jaspers limits the normative aspect
to the process of forming a scientific perspective, excluding the interpretative process from the inevitably result-impacting framework of values. This is precisely what
Weber does not do in his epistemological considerations.[428]

   If one follows Kurt Salamun in seeking reasons for the "narrowly defined concept of science",[429] one can certainly agree that the resistance against ideological
instrumentalization was a central motive for Jaspers. The anti-ideological tendency
of this restrictive understanding of science was already commented on in a detailed
analysis conducted by Otto Friedrich Bollnow in 1938. The young *Privatdozent*
more or less advocated the dominating spirit of the age in regretting that Jaspers did
not allow any "creative", i.e. practical value judgments to be made in the sense of a
nationalistic philosophy of history.[430]

   Bollnow was right in pointing out that Jaspers did not primarily reject the cou-
pling of scientific study with value judgments for metascientific reasons, but rather
on the basis of his existence-philosophical approach. For the "purity" of individually

---

[423] MMA, pg. 159; cf. GS, pg. 161.
[424] MMA, pg. 159; cf. GS, pg. 161.
[425] MMA, pg. 159; cf. GS, pg. 161.
[426] Jaspers (1932a), pg. 87.
[427] Jaspers (1938), pg. 6.
[428] Cf. this study, pp. 64-66.
[429] Salamun (1985), pp. 127-32, pg. 127.
[430] Bollnow (1938), pg. 203.

based existence-philosophical faith would be endangered were science to extend into this area with its compelling claim to validity, thus suspending the constitutive "uncertainty" of ontological statements about concealed transcendence.[431]

As already indicated earlier, existence-philosophical experiences of transcendence are envisioned as being based on incommunicable "mystic" evidence which need not enter into intellectual conflict with objectifiable knowledge.[432] To be sure, such – as it were – mystical faith can appear to someone who has never seen evidence of it, i.e. someone who is lacking in the necessary religious musicality,[433] as a sterile notion. This seems to be the case with Bollnow, who refers to Jaspers' existence philosophy as an "abstract alternative" to a nationalistic philosophy of history.[434] In the ideologized era of National Socialism, the existence-philosophical orientation towards unfixed statements in the sense of "ciphers of transcendence" offered no possibilities for tapping into and legitimizing norms in any substantial way. And yet Jaspers did not fail to "satisfactorily observe the role played by the principle of value freedom as an ideal to at least strive for"; the sharp distinction made between objective science and subjective values was motivated by the program laid out by his existence philosophy, which did not see ultimate value ascriptions as connected with scientific certainties.[435]

Psychoanalysis and Otto Gross' 'Erotic Movement'

If one considers the specific criticism of psychoanalysis which Jaspers formulates in concentrated, sentential form on two pages of his *Man in the Modern Age*,[436] three thematic lines of attack emerge which echo those to be found in the *General Psychopathology* of 1920. For one, Jaspers sketches out his epistemological critique; secondly, he contrasts psychoanalytic self-reflection to its disadvantage with the philosophical tradition; and thirdly and most pronouncedly, he addresses its criticism of bourgeois sexual morality.

The terse epistemological misgivings which Jaspers airs orient themselves towards Weber. Jaspers relativizes the "merit" by pointing out the lack of "a convincing record of cases".[437] In a similar vein, Weber had written to Gross demanding the "creation of exact casuistics", these being, as he wrote, necessary in order to adequately assess psychoanalytic theories.[438] In the course of Jaspers' considerations formulated in *Man in the Modern Age*, he increasingly condenses the passages

---

[431] Cf. Bollnow (1938), p. 206 and Ph 3, pg. 157.

[432] Cf. this study, pg. 47f. Also cf. Weber (1991), pg. 352; Weber (1920a), pg. 566.

[433] Cf. Weber (1989), pg. 28; Weber (1919b), pg. 610.

[434] Bollnow (1938), pg. 203.

[435] Salamun (1985), pg. 130. From a purely epistemological perspective, Jaspers follows Kant in assuming that "all cognizing subjects [possess] mutual formal conditions for cognition irrespective of their individual-subjective particularities", these being conditions broad enough to provide grounds for positing general and compelling validity.

[436] Cf. MMA, pg. 154f..

[437] MMA, pg. 153; cf. GS, pg. 154.

[438] Marianne Weber (1926), pp. 378-384, pg. 379f..

which explain certain aspects of psychoanalysis – already to be found in the 1920 edition of his *General Psychopathology* – without any further comment. Unquestionably, psychopathological aspects play only a marginal role here.

Psychoanalytic self-reflection is contrasted with the existence-philosophical approach in a manner as derogatory as that adopted in the 1920 *Psychopathology*. As Jaspers writes, the latter may invoke the notion of "the self-examination of a sincere thinker" as put forward by Kierkegaard and Nietzsche, they having elevated it as far as possible after a "long-lasting Christian interlude".[439] Jaspers contends that in psychoanalysis, such self-examination had been "degraded into the discovery of sexual longings".[440] According to Jaspers, "genuine but hazardous self-examination" is "masked [...] by the mere rediscovery of familiar types in a realm of reputed necessity wherein the lower levels of human life are regarded as having an absolute validity".[441] Once again, Freud is excluded to a considerable degree from Jaspers' criticism, being called a "restrained" and "gentelly reserved personality" with a sometimes quite fascinating style.[442] To be sure, Jaspers remarks, he did not prevent his students from living their Bohemian lifestyle, whose aim was to "liberate themselves from the fetters without the bathos of new fetters".[443] Without a doubt, Otto Gross, as a distinguished representative of the Schwabing *bohème* after 1900, stands for this group of Freud students, as Jaspers' further commentaries on the psychoanalytic critique of bourgeois sexual morality show, they using Weber's remarks on Otto Gross as their point of departure.

In this context, Jaspers speaks of the instinctive "affirmation of the human being in his all-too-human aspect" and the "self-justification of existence in its naked facticity". According to Jaspers, psychoanalysis aims to achieve a situation in which "from the cleavage and coercion through which man could come to himself, he is to return to that nature in which he no longer needs to be man".[444] Jaspers places these remarks in the pejorative context of his critique of the age, writing: "Thus in psychoanalysis there are gathered together various elements intended to show the perplexed masses what man really is."[445] In terms of existence philosophy, *Man in the Modern Age* follows Weber's assessment, expressed vis-a-vis Otto Gross in 1907, an assessment Jaspers was well familiar with, having found it cited in the Weber biography from the year 1926.[446]

Weber's 1907 critique of psychoanalysis had distinguished two polar, mutually exclusive ethical concepts: a Kantian, duty-oriented "heroic ethics" and an inclination-oriented "average ethics". According to Weber's early notions, the individual acts in accordance with duty in a Kantian sense and is moreover guided by a clear definition of values to help him resist the pull of natural inclination and mood in a

---

[439] MMA, pg. 153; cf. GS, pg. 155.
[440] MMA, pg. 153; cf. GS, pg. 155.
[441] MMA, pg. 153; cf. GS, pg. 155.
[442] AP 2, pg. 293.
[443] AP 2, pg. 293.
[444] MMA, pg. 154; cf. GS, pg. 155.
[445] MMA, pg. 153; cf. GS, pg. 155.
[446] Cf. this study, pg. 59f..

culturally calculatable manner.[447] In the sense of this distinction, he criticizes the naturalistic ethics of Otto Gross which maintains that human nature is straitjacketed by culture – particularly through its sexual morals – and that it requires freedom if the human being is to harmonize with life.

> Only the first category, 'heroic ethics', can call itself 'idealism', and the ethics of old, intact Christianity as well as Kantian ethics both belong to this category. Both subscribe to such a pessimistic assessment of the 'nature' of the average individual – in keeping with their ideals – that Freud's discoveries from the realm of the unconscious could add no new 'terrible' aspects. – Insofar as 'psychiatric ethics' only demands that one 'admit what one is and what one has desired', it truly makes no new ethic demands of any kind.[448]

Weber contrasts Gross' ideal, i.e. the elimination of cultural repression in the service of fulfilled personalities, with a skeptical view of human nature as put forth by Kantian-Christian heroic ethics. Weber's notion of how best to deal with human nature – at this time in any case – is to subject it to ultimate norms in the sense of an individualistic heroic ethics which does *not* affirm natural inclinations. Jaspers is no doubt personally fascinated by this view, and *Man in the Modern Age* adopts it as an indirect criticism of Otto Gross, whom Freud and C.G. Jung had given up as lost for psychoanalysis in 1908 after diagnosing him with "Dementia praecox".[449]

Jaspers most probably never read Freud's famous essay entitled *Civilization and its Discontents* (*Das Unbehagen in der Kultur*), which was published one year before *Man in the Modern Age*. But on the basis of his reading of Freud's *Introductory Lectures to Psychoanalysis*, it was clear to Jaspers in 1931 that Freud's criticism of sexual morality as it prevailed at the time did not imply its radical nivellation, as sometimes-student Otto Gross had envisioned. For in his lectures, Freud also wrote in a pronounced cultural-pessimistic vein and in this sense he viewed the cultural repression of human drives as an endeavor which was indispensible, if also uncertain in terms of its ultimate effects, contending that it should be undertaken in the interests of social existence. One central task of psychoanalysis, so Freud would seem to be saying, is to weigh the "psychical constitution" of the individual against the dominant culture using as one's measure a compromise tolerable for both sides.[450]

---

[447] Weber's heroic-ethical "idealism" is described by Schluchter as a conflict between "naturality and culturality"; the human being is to escape his "naturality" by the connection to "supraempirical values". Cf. Schluchter (1988), pg. 192.

[448] Marianne Weber (1926), pg. 382 and Weber (1990), pg. 399f. Cf. Schluchter's interpretation (Schluchter, 1988, pp. 188-194).

[449] Cf. Freud/Jung, Letters (1974), pp. 155-161; Freud/Jung, Briefe (1974), pp. 172-178. Gross was indeed dependent on cocain for many years despite several withdrawal treatments. In 1913 he was confined in an institution as a result of efforts taken by his father, the famous criminal psychologist Hans Gross from Graz. This led to heated protests on the part of artists and writers. Gross' persistent drug abuse was a contributing factor to his death in Berlin in 1920. Cf. Hurwitz (1979), pp. 302-306.

[450] Freud, Works XXI, pg. 83; cf. Freud (1930), pg. 442.

CHAPTER 5

CRITIQUE OF PSYCHOANALYSIS IN 1941

> Psychoanalysis! Diagnoses! Formulas! I would bite any
> psychiatrist in the hand who got it into his mind to eviscerate
> my inner life.
>
> Witold Gombrowicz[451]

Jaspers wrote his new *General Psychopathology* during the war years, between June 1941 and July 1942. Various reasons can be offered to explain the fact that after almost twenty years of silence in this respect – not taking into account the "pathographic analyses" and the chapter on illness in his Nietzsche-book,[452] he was personally confident enough again, and still scientifically confident enough to address psychiatric issues in a comprehensive analysis. For one, the third edition from 1923 was now out of print and the publisher had expressed the wish for a "new revision" by Jaspers.[453] Secondly, he now felt he could compensate for his lack of clinical experience, which had been criticized since the publication of the second edition, through his philosophically sharpened methodological sensibility. As he writes:

> One danger posed by having me do the new revision is of course the dearth which re-
> sults from my current lack of demonstration. This will create an even greater distance
> from the concrete than before. On the other hand I believe that my long years of study
> for my main works which are now in progress (*On Philosophical Logic* and *Universal
> History of Philosophy*) are not a disadvantage, but rather a benefit. The methodological
> foundation of the book will hopefully present itself as more lucid and richer.[454]

And thirdly, he had in Kurt Schneider, who had rendered an original version of his psychopathological concept, a competent consultant in regard to the state of psychiatric research. As their extensive correspondance from the time when the *General Psychopathology* was being written between June 1941 and July 1942 documents, Jaspers' sense of indebtedness to the "fierce criticism" and "valuable comments" is completely justified.[455]

A further help, but one which in retrospect must be viewed with ambivalence, was the fact that Jaspers had unlimited access to the library of the Heidelberg

---

[451] Gombrowicz (1988), pg. 238.
[452] Cf. Jaspers (1926) and Jaspers (1936), pp. 91-119.
[453] Cf. letter from Karl Jaspers to Kurt Schneider from June 11, 1941, JLE-GLA.
[454] Letter from Karl Jaspers to Kurt Schneider from June 11, 1941, PPJ-GLA.
[455] Cf. letter from Kurt Schneider to Karl Jaspers from October 11, 1946, PPJ-GLA.

Clinic.[456] Carl Schneider, professor in Heidelberg at the time, was one of those physicians whose research projects had quite directly profited from the killing of patients in the course of so-called euthanasia. Since the 'Crystal Night' in November of 1938, Jaspers and his Jewish wife were certainly aware that they were in "constant life danger".[457] The life-threatening situation was one of the most compelling reasons for Jaspers to take the enormous task of refamiliarizing himself with the psychiatric subject matter in the first place. For when his chances of emigrating to Switzerland proved futile in 1941, one of the few possibilities for averting persecution was to increase his reputation as a scientist. Apart from possible translations of his philosophical writings in Japan and Italy, the perspective of heightening his renown as a psychiatrist provided him with an opportunity which – in light of the official ban on speaking and writing as a philosopher – had to be seized upon. When the manuscript was completed in 1942, the paper needed to print it was not alloted. This had to have been a disappointment for Jaspers. As he writes, "this would have been a highly desirable time to increase my prestige through the appearance of my book".[458] In 1943 he also informed Ludwig Binswanger of the existence of his book, but Binswanger's offer to help him find a publisher in Switzerland failed – probably due to the hurdles of National Socialist censorship.[459] As it happened, the book did not appear until the end of 1946, "without any alterations or abridgement".[460]

The chronology of the emergence and publication of the new *Psychopathology* must be supplemented by several remarks on Jaspers' relationship to Mitscherlich, who was to become the most important pioneer to achieve recognition of psychoanalysis at the university level and in society at large in the Federal Republic of Germany. Mitscherlich, who had studied medicine in Heidelberg since 1938 and had held a position as an assistant physician in neurology at the Heidelberg Clinic since 1941, belonged to the political resistance grouped around Emil Henk during the war years. Henk had offered Jaspers a refuge in case his wife were to be in danger of deportment.[461] In his biography *A Life Devoted to Psychoanalysis* (*Ein Leben für die Psychoanalyse*), Mitscherlich writes:

> I had gotten to know Jaspers through a circle of Anti-Nazis. At the time we were getting a refuge ready for Mrs. Jaspers, to which she probably could have retreated any time without putting herself into danger. During the entire war years, I went to have one- or two-hour-long talks with Jaspers on many Thursday afternoons. He introduced me to many problems concerning the history of philosophy. [...] Our relationship was overshadowed by Jaspers' frenetic disdain for psychoanalysis, however.[462]

---

[456] Cf. GP 4, pg. xx; AP 4, pg. V.

[457] Jaspers (1967b), pg. 35.

[458] Draft of letter from Karl Jaspers to Viktor v.Weizsäcker from November 7, 1942, PP-GLA.

[459] Cf. letter from Karl Jaspers to Ludwig Binswanger from March 8, 1943, JLE-GLA and copy of letter from Ludwig Binswanger to Karl Jaspers from March 16, 1943, Binswanger estate, UA Tübingen.

[460] GP 4, pg. xx; AP 4, pg. V.

[461] Cf. Saner (1970), pg. 48.

[462] Cf. Mitscherlich (1982), pg. 123f..

For Mitscherlich, their discussions took on such a personal character that he in part compared them with "psychotherapeutic sessions", which he welcomed not without inner resistance. As he writes in a letter to Jaspers,

> [i]n the school of psychoanalysis it is often observed that the acceptance of the psychotherapist's help on the part of the patient generates a guilty conscience. I had never understood this until I experienced it today. Naturally it is difficult if one has to grant the therapist such a winning margin in regard to the issues in question. But in my case I received a great gift, being allowed, as I was, to see myself through your medium. Nevertheless I would prefer to spare myself talks of this kind in the future.[463]

Before this time – so we infer from Mitscherlich's autobiography – an attempt had been made to convince Jaspers to revise his view of psychoanalysis during the time the author was working on the new edition of his *General Psychopathology*. Mitscherlich's request had been turned down, however; the "foolish passages" on psychoanalysis had not vanished when the book finally came out in 1946. Thus Mitscherlich sums up the issue with bitterness and wrath in 1980, writing, "I have never forgiven him for this betrayal – and I must use this word – to this very day."[464] Mitscherlich accounts for the fact that his advice had been rejected by issuing a psychodynamic judgment on Jaspers, calling him a typical representative of the "emotional resistance" against Freud and psychoanalysis in the "academic world".[465]

Irrespective of the way this interpretation is to be taken, Mitscherlich certainly makes an error when he retrospectively claims to have found no traces of his influence in the *Psychopathology*. After all, the extremely detailed and extensive discussion of psychotherapy is certainly indebted in no small part to the ideas and information provided by Mitscherlich, who had contacts to many representatives of the psychotherapeutic realm in Germany and Switzerland from various persuasions. Thus the particular attention which was paid to the psychosomatic approach taken by his teacher Viktor von Weizsäcker in the *General Psychopathology* also seemed to be the result of week-long discussions which Mitscherlich had conducted with Jaspers during the war years.

Jaspers judges psychoanalysis itself even more critically than before, however, albeit as a phenomenon of the past. His growing self-identity as a philosopher certainly played a crucial role in this development, a factor which also expressed itself in the "complete re-writing" of the textbook with the "deepening" of its philosophical "basic knowledge".[466] This change yielded skeptical remarks among psychiatrists with a similar psychopathological bent in particular. The philosophical perspective does indeed influence the conceptualization of the *General Psychopathology* considerably, especially when it comes to the substantially expanded passages on psychoanalysis and psychotherapy.[467] This "overgrowth of the philosophical aspect"[468] which Kurt Schneider makes critical note of, or, to use an image coined

---

[463] Letter from Alexander Mitscherlich to Karl Jaspers from February 27, 1943, JLE-GLA.
[464] Mitscherlich (1980), pg. 124f..
[465] Cf. Mitscherlich (1980), pg. 125.
[466] GP 4, pg. xix; cf. AP 4, pg. IV.
[467] Cf. GP 4, pp. 768-779 and 790-822; cf. AP 4, pp. 641-651 and pp. 663-686.
[468] Letter from Kurt Schneider to Karl Jaspers from June 24, 1942, JLE-GLA.

by Hans Gruhle, the philosophical saturation of the fourth edition of the *Psychopathology*,[469] is particularly pronounced in Jaspers' draft of an institutionalized form of psychotherapy, or rather, more specifically, in his recommendations for existence-philosophical "self-reflection". Thus this chapter will begin by depicting an historicizing critique of psychoanalysis and then go on to elucidate Jaspers' philosphically motivated ideas on psychotherapeutic practices. Last of all, it will discuss the benevolent reception of Viktor von Weizsäcker's psychosomatics, which seems to evidence quite a close affinity to the existence-philosophical perspective at this time.

HISTORICAL IDEOTYPE? PSYCHOANALYSIS
DURING NATIONAL SOCIALISM

The *General Psychopathology* of 1941/42 brings forth well-known arguments against psychoanalysis but within a different framework. Jaspers' discussion is informed by the view that psychoanalysis is to be looked upon as an historical phenomenon. As Jaspers writes, "[t]he famous example from the past is Freud and the movement which he founded and led; [...]. In 1919 I characterised this movement [...]".[470]

The earlier passage from 1919 introduces a sociological critique of "Freudianism" as a kind of sectarian "movement of faith";[471] the new, expanded text offers no new arguments, merely putting forth the familiar ones in more condensed form. Now Jaspers no longer claims that he wishes to warn his readers of psychoanalysis as an imminent danger, however. His critique sketches psychoanalysis as an historical ideotype deriving from a psychotherapeutic sect whose more salient characteristics were deemed to be suitable for sharpening the focus on possibile future phenomena of a similar kind. As Jaspers writes:

> Freudianism as a whole is an existing fact which has made it universally clear that psychotherapeutic sects as such must be something like substitute-religions; their teaching becomes a dogma of salvation and their therapy a redemption.[472]

In his sketch of such an ideotype, Jaspers repeats and intensifies his apodictic judgments of the anti-traditional strain of psychoanalysis. He speaks of the "existential ruin" it "worked to" in terms of the mentality of the individual, leading to "nihilism, a callous fanaticism and an arbitrary scepticism".[473]

But what gives Jaspers the right to view psychoanalysis in 1941/42 as a phenomenon whose epoch-making influence belongs to the past and which now only merits mention as a pejoratively exemplary ideotype for psychotherapeutic sects? The decisive reason given by Jaspers for his historicization of psychoanalysis is its institutional consolidation during National Socialism, in the course of which it was completely swallowed up by the blanket organization of psychotherapeutic

---

[469] Cf. Gruhle (1953), pg. 167.
[470] GP 4, pg. 773; cf. AP 4, pg. 646.
[471] GP 4, pg. 774; cf. AP 4, pg. 647.
[472] GP 4, pg. 774; Cf. AP 4, pg. 647
[473] GP 4, pg. 774; Cf. AP 4, pg. 646.

approaches. Furthermore, Jaspers points to the developments in the 1920's. During this time, the institutionalization of medical psychotherapy had progressed alongside that of psychoanalysis. As Jaspers reports, journals were established and conferences were held, and this resulted in the emergence of a "scientifically and philosophically sound psychotherapy"[474] which offered an alternative to psychoanalysis. Here Jaspers is alluding to the internationally anchored *General Medical Society for Psychotherapy (Allgemeine Ärztliche Gesellschaft für Psychotherapie [AÄGP])* which was founded in 1926.[475]

From 1926 on, this society held almost annual conferences which were open to all medical disciplines involved in psychotherapeutic approaches. Thus it had a throng of prominent representatives from various medical disciplines to show for itself. Among others, Alexander Mitscherlich's future teacher, Viktor von Weizsäcker, became a member. Soon an organ was also established, which bore the title *Zentralblatt für Psychotherapie (Central Organ for Psychotherapy)* and published regular issues from 1930 on.[476] The *Deutsche Psychoanalytische Vereinigung (German Psychoanalytic Society)*, to which the *Berliner Psychoanalytisches Institut (Berlin Psychoanalytic Institute)*, founded in 1920, belonged, refused to recognize the existence of the *Allgemeine Ärztliche Gesellschaft für Psychotherapie* on the grounds that it deemed their pragmatic criteria for membership to be theoretically insufficient. For this reason, the two organizations initially remained independent.[477]

During National Socialism, the *Ärztliche Psychotherapeutische Gesellschaft* reacted to the hostility towards "Jewish" psychology with the establishment of a national chapter, the so-called *Deutsche allgemeine ärztliche Gesellschaft für Psychotherapie (General German Medical Society for Psychotherapy)*. Matthias Heinrich Göring was elected as its "Führer"; as the cousin of the high-ranking party functionary Hermann Göring, he was in a position to offer excellent 'protection' for psychotherapy in an increasingly dictatorial environment. C.G. Jung took over the chairmanship of the international umbrella association and the editorship of the *Zentralblatt für Psychotherapie* from Ernst Kretschmer, a proponent of psychiatrically monitored psychotherapy.[478] In this journal, Jung confirmed the National Socialistic race clichés by distinguishing between the "Jewish and Arian unconscious".[479]

The *Deutsche Psychoanalytische Gesellschaft (German Psychoanalytic Society)* had complied with the legislatively decreed 'arianization' in April of 1933 and

---

[474] GP 4, pg. 678; cf. AP 4, pg. 810.
[475] Concerning the history of the AÄGP, see Cocks (1983), pg. 1099ff., Cocks (1985), pp. 43-49 and Lockot (1985), pp. 134-183
[476] Cf. Cocks (1983), pg. 1062f..
[477] Lockot gives an overview of the history of the Berlin Psychoanalytic Institute. Cf. pp. 39-48.
[478] Lockot describes the transition from Kretschmer to Göring and C.G. Jung in great detail. Lockot (1985), pp. 74-93.
[479] The controversy is depicted by Lockot (1985), pp. 93-99. Concerning Jung's role in the development of psychology under National Socialism see Cocks (1985), pp. 127-135 and Hermanns (1994).

dismissed all Jewish members by 1935. In 1936 the psychoanalysts who were left had to tolerate the fact that the Psychoanalytic Institute of Berlin was completely incorporated by the newly founded 'Göring Institute', which meant the members of the psychoanalytic institution were forced to join by 1938 after the ultimate dissolution from their own institution.[480] Thus the psychoanalytic "torso" succeeded in surviving by means of a compulsory fusion. Officially, the institutional 'homogenization' of psychoanalysis in the German-speaking world since 1938 robbed it of all its opportunities – apart from those in Switzerland – to take action in the public sphere, except for certain efforts made under the cloak of the 'Göring Institute'.[481] The American historian Geoffry Cocks, who can be viewed as an unbiased and well-informed expert on psychotherapy during the Third Reich, having published a book with that title, formulates it pointedly in this way. "Der Aufmarsch Hitlers eliminierte Berlin und Wien als psychoanalytische Zentren und verlagerte den Schwerpunkt der Bewegung nach London und New York."[482] Peter Gay, an American historian with an interest in psychoanalysis, depicts the politically caused hiatus apologetically as a kind of inner emigration at the high price of intellectual and moral self-denial.[483] Walter Bräutigam, who received psychoanalytical training in Berlin in 1942, speaks of an opportunistic "compromise" which had consisted in tolerating the "increasing discrimination" of Jewish colleagues and refraining from mentioning Sigmund Freud by name.[484]

However one assesses the role played by psychoanalysis during this time, the dissolution of the psychoanalytic movement effected by the National Socialist State through its compulsory integration into the 'Göring Institute' is in Jaspers' eye a quite fortunate development, especially considering the fact that in his view the establishment of a centralized institution increased the chances of setting up scientifically standardized psychotherapy considerably. In comparison to efforts made to institutionalize the field before 1933, he describes the founding of the Berlin Institute in positive terms as a serious hiatus in the history of psychotherapeutic professionalization. He writes:

> In 1936 something happened that was fundamentally new. The 'Deutsche Institut für Psychologische Forschung und Psychotherapie' was founded in Berlin under M. H. Göring. This was the last step whereby psychotherapy became institutionalised.[485]

Cooks agrees with Jaspers in his view that the "favorable" constellation of the 'Göring Institute' had resulted in a degree of "professionelle Konsolidierung und Etablierung" of psychotherapy which had never been achieved before and was not reached after 1945 either.[486]

---

[480] Cf. Brainin/Kaminer (1994) and on the 'Göring Institute' in particular, Cocks (1985), pp. 176-230.
[481] Cf. Cocks (1983), pg. 1064f..
[482] Cf. Cocks (1983), pg. 1075.
[483] Cf. Gay (1988), pg. 719.
[484] Cf. Bräutigam (1984), pg. 905.
[485] GP 4, pg. 811; cf. AP 4, pg. 678.
[486] Cocks (1983), pg. 1067 and 1069. On the basis of a passage of the *General Psychopathology* (fourth edition) published in 1955, Cocks dates Jaspers' statement as

The benevolence with which Jaspers watched the institutional consolidation of psychotherapy seems to have been so pronounced that he did not even problematize the fact of its having been the result of political coersion demanding the fusion. As Jaspers writes:

> Everything that has been initiated by individual endeavour and developed within cliques and schools must now shape itself into some integrated whole. The Institute tries to establish an interchange of mutual influence between all the forces of psychological knowledge and skill. The intention is to bridge the opposites, establish the idea.[487]

In airing such sentiments, Jaspers hopes that it will be possible, in the centralized institution, to establish a more coordinated and standardized form of collecting empirical data in order to eliminate the problem which Weber had already pointed out, namely the lack of casuistics in psychotherapy. As Jaspers writes,

> [a]n out-patient department serves a practice which increases steadily. It is hoped to gain an extensive basis for research by regularly working through the case-histories. In this way, perhaps for the first time, it would prove possible to amass a number of psychotherapeutic biographies.[488]

Furthermore, Jaspers expects the institution to develop clear "rules and regulations" which would "embody the whole scientific and professional tradition" and protect against the danger of abuse.[489]

Cocks' retrospective assessment of the relatively modest "theoretical progress" of psychotherapy during the Third Reich does not correspond with the hopes which Jaspers still entertained in 1942.[490] Furthermore, Cocks assessed the situation which psychoanalysis found itself in as not quite so desolate and devastating as Jaspers had in his historical treatment of it.[491] As he maintains, not the conceptual integration of all schools of psychotherapy apostrophized by Jaspers was realized by the institutional fusion. Despite all coerced compromises and new impulses which might have come about as a result of the process, one must realistically speak of an unvoluntary coexistence of various schools of psychotherapy under one institutional roof. Sociologically speaking, the fortunate result of this consisted in the high degree of "professional identity" which psychotherapy enjoyed as never before despite the difficult political conditions under which it had emerged, Cocks observes.[492]

---

having been made in the post-war period. The quoted passage is to be found in Jaspers (1955), pg. 46 and GP 4, pg. 678.

[487] GP 4, pg. 811; cf. AP 4, pg. 678.

[488] GP 4, pg. 811; cf. AP 4, pg. 678.

[489] GP 4, pg. 812; cf. AP 4, pg. 679.

[490] Cocks (1983), pg. 1067. Apart from the rapid decrease in the frequency with which publications of the periodical for psychotherapy, *Zentralblatt für Psychotherapie,* came out, and the noticeable reduction in the number of conferences held – these being superficial indications of certain developments – the emigration of eminent psychotherapists and the lack of international contacts within the association together with the repressive, race-ideologically saturated intellectual climate in Germany had a devastating effect on the quality of the professional discourse. Cf. Cocks (1983), pg. 1078.

[491] Cf. Cocks (1983), pp. 1068 and 1077.

[492] Cf. Cocks (1983), pg. 1065.

Matthias Göring suspended the exclusive right of the medical profession to practice the profession of psychotherapy in 1933, however, so that in the later institute
the medical laymen constituted the majority of the members. Jaspers comments on
this fact quite critically in 1941/42, writing:

> The main deficiency of this initial institution is that it functions apart from any psychiat
> ric clinic. Psychotherapists who have no sound knowledge of the psychoses gained from
> their own experience and no contact with them in institutional practice can easily make
> fatal mistakes of diganosis; they also fall victims to the fantastic nonsense which occu
> pies so much space in the psychotherapeutic literature.[493]

Jaspers' objection is representative of the opinion largely held among psychiatrists at universities and it corresponds with that of Ernst Kretschmer, who made
endeavors to incorporate psychotherapy into the field of psychiatry while serving as
chairman of the AÄGP until 1933.[494] Irrespective of how well Jaspers' assessment
stands up to present-day historical reconstructions of the situation psychotherapy
found itself in under the National Socialists, one must ascertain that Jaspers' *General Psychopathology* of 1941/42 historicizes psychoanalysis as the ideal paradigm
of a psychotherapeutic sect and that he applauds the compulsory fusion of various
forms of psychotherapy in Berlin.

'EXISTENTIAL' SELF-REFLECTION AND
FACULTATIVE 'TRAINING ANALYSIS'

The professionalization of psychotherapy under the National Socialists as it was
realized at the Berlin Institute is described by Jaspers as a "crucial situation of transition" to the institutional phase. "A young profession in process of establishing
itself may have unrestricted possibilities but it may become limited by the choice of
its initial organisation," he writes.[495] In this connection he shows a certain degree of
understanding for the function which psychotherapy was forced to fulfill in an "age
poor in faith", noting:

> Psychotherapy nowadays not only wants to help the neurotic but mankind itself in all its
> spiritual and personal needs. It is significantly, though not traditionally, linked with con
> fession, unburdening of the soul, the care of souls as in the ages of faith. Psychotherapy
> makes demands and gives promises which extend to mankind in general. We cannot yet
> foresee what will come of it.[496]

Here Jaspers views modern psychotherapy as a continuation of philosophical
schools in antiquity, its goal being to help the individual lead a meaningful life. In
taking this view, Jaspers posits that psychotherapy defines the "human being as a
whole" as its frame of reference, thus adopting, as he himself writes, a "radically
different and much more comprehensive [view] than the purely psychopathological
one".[497]

---

[493] GP 4, pg. 811; cf. AP 4, pg. 678.
[494] Cf. Cocks (1983), pg. 1099f..
[495] GP 4, pg. 814f.; cf. AP 4, pg. 681.
[496] GP 4, pg. 811f.; cf. AP 4, pg. 678f..
[497] GP 4, pg. 812; cf. AP 4, pg. 679.

According to Jaspers, the integration of various forms of psychotherapy should culminate in a two-phase concept for treatment so that on the basis of mutual "psychological techniques" like hypnosis and autogenic training, the various "illuminating deep psychologies" could be used in addition to illuminate personal, biographical aspects of the emotional disorder in question.

Thus Jaspers recognizes 'self-illumination' as the "only unconditional requirement" of psychotherapeutic training but he rejects quite decidedly the obligatory "training analysis" as it was discussed in the *Zentralblatt für Psychotherapie* in 1938, a measure which was to encompass some 100 to 150 hours.[498] He unequivocally expresses his eminent reservations in regard to socialization processes which aimed to influence the individual via technically, burocratically and conceptionally standardized procedures, arguing that "the content of the established institutional training would have to be what is accessible to all and objectively valid, although in practice everything decisive will depend on the personalities who make use of what they have been taught".[499] For this reason his concept sees in psychotherapeutic training no more than a facultative possibility for "depth-psychological analysis". In concrete terms, he favorizes a plurality of training models for the individual to choose from. The selection process should not be limited by external regulations, he emphasizes.

But in advocating tolerance Jaspers did not mean that he shared the opinion of those who believed that successful training treatment constituted an "objective" measure for controlling the qualification process. In his eye, all efforts to certify in any way an individual's competence as a psychotherapist, for example through the establishment of a teachable and testable psychodynamic understanding of self and others was dangerous. As he argues, such schooling and socialization would progressively suppress individuality and ultimately eliminate it as a decisive factor in making treatment effective. "To choose a training analysis as an arbitrary criterion for admission to the profession would lead to the restrictedness of several mutually exclusive and opportunistically tolerant schools and finally to the extinction of the profession itself," Jaspers writes.[500] Considering the position he takes here, Jaspers' tolerance in regard to facultative training analysis must be interpreted as a pragmatic concession made in order to achieve the goal of institutionalized psychotherapeutic training. For Jaspers, obligatory training analysis would be inacceptible because it would prove absolutely irreconcilable with the demand he makes for independence in terms of self-reflection as he envisions it.

As opposed to the models of self-reflection propagated by the schools, all of which depended upon training analysts, Jaspers' existence-philosophical concept of self-reflection aimed to protect the deeper, more unconscious realms of the psyche from interpretation by others of whatever kind, this being necessary, as Jaspers argues, to avoid impairing the free emergence of personality from its individual sources.

---

[498] GP 4, pg. 814f.; cf. AP 4, pg. 680.
[499] GP 4, pg. 814; cf. AP 4, pg. 681.
[500] GP 4, pg. 814; cf. AP 4, pg. 681.

> Success depends on our confronting the unconscious depths with an enhanced respect. We have to avoid turning everything into a technique if we are to keep open communication with our own nature. We must not expect that the personal qualities of the psychotherapist will spring from formal instruction; the professional demands are much more far-reaching and among them there is something essential that most decisively cannot be taught.[501]

Jaspers aims to safeguard the existential process, which is for him "always [...] unique and unrepeatable" from the demand for a methodical procedure which is monitored by a training analyst.[502] His psychotherapeutic training ideal as he outlines it in the new edition of the *General Psychopathology* is individualized 'self-illumination' in the sense of his existence philosophy.

This form of "self-reflection" is to increasingly integrate the individual "unconscious" into the consciousness of the personality. Jaspers assumes there are unconscious premises which are inherent to every human being and which are constitutive for the development of that human being's personality. Thus individuals can never completely understand the "reality of existence," he says. "[...] meaningful interpretation of myself is [...] endless and always relative. In the last resort I neither know what I am nor what moves me nor which motives are the decisive ones."[503] Jaspers envisions a "gradual transformation of this relationship between the conscious and the unconscious" in which both sides are mutually dependent. In developing this idea, Jaspers distinguishes between psychologically possible knowledge about social role patterns and knowledge about psychodynamically decisive pre-conditions which define the core of an individual's personality.

> Psychology cannot answer the question as to *what the individual person really is*. We understand how almost all roles can be separated from the person himself. He stands outside them, they are not he, himself. But what this self then is remains inaccessible to us, a mere point outside. Or else it is – something which cannot be grasped psychologically – his innermost nature which never presents itself, the inward element which never becomes the outer and therefore empirically does not exist.[504]

The limits set on understanding as concerns the unconscious core of a human being are elucidated by Jaspers suggestively using the metaphor of the ocean. He writes:

> To get to know the individual is comparable to a sea-voyage over limitless seas to discover a continent; every landing on a shore or island will teach certain facts but the possibility of further knowledge vanishes if one maintains that here one is at the centre of things; one's theories are then like so many sandbanks on which we stay fast without really winning land.[505]

The ocean of the personal unconscious is unfathomable, says Jaspers, and the "enigma of the individual" in the unconscious core of the personality cannot be solved. As Jaspers puts it:

---

[501] GP 4, pg. 815; cf. AP 4, pg. 681.
[502] GP 4, pg. 813; cf. AP 4, pg. 680.
[503] GP 4, pg. 349f.; cf. AP 4, pg. 291.
[504] GP 4, pg. 354; cf. AP 4, pg. 295.
[505] GP 4, pg. 751; cf. AP 4, pg. 627.

Dissected though it may be into something biological in genetics and into something psychological in human society and culture, and thus as it were at the cross-roads of heredity and environment, individuality is never just the point of transit but always a mystery, somehow itself, unique, existing for itself in an historic concreteness as present riches; a single incomparable wave in the infinity of waves that mirror the whole.[506]

For Jaspers, self-reflection, as a process whose point of departure is the unconscious, is equivalent to that which he refers to in a philosophical context as 'self-illumination', which culminates in 'self-revelation'. For Jaspers, this is a process which is determined philosophically and not psychologically.[507] Like philosophical knowledge in Jaspers' sense of the word, it can never be really objectified. As we read, it is insight "in suspension" and is based on the "unlimited flow of possible interpretation". As Jaspers writes, "[i]f we desire final knowledge in the field of self-understanding, we have made a completely wrong start."[508]

But as uncertain knowledge about an individual's personal core is, Jaspers feels certain that any self-reflective individual, by virtue of "the fundamentals of his nature", can "extend to godhead, in the Transcendence whereby he knows he is given to himself in freedom". For Jaspers, this is what guarantees his self-understanding in a philosophical sense.[509] The *General Psychopathology* also unequivocally posits the concealed but nonetheless real presence of transcendence, which Jaspers – following the Biblical tradition – calls "God". The author emphasizes that God is not a relative construct fashioned from a this-worldly immanent perspective. He writes:

Man himself [...] knows that he has not created God through his ideas and that the first statement holds: God is. This was enough for man whenever he foundered (as with Jeremiah). The finitude of man finds rest in this faith in the Being of God.[510]

Jaspers speaks critically of a "circle of immanence". This constructivist notion implies that the relativity of our own cognition makes it impossible to assume the existence of a transcendent sphere, for all ascriptions of transcendence ultimately fall back on human beings as their cultural producers. Jaspers evaluates this position here, as he did indirectly in *Man in the Modern Age*, as issuing from the hybris of modern man and the absolutization of his position in historic time. Against this tendency Jaspers sets his existence-philosophical creed, which reads as follows:

He does not contrive his deepest freedom but it is just this which gives him knowledge of Transcendence, his means for freedom in the world. Man can create himself only by [...] trusting one thing else, Transcendence.[511]

By formulating this position, Jaspers divorces himself from the notion of secularization which dominates the Modern Age, a notion which, as Koselleck maintains, evaluated all ideas and actions according to this-worldy criteria.[512] In some respects, Jaspers' approach is individualistic and thus also modern, but in formulating

---

[506] GP 4, pg. 754; cf. AP 4, pg. 630.
[507] GP 4, pg. 349; cf. AP 4, pg. 291.
[508] GP 4, pg. 350; cf. AP 4, pg. 292.
[509] GP 4, pg. 766; cf. AP 4, pg. 640.
[510] GP 4, pg. 764; cf. AP 4, pg. 638.
[511] GP 4, pg. 763; cf. AP 4, pg. 637f..
[512] Koselleck (1985), pg. 183.

his transcendence postulate he shows his affinity to the metaphysical tradition as well. Thus when Jaspers speaks of individual self-reflection which is to illuminate the unconscious core of the personality, he places his notion of individualism within a transcendental frame of reference.

In Jaspers' thinking, the individual incommensurability which lies in the unfathomable unconscious affords the freedom of self-determination in the light of transcendence. Furthermore, Jaspers expands the room for interpretation as far as philosophical self-determination is concerned by rejecting any scientific demand for ultimately causal determination. "The individual not only lives and experiences but knows he does so. In his attitudes to himself he can somehow go beyond himself."[513] Jaspers founds this on the complexity of possible causal connections in terms of human cognizance. The endless combination of possible connections[514] prevents definitive ascriptions, Jaspers argues,[515] and in another passage we read:

> So far as the human being is empirically explorable as an object for knowledge he is unfree. But in so far as we ourselves experience, act and investigate we are free in our own self-certainty and hence more than we can ever discover.[516]

The possibility of "freedom" and the "exceptional status of the human being in nature" which it establishes is a philosphical idea which Jaspers expressly incorporates into the new conception of his *General Psychopathology*. The *Psychopathology* bases its argument on the assumption that individual self-determination is relatively independent of somatic and psychic conditions and describes the "existence of freedom" of the human being as a quality *sui generis* alongside the concept of nature.[517] Jaspers posits:

> It is wrong to put Nature and Freedom (Life and Mind) side by side as if they were factors on the same plane and as if they interacted. Rather it is that the one form of approach – whether that of the Natural Sciences or that of Understanding and its accompanying Illumination – comes up against its respective limits, not however to absorb new factors of explanation but to become aware of its own limitations in the face of Being as a whole. Thus causality comes up against freedom and, vice versa, understanding comes up against the meaningless (the ununderstandable) in the form of the causal connections of biology or in the form of Existence itself.[518]

Jaspers does not clarify the question as to how the personal unconscious, as something predetermined, equates with the postulated freedom of self-determination. For him it fundamentally functions as a metaphor for all aspects of human existence which escape clear signification and definition.

In view of this conception it is not surprising that Jaspers rejects all other psychodynamic models of understanding, for the seemingly assured claims they make concerning unconscious drives and motivations had to seem suspicious to him. In Jaspers' way of thinking, the notion of psychological self-awareness could only

---

[513] GP 4, pg. 755; cf. AP 4, pg. 631.
[514] Cf. GP 4, pg. 758; AP 4, pg. 633.
[515] GP 4, pg. 754f.; cf. AP 4, pg. 630.
[516] GP 4, pg. 758; cf. AP 4, pg. 633.
[517] GP 4, pg. 749; cf. AP 4, pg. 626.
[518] GP 4, pg. 755f.; cf. AP 4, pg. 631.

apply to conventional roles in social contexts, not to the deepest drives of life. For Jaspers, existence-philosophical self-reflection constitutes a necessary supplement to psychotherapy, which in his eyes no longer belongs in any way to the realm of psychiatry. Psychology of understanding, which he assigns to the realm of scientific psychotherapy, no longer plays an important role in the new edition of the *General Psychopathology*, at least not for psychotherapy, for as Jaspers posits, the processes of understanding which are of decisive importance for an individual's personality are completely dependent on existential hermeneutics. Psychology of understanding not only stops at the somatic limits of character, the "organic diseases" and "psychoses", – so the position Jaspers had already taken in earlier editions of the *General Psychopathology* –, but it is also confronted with the limits of existential understanding, whose exclusive task it is to illuminate the "reality of existence".[519]

Thus Jaspers can claim: "The *limits* of every psychology of meaningful connections must necessarily remain the same for psychoanalysis in so far as the latter is meaningful."[520] In Jaspers' view, all "illumination of psychoanalysis" is "pseudo-illumination" which erroneously deems itself capable of illuminating the unconscious, this non-objectifiable challenge for the process of self-reflection. From his historicizing perspective of psychoanalysis, Jaspers formulates his concluding judgment as follows: "Psychoanalysis has always *shut its eyes* to these limitations and has *wanted to understand everything*."[521] On the basis of the existence-philosophical norm of self-reflection, Jaspers consistently rejects all large schools of psychotherapy and the methods they apply. He views them to be scientific ideologies, calling them 'weltanschaulich', but is forced to tolerate them as facultative possibilities for pragmatic reasons having to do with the establishment of the institute in Berlin. As Jaspers writes, "no movement of this high order could ever be based on Freud, Adler and Jung, and because one grows dependent on one's opponents, no successful engagement with them along their own lines will ever find the way".[522]

Jaspers' critique of so-called 'Daseinsanalyse' ('analysis of existence') is more benevolent; Jaspers at least recognizes it as an "intellectual movement in psychiatry". In the short critical discussion of its main representatives, Viktor v. Gebsattel and Ludwig Binswanger, who are now viewed as the founding fathers of "anthropological psychiatry",[523] Jaspers raises his fundamental objection against their philosophically ambitious hermeneutics, maintaining that "[t]he totality of human life and its ultimate origin cannot be the object of any scientific research".[524] He shows appreciation of their "descriptive accomplishments" but dismisses their aetiological explanations. The arguments Jaspers uses reflect the self-understanding of his now apodictic treatment of psychopathology and its now apodictic nature, which only

---

[519] GP 4, pg. 363; cf. AP 4, pg. 302.

[520] GP 4, pg. 363; cf. AP 4, pg. 302.

[521] GP 4, pg. 363; cf. AP 4, pg. 302.

[522] GP 4, pg. 815; cf. AP 4, pg. 681.

[523] Concerning the present-day status of this approach see Schmidt-Degenhards 1997 study *Standortbestimmung einer anthropologischen Psychiatrie* and Schmidt-Degenhard (2000).

[524] GP 4, pg. 543; cf. AP 4, pg. 455.

deems symptomatically oriented, descriptive approaches to be useful within its hermeneutic framework and which rejects all aetiological approaches as a speculative overstepping of the boundaries of the physician's competence. As Jaspers does not recognize any connection between aetiology and psychological hermeneutics, he ironically designates the psychologico-philosophical interpretations offered by *Daseinsanalyse* as attempts at understanding which create an unspecifically human climate without doing any real damage. "[I]nterpretations are soothing yet interpretations are nothing but interpretations," he writes.[525]

In his *General Psychopathology* Jaspers concedes that his own approach of understanding is primarily motivated by philosophical concerns which had remained unrecognized in the "darkness of the unconscious" of his thought for a long time.[526] The concept of existential self-reflection, which culminates in "self-revelation", informs this existence-philosophical orientation of understanding in Jaspers' thought. What Kurt Schneider and Hans Gruhle criticize as an "overgrowth" or "saturation" of the book with philosophical considerations lies in this fact. Schneider in particular, who had held Jaspers' *Philosophy* in high esteem since it came out in 1932,[527] was alienated by the fact that Jaspers introduced the concept of existential self-reflection as a quality *sui generis*, declaring it to be a fixed variable in psychiatric thought alongside the somatic conditions of emotional disorders. After 1946, Schneider recommended to his staff that they read the 1913 edition of *General Psychopathology* rather than the new, existence-philosophically oriented one.[528]

DEFINITIVE AND INSTRUMENTAL GOALS OF PSYCHOTHERAPY

The *General Psychopathology* proposes a two-phase model of psychotherapy which includes an "external praxis" of psychotechnical methods and the actual "internal praxis".[529] Conceptually speaking, this center of psychotherapy is to a large extent congruent with Jaspers' notion of existence-philosophical self-reflection, since he emphasizes the special status of psychiatric psychotherapy "*within the art and practice of medicine*" and describes it as a "'revelation'" of the patient far beyond any "psychotherapeutic plan", the goal being the "philosophical realm of the individual growth of a self". In "establishing and filling out the revelation of himself in the course of existential communication" with the physician during psychotherapeutic treatment, the patient leaves the medical sphere in the genuine sense of the word behind him, says Jaspers, writing:

> One questions and gropes from one freedom to another within the concreteness of the actual situation, taking no responsibility for the other nor making any abstract demands. [...] Doctor and patient are both human beings and as such are fellow-travellers in

---

[525] GP 4, pg. 546; cf. AP 4, pg. 458.
[526] GP 4, pg. 349; cf. AP 4, pg. 290.
[527] Cf. letter from Kurt Schneider to Karl Jaspers from September 4, 1932, JLE-GLA.
[528] Cf. Janzarik (1986), pg. 122.
[529] Cf. GP 4, pg. 793; AP 4, pg. 664.

destiny. The doctor is not a pure technician nor pure authority, but Existence itself for its own sake[...].[530]

In medico-ethical terms, Jaspers looks upon this "existential communication" as it was first described in 1915 in a manuscript entitled *Solitude* (*Einsamkeit*) and developed systematically in Jaspers' 1932 *Philosophy*, as unproblematical, for, as he contends, it does not patronize the patient through suggestive or seemingly clear statements.

As Jaspers emphasizes, the interaction between physician and patient is typically characterized by an asymmetrical relationship between a support-giving expert and a layman in need of help. In his *General Psychopathology* Jaspers reflects on this situation indirectly when he points out that every human being feels the impulse to resist medical help despite his need for it due to his natural striving for autonomy; the sometimes unavoidable dependence upon physicians can injure his pride, Jaspers observes. Particularly in cases where the integrity of a patient's psyche is vulnerable, patients find it very hard to assert their interests vis-a-vis a physician unselfconsciously, Jaspers says. In the case of physical diseases, the situation is easier, for the patient is better able to distance himself from the condition and therefore has an easier time demonstrating self-confidence in his interaction with the care-giver. According to Jaspers, a person only seeks psychotherapeutic help if the distress weighs more heavily than the resistance against receiving help and the person does not know how else to come to terms with the situation.[531]

As Jaspers sees it, a completely different situation presents itself if, on the basis of changes in a person's cultural self-understanding, the resistance against the asymmetrical relationship to the physician has been considerably reduced so that the person's self-confidence is barely affected by the need for "some sort of inner guidance" by a "personal counsellor". But Jaspers distances himself from this cultural development, which issued from the modern crisis of orientation, when he writes, "[a] need for therapy here signifies acceptance of loss of freedom, though in fact freedom is still there and maintains its rights at the same time as it renounces them". From Jaspers' cultural perspective, anyone who wants to be an independent individual "recoils from psychotherapeutic ways which penetrate the psychic depths and concern themselves with the person as a whole", making out of "the entire being" an object of the treatment relationship.[532]

In medico-ethical terms, Dieter Birnbacher and Leonore Kottje-Birnbacher have recently come to distinguish between "instrumental" and "financial" goals in psychotherapy. They point out to what great extent they are determined by individual forms of psychotherapy.[533] As they contend, the goal of treatment must generally be measured according to "how deep the realization of the goal [impacts] the personality and life conduct of the patient".[534] The decision as to which goal is to be chosen is not a medical decision but rather a private one, they say. A definitive goal of

---

[530] GP 4, pg. 798f.; cf. AP 4, pg. 668.
[531] Cf. GP 4, pg. 801; AP 4, pg. 670.
[532] GP 4, pg. 801; cf. AP 4, pg. 670.
[533] Birnbacher/Kottje-Birnbacher (1998), pp. 184-188.
[534] Birnbacher/Kottje-Birnbacher (1998), pp. 185.

therapy such as the development of a patient's personality, the aim being to realize a purely instrumental therapy goal such as the extinction of symptoms using behavioral therapy, has considerable consequences for individual life conduct. For this reason these authors regard decisions made in favor of a definitive therapeutic goal as ethically unobjectionable if, and only if, the individual in question has been informed over potentially far-reaching changes in the patterns of his life conduct and he strives voluntarily to subject himself to the treatment. In a similar vein, Jaspers' *General Psychopathology* pointed out the medico-ethical repercussions of psychotherapy. As we read:

> In any case we cannot deny that the decision to undergo psychotherapy is a decision indeed and means something like an irrevocable choice in anyone's life, for better or for worse.[535]

Jaspers has fewer misgivings about instrumental goals which use psychotechnical methods in order to effect changes on the symptomatic level – relatively far removed from personal motivational structures. In his eye, such measures at best eliminate limitations on self-fulfilment without intending to have any substantial normative influence in themselves.

Jaspers' position is also conform with that of more contemporary medical ethics insofar as he demands of the therapist that he refrain from asserting his "professional authority" when it comes to formulating "the treatment-goal", speaking only on "personal authority". As Jaspers writes,

> [in] the *doctor-patient relationship, authority* is always present and may have beneficial effects. In the rare case where true communication is achieved, this is lost again immediately, unless authority is entirely discarded.[536]

In other words, more recent medico-ethical positions as well as that advocated by Jaspers expect of the psychotherapist that he be versed enough in philosophy to be able to clearly explain the normative premises of his psychodynamic theory to others when it comes to questions of laying down definitive goals such as certain personality ideals. But even if a psychoanalyst elucidates the normative implications of his therapy goal to the patient before beginning with the treatment, for example, Jaspers would still view psychoanalysis as questionable in comparison to his philosophical position. He perforce had to tolerate depth-psychological analyses, indicating as much in the course of formulating his psychotherapeutic concept. He did not subscribe to the kind of tolerance which Birnbacher and Kottje-Birnbacher advocate with conviction on the basis of their pluralistic stance on value orientation, however. The hippocratic oath which Jaspers likes to cite – "iatros philosophos isotheos" – implies a physician's philosophy which adopts the traditional category of transcendence as something self-evident.[537]

---

[535] GP 4, pg. 801; cf. AP 4, pg. 670.
[536] GP 4, pg. 805; cf. AP 4, pg. 673.
[537] GP 4, pg. 805; cf. AP 4, pg. 673.

PRAISE OF PSYCHOSOMATICS

After 1945 Jaspers will come to criticize psychoanalysis primarily by correlating it with the psychosomatic medicine practiced by Viktor von Weizsäcker. For this reason it is illuminating to compare the various editions of Jaspers' *General Psychopathology* and note that the new edition of the textbook had expressly prized von Weizsäcker's psychosomatic approach, namely as long as it was not associated with Freud's thought.[538]

The fact that von Weizsäcker no longer made any explicit reference to psychoanalysis after 1933[539] is most probably a heavily weighing reason for Jaspers to mention only those publications on psychosomatics without reservations which appeared during the late 1930's.[540] Moreover, Jaspers had no difficulty giving a positive depiction of von Weizsäcker's concerns as he thought he discerned a skeptical tenor in regard to psychodynamic interpretations in von Weizsäcker's work after 1933 which quite likened his own skepsis towards "compelling verification" as concerned the "psychogenesis of organic disease". To Jaspers, von Weizsäcker appears to be a researcher who takes the biographies of his patients into account in his methodological investigations. In addressing his work, Jaspers formulated three objections to erroneously simplifying interpretations, which read as follows:

> He [Viktor von Weizsäcker] finds it hard to be convinced because firstly, positive and negative cases can be found side by side. For instance, if one finds positive evidence of psychogenicity in one case, the next case fails to show it and nothing psychic can be found of any importance. Secondly, we are ignorant of the significance of inner organs for psychic life. [...] Thirdly, the relationship between the physical and psychic factors seems an extremely irregular one.[541]

It is quite in keeping with Jaspers' epistemological skepsis that von Weizsäcker does not, as he expressly states, view the "biographical method" as a form of scientific "explanation", but rather as a form of "observing perception" which was as such not intended to deliver any objective, "tangible 'results'". In accordance with von Weizsäcker's biographic approach, the physician should actively accompany the process of self-reflection oriented toward the entire biographic framework, participating as a "personality" in the "destiny of the patient". Here Jaspers is still willing to concede that the somatic findings act as crisis indicators which the physician

---

[538] For the first time, Jaspers devotes a complete chapter to questions of psychosomatics in his psychopathological textbook. Cf. AP 4, pp. 188-211. The term 'somatopsychology' was suggested by Kurt Schneider. Cf. letter from Kurt Schneider to Karl Jaspers from February 27, 1942, JLE-GLA.

[539] As Mitscherlich emphasizes, von Weizsäcker purchased the complete writings of Freud for his clinical department in Heidelberg, but on the other hand one must not forget that he was the one to throw Freud's work *The Future of an Illusion* (*Die Zukunft einer Illusion*) into the fire in May 1933 in the framework of book burnings organized by the National Socialists, calling it "self-glorification of doubt" and moreover feeling the necessity to knuckle under political coersion by demonstrably severing his ties to Freud. Cf. Wein (1988), pg. 391f.

[540] Jaspers refers to von Weizsäcker's publications *Physicians' Questions* (*Ärztliche Fragen*) and *Studies on Pathogenesis* (*Studien zur Pathogenese*). Cf. von Weizsäcker (1934) and von Weizsäcker (1935).

[541] GP 4, pg. 240; cf. AP 4, pg. 203.

interprets biographically together with the patient. This "introduction of the subject" into the process of participating observation on the part of the physician in von Weizsäcker's model is interpreted by Jaspers in his *Psychopathology* as approximating what he himself indicates as a possibility for psychotherapeutic communication, namely an "approach of mutual living engagement, of existential and metaphysical experience".[542]

As Jaspers sees it, interaction on the part of the physician in the course of "participatory observation" in psychotherapy involves the physician giving the patient suggestions as to how to place the disorder in the framework of his biography as a whole but without intending to objectify the incommensurable individual connections. We read:

> There is a radical difference between our perceiving in a case an instance of something general (the scientific approach) and perceiving something which immediately confronts us as unique, an enigma which can never be turned to good account by the use of general statements [...].[543]

Jaspers accentuates the metascientific distinction which results from the differing conditions under which the objectifying scientist and the subjectively engaged psychotherapist make observations respectively. On the basis of his claim to objectivity, the distanced scientist is justified in making generalized statements, whereas the personal statements of the self-involved therapist correspond to the subjective aspect of the biographic self-clarification process and because of this individual assistance in the process of incommensurable 'self-revelation', no claim can be made to generalizability whatsoever, Jaspers argues.

Jaspers also clearly distances himself from von Weizsäcker, however, because in his eye, von Weizsäcker does not entertain the same strict notion of epistemological relativity in regard to biographic-subjective hermeneutics which he himself subscribes to. On the one hand, von Weizsäcker speaks of the fact that "the most important impulses cannot be conceptually tangible", while maintaining on the other that "conceptual determination [should not] be neglected". For this reason, Jaspers views von Weizsäcker as a pioneer of 'biographics' as a psychopathological method,[544] but at the same time he formulates epistemologically skeptical objections against the expectation that it would be possible to write an "absolute biography", these objections likening those targeted at the expectations which psychoanalysis places in hermeneutics. As Jaspers writes,

> [a]n empirical biography which believes it knows something about an individual and tries as it were to strike a balance would always contain the individual within biographical categories of a particular kind which it would be wrong to take as exhaustive.[545]

---

[542] GP 4, pg. 677; cf. AP 4, pg. 567f..
[543] GP 4, pg. 677; cf. AP 4, pg. 568.
[544] GP 4, pg. 676; cf. AP 4, pg. 567.
[545] GP 4, pg. 673; cf. AP 4, pg. 565.

Jaspers' aim is to preserve a space for comprehensive existential self-reflection which is sheltered from all scientifically sanctioned rational analysis. He posits:

> As scientists we must stand by the biography that is inconclusive, which leaves the essential reality of the whole untrammelled, those depths of human life which can no longer be psychologically explained but which only the poets and philosophers can illumine.[546]

Benevolently, but sceptically, Jaspers is indecisive about how to judge the epistemological claims made by psychosomatics, asking:

> But is it true that all somatic illnesses – even the severe, organic ones – are penetrated by the psyche? Could this be shown convincingly, not only would new fields of human knowledge open up, but a radically new sort of knowledge of physical events would be constituted. I doubt however, that this is possible yet suspect that there are rather close boundaries here, in spite of everything. The question, however, retains some justification.[547]

---

[546] GP 4, pg. 673f.; cf. AP 4, pg. 565.
[547] GP 4, pg. 236; cf. AP 4, pg. 199.

CHAPTER 6

THE FOUNDING OF THE PSYCHOSOMATIC CLINIC IN HEIDELBERG 1946-1949

> There is no forgetfulness which would not have been buried in slips of the tongue and delusions of significance.
>
> Ingeborg Bachmann[548]

Jaspers' contention that psychoanalysis had become an historical phenomenon as a result of the compulsory integration into the 'Göring Institute' did not prove true after 1945. In fact, Heidelberg became the center of a psychoanalytic psychosomatics which played a decisive role in the establishment of chairs for psychosomatic medicine and psychotherapy in 1970 all over the Federal Republic, – chairs which were filled with psychoanalysts.[549] The basis for this was the foundation of what would become the Heidelberg Psychosomatic Clinic in 1949 by Viktor von Weizsäcker and Alexander Mitscherlich. Mitscherlich also endeavored to convince psychoanalysts who had emigrated to North America and England to return to Germany, and these efforts were crucial for the resinstitutionalization of psychoanalysis in the Federal Republic,[550] leading to the foundation of the Sigmund-Freud-Institute in Frankfurt in 1960. These circumstances, along with the promotion of psychoanalysis by Critical Theory, in particular through Jürgen Habermas, created the prerequisites which allowed psychoanalysis to become one of the leading sociophilosophical theories guiding intellectuals in the Federal Republic from the 1960's on.[551] Thus it must almost appear as an ironical twist of history that Jaspers had served as mentor for the one who played the most crucial role in efforts to institutionalize psychoanalysis in the Federal Republic during that person's first years as a researcher and instructor at the university from 1940 to 1950. As Mitscherlich himself writes, Jaspers had been – personally speaking – a "benevolent, paternal friend".[552] The following will depict the controversy over the process of institutionalizing

---

[548] Cf. Bachmann (1979), pg. 407.

[549] Cf. Hoffmann (1999), pg. 7f.. Preliminary activities included a publication commissioned by the DFG (German Research Society) in 1964 entitled *Denkschrift zur Psychotherapie und Psychosomatischen Medizin (Exposé on Psychotherapy and Psychosomatic Medicine)*, which Mitscherlich was involved in.

[550] Cf. Bräutigam (1967), pg. 395.

[551] Cf. this study, pp. 153-155.

[552] Cf. letter from Alexander Mitscherlich to Karl Jaspers from May 10, 1946, JLE-GLA.

psychoanalysis after 1945 as it was conducted in Heidelberg. Here we find many arguments against psychoanalysis which Jaspers would put forth in his later publications. Furthermore, both sides make reference to the criminal actions of the medical profession during National Socialism to discredit either natural-science or psychosomatically oriented medicine.

EXPOSÉ (*DENKSCHRIFT*) ON PSYCHOSOMATIC MEDICINE

Von Weizsäcker and Mitscherlich are to be given the credit for the fact that psychoanalysis succeeded in getting a foothold in the first years after 1945 at the University of Heidelberg. They acted as such convincing advocates of psychoanalytic and psychosomatic medicine that Mitscherlich could begin with the establishment of a Department for General Therapy, later to be called the Psychosomatic Clinic, in the Summer Semester of 1949. When von Weizsäcker returned to Heidelberg after a short period of war captivity in the late summer of 1945, demoralized and with hardly anything in his suitcase but autobiographical writings, Alexander Mitscherlich soon became a close colleague and personal interlocutor. They had known each other for a longer time, for von Weizsäcker had acted as doctoral advisor for Mitscherlich before he took a chair in neurology in Wroclaw. Mitscherlich's thesis, completed in 1941, was entitled *On Characterizing Synaesthetic Perception* (*Zur Wesensbestimmung der synästhetischen Wahrnehmung*). During von Weizsäcker's absence, Mitscherlich wrote a study on psychosomatics under the advisorship of von Weizsäcker's successor Paul Vogel, entitled *On the Origin of Addiction* (*Vom Ursprung der Sucht*). The *Habilitation* study evidenced psychoanalytic leanings in some of its interpretations.[553] For von Weizsäcker, the manuscript constituted one of the "few great gratifications" of this period and he viewed it as a very promising new beginning for Freudian medicine. He did concede, however, that an "epoch" had come to an end since his own efforts to establish psychoanalysis,[554] for von Weizsäcker had not made any theoretical connections between his psychosomatics and Freud's thoughts between 1933 and 1945.

As of January 1946, von Weizsäcker held a chair for "General Clinical Medicine" in Heidelberg which allowed him to carry out clinical research to a modest extent. Furthermore, what is of interest in this context is the fact that he had a vote in the Faculty of Medicine.[555] As early as Spring 1946, he and Mitscherlich presented separate exposés (*Denkschriften*) to the academic public in which they called for institutionalization of psychosomatic and psychoanalytic thought. Within the Faculty of Medicine, their request came up against the resistance of Kurt Schneider, who formulated a wholesale rejection of psychoanalysis. In the course of the controversy, Jaspers was called in to draw up an extensive expertise on psychoanalysis on behalf of the university as a whole. His depiction critically addresses the writings of von Weizsäcker and Mitscherlich, whose argumentative strategies clearly differ.

---

[553] Mitscherlich (1947).
[554] Letter from von Weizsäcker to Alexander Mitscherlich from July 28, 1945, Mitscherlich estate, UA Frankfurt am Main.
[555] Cf. Henkelmann (1992), pg. 177.

This internal discussion already offers many arguments which were to shape the writerly controversy over psychoanalysis from 1950 on.

Von Weizsäcker: "Retribution" and Psychoanalysis

Von Weizsäcker's *Denkschrift* entitled *Recommendations and Application for Designing the Chair for General Clinical Medicine* from April of 1946 begins with fundamental considerations. He emphatically suggests three quite concrete innovations, writing: "Psychoanalysis is the most perfected process in the transformation of medicine, the social orientation of medicine is the most universal, and psychosomatics is the most purposeful."[556] Viktor von Weizsäcker prizes psychoanalysis above social medicine and psychosomatics because, as he contends, the "technique of so-called transference therapy" exerts a particularly ethical effect on the physician-patient relationship, making it the "ideal paradigm for the reform of medicine as a whole". Von Weizsäcker makes not only the widespread rejection of traditional medicine responsible for the lacking effectiveness of psychoanalysis, but also and primarily National Socialist scientific policies. As von Weizsäcker writes, "For well-known reasons, it [psychoanalysis] practically vanished in Germany after 1933."[557] Thus in a later letter he comes to the following conclusion: "After the recent persecution of many representatives of psychoanalysis we even have the obligation to make amends."[558]

Alexander Mitscherlich: Syncreticism of Psychoanalysis at the 'Göring Institute'

In contrast, Mitscherlich's *Denkschriften* from March and May of 1946 do not retrospectively treat psychoanalysis as a guiding theory of psychosomatics. These documents get by almost completely without even using the term and speak in a dissociating manner of "so-called 'psychoanalysis'". Mitscherlich only mentions psychoanalysis explicitly and without any relativizing sentiments in passages where he calls attention to its politically caused suppression during the Third Reich. Thus, in a *Denkschrift* addressed to all professors involved in university policy entitled *Concerning the establishment of an Institute for Biographic Medicine* from March 1946 he writes: "Even during the past decade, individual voices which resisted psychoanalysis for quite noteworthy reasons did not succeed in squelching the interest [in psychoanalysis], which began to evidence itself all over the world once it had awakened."[559] Like von Weizsäcker, he was aware that in the framework of denazification efforts on the part of the allies, it would be hard for the university to reject a

---

[556] Letter from Viktor von Weizsäcker to the Ministery of Culture in Württemberg and Baden, from April 4, 1946, PA Mitscherlich, UA Heidelberg.

[557] Letter from Viktor von Weizsäcker to the Ministery of Culture in Württemberg and Baden, from April 4, 1946, PA Mitscherlich, UA Heidelberg.

[558] Letter from Viktor von Weizsäcker to Dean Engelking from May 25, 1946, PA Viktor von Weizsäcker, UA Heidelberg.

[559] Mitscherlich, manuscript entitled *Recommendations for the Establishment of an Institute for Biographic Medicine (Vorschlag zur Errichtung eines Instituts für biographische Medizin)* from March 6, 1946, Mitscherlich, UA Heidelberg.

discipline which had been attacked by the National Socialists. Furthermore, his status as a "politically 'uninvolved'" and "persecuted person" gave him an advantageous position as concerned university policy-making processes because in light of the large number of politically suspicious members of the university, there was interest in presenting persons like Mitscherlich to the allies as proof of the integrity of the academic community.[560] Mitscherlich himself calls these reasons decisive for the approval of the reestablishment of the Psychosomatic Clinic.[561]

The relatively strong rejection of psychoanalysis expresses itself in the fact that in 1946, Mitscherlich retrospectively praises the 'Göring Institute' in Berlin as an exemplar for the very fact that it had integrated various schools of psychotherapy to form a "syncretic" institution whose aim had been to unite "all schools" such as those of Freud, Adler and Jung with "decidedly mutual treatment methods". The fact that the fusion of various schools of psychotherapy in the form of the 'Göring Institute' of Berlin had been an act of political coersion and was thus questionable was not problematized by Mitscherlich until two decades later.[562]

Without a doubt we can assume that in 1946 Mitscherlich did not favor the exemplary "syncretic" institution in Berlin over psychoanalysis in 1946 for purely pragmatic and tactical reasons.[563] After all, his psychotherapeutic concept is characterized by strong existential leanings and an orientation towards *Daseinsanalyse*. As concerns Mitscherlich's theory of medicine, Jürgen Habermas will later aptly remark:

> When a person becomes ill, he relinquishes part of his freedom. The almost existential motivation for becoming well i.e. the reprocurement of one's freedom, shaped Mitscherlich's understanding and appropriation of psychoanalysis.[564]

Mitscherlich envisions a two-phase model of psychotherapeutic professionalization. He speaks of the psychotherapeutic "specialist" and of the "lay analyst" who, as a psychologist, sociologist or scholar of philosophy was to receive the same training but would only be permitted to work in the psychagogic realm of "educational counselling" and "ministrative education".

Although the praised Berlin Institute had demanded training analysis as a central feature of its training program, Mitscherlich does not mention this at all. To be more precise, his formulations adeptly evade the differentiaton of various training elements without decidedly ruling out the possibility of training analysis. As he writes:

---

[560] Volker Roelcke investigates in great detail the enormous efforts made by the surgeon Karl Heinrich Bauer to recruit Mitscherlich, as one of the few members of the university who had been persecuted by the National Socialists, for the 'Denazification Committee' of those willing and capable of rehabilitating themselves, and shows how Mitscherlich, in a diplomatically wise move, made his membership in the committee indiscretely contingent upon approval of the establishment of the psychotherapeutic institute. Cf. Roelcke (1995), pg. 137f..

[561] Cf Mitscherlich (1980), pg. 187

[562] Cf. Mitscherlich (1983b), pg. 550f..

[563] Cf. Mitscherlich, manuscript entitled *Vorschlag zur Errichtung eines Instituts für biographische Medizin (Recommendations on the Establishment of an Institute for Biographic Medicine)* from March 6, 1943, PA Mitscherlich, UA Heidelberg.

[564] Habermas (1982), pg. 1060; cf. Henkelmannn (1992), pg. 177 as well.

Training programs for candidates previously included practical training and a theoretical introduction to the theory of neurosis, etc., lectures in philosophy, normal psychology and psychiatry along with some special lectures. It is clear that all of this could be best provided for within the framework of an institute of higher education.[565]

Mitscherlich only speaks of "closed seminar exercises" and "special training issues". Apart from the prejudice which he presumed Kurt Schneider – most eminently – to have, a further reason for this obvious secrecy concerning training analysis lies in the fact that neither he nor his teacher, von Weizsäcker, had themselves undergone any training analysis, so this meant that the demand for such a measure would give them little credibility in their dealings with the faculty.[566]

The *Denkschrift* shows that Mitscherlich was well familiar with the *General Psychopathology* through his close contact with Jaspers. For in the passages where he sketches the antagonistic relationship of academic psychiatry to "the psychology of the unconscious", he aptly outlines the psychopathological position held by Jaspers, albeit without making any mention of his name. He writes, "psychology as it has emerged from the schools of psychiatry constitutes without exception psychology of consciousness or phenomenology of psychopathological syndromes without immersion into any special aetiological or therapeutic considerations."[567]

DISPUTE BETWEEN THE FACULTIES – "... THE CAT OUT OF THE SACK"

Kurt Schneider, who had served as director of the Psychiatric Clinic in Heidelberg since March 1946, is the inner-facultative opponent of von Weizsäcker and Mitscherlich. His fear is that psychosomatic psychotherapy will penetrate too far into his own discipline and primarily treat neurotic disorders without somatic symptoms. And indeed, this later came to be the case. As Schneider writes:

Thus I can only vote in favor of the establishment of an institute for psychotherapy if it is exclusively limited to counselling and treatment of non-psychiatric conditions and would under no conditions take on cases of psychogenic disorders (misunderstandably referred to by many as 'neuroses').[568]

Kurt Schneider does not want to relinquish the less seriously afflicted patients, turning his clinic into a "complete mental institution" reduced to presenting only "the insane" in lectures and seminars.[569]

---

[565] *Denkschrift* in letter form from Alexander Mitscherlich to Dean Engelking from May 3, 1946, PA Mitscherlich, UA Heidelberg. Henkelmann claims that Mitscherlich did not fail to address the "topic of training analysis", which he felt to be indispensible. But in my opinion one can not infer from the mention of a "training analyst" that "training analysis" was envisioned as part of the training program. Cf. Henkelmann (1992), pg. 180.

[566] Cf. von Weizsäcker (1954), pg. 44. Mitscherlich did not acquire competence in training analysis until he spent some time of study in England in 1958. Cf. Henkelmann (1992), pg. 183.

[567] *Denkschrift* in letter form from Alexander Mitscherlich to Dean Engelking from May 3, 1946, PA Mitscherlich, UA Heidelberg.

[568] Copy of letter from Kurt Schneider to Dean Engelking from May 6, 1946, JLE-GLA.

[569] Copy of letter from Kurt Schneider to Dean Engelking from May 6, 1946, JLE-GLA.

In response to Schneider, Viktor von Weizsäcker once again clearly advocates psychoanalytic psychotherapy for neuroses by accentuating psychoanalysis as an important original theory from which psychotherapy had emerged.[570] In doing so he emphasizes the cultural-critical impetus of psychoanalysis as a necessary "intellectual revolution" which, as he feels, should continue to be promoted by the university in accordance with psychotherapeutic necessities. Furthermore, in an excursus on the history of psychiatry, von Weizsäcker criticizes "traditional psychiatry", depicting it as antagonistic towards psychoanalysis and deep psychology.[571] Mutual provocations incite the disputants. Kurt Schneider reproaches von Weizsäcker for simply negating "deep psychology" rather than adopting a "more moderate form of it".[572] Von Weizsäcker's foregrounding of psychoanalysis leads Kurt Schneider to claim that now "the cat has been let out of the sack". He candidly cautions the faculty against "establishing an institute built on such a world view".[573] Later he writes:

> As one can see, I operate on the assumption that the planned Institute for Psychotherapy will be engaged in Freud's psychoanalysis. If that were not the case, and were all psychotherapeutic schools to have their place in the institute, I would take a different view of the issue.[574]

Mitscherlich's strategy, which was to play down the image of psychoanalysis as something which evoked antagonism on the part of academic psychiatry by championing a syncretistic training institute modeled after the Berlin Institute had not been successful. Von Weizsäcker's passionate, compensatory determination to defend psychoanalysis against its persistent dispraisers after the years during which he had ignored it, was in no small part responsible for the failure of Mitscherlich's strategy to bear fruit.

Kurt Schneider now attempted to get Jaspers involved in the discussion via the Senate since he justifiably sensed that he would not be able to establish a lobby within the Faculty of Medicine large enough to resist the foundation of the institute. Mitscherlich had expressed his disapproval of Schneider's blockade tactics in a letter to Jaspers and insinuated, "[a]s far as I can see, he will find himself confronted with quite a united front at the next faculty meeting."[575]

---

[570] Cf. letter from Viktor von Weizsäcker to Dean Engelking from May 25, 1946, PA Viktor von Weizsäcker, UA Heidelberg.
[571] Cf. letter from Viktor von Weizsäcker to Dean Engelking from May 25, 1946, PA von Weizsäcker, UA Heidelberg.
[572] Cf. letter from Viktor von Weizsäcker to Dean Engelking from May 25, 1946, PA von Weizsäcker, UA Heidelberg.
[573] These words were spoken at the faculty meeting on April 25, 1946. Parts of the minutes of this meeting with verbatim quotes of participants are to be found in the PA Mitscherlich of the UA Heidelberg. Cited from Henkelmann (1992), pg. 179.
[574] Letter from Kurt Schneider to Dean Engelking from June 13, 1946, PA Alexander Mitscherlich, UA Heidelberg.
[575] Letter from Alexander Mitscherlich to Karl Jaspers from May 12, 1946, JLE-GLA.

JASPERS' ADVOCATION OF PSYCHOANALYSIS UNDER THE SUPERVISION OF MITSCHERLICH

Before the dispute over psychoanalysis made the establishment of the institute an issue for the Senate, Jaspers had, in personal communication with Mitscherlich, advocated the "founding of an institute" connected with Schneider's clinic.[576] In accordance with this preference, he rejected an independent institute in the expertise commissioned by the Senate and spoke out in favor of one which would be connected to the psychiatric clinic supervised by Kurt Schneider. To be sure, Jaspers recommended that the psychotherapeutic institution become independent at a later date if it were to produce convincing results. Because he felt that Mitscherlich was the only one capable of producing such results, Jaspers made the potential establishment of the new department dependent upon him as a "personality of high intellectual rank, comprehensive education and Aesculapian passion".[577] The fact that Mitscherlich's *Habilitation* had been granted solely on the basis of "works of a psychoanalytic nature" without any further scientific accomplishments raised skepsis, however. In part, the expertise declared this shortcoming to be a virtue in that it requested of the faculty that they resolutely initiate the second innovation and let Mitscherlich "research and teach in the discipline he aims to establish".[578] Previously, Mitscherlich had been only moderately successful in establishing a scientific reputation and for Jaspers, this fact is only compensated for to a limited degree by personal qualities. For this reason he makes a case for a contingent department, writing that

> Mr. Mitscherlich's research performance is limited. His personality counts more than what he has to show for himself in the way of publications. He will have to continue to prove himself. If the institute is not founded now, this step could be taken at a later date as affirmation of a second course of action after Mr. Mitscherlich has implemented therapy as a reality and created visible research results.[579]

Apart from commenting on the concrete issue of whether to establish an institute or not, Jaspers addresses fundamental questions concerning psychoanalysis. He contradicts von Weizsäcker's view that it now belonged to the "base stock" of academic knowledge by contesting the neurosis-aetiological claims made by psychoanalysis which strived to prove the validity of its theories by presenting successfully treated cases.[580] Looking upon himself as an "administrator of philosophical traditions", Jaspers debases psychoanalysis as an "undeveloped philosophy with no clear consciousness of itself".[581] Freud is also subjected to wholesale denunciation with

---

[576] Letter from Karl Jaspers to Alexander Mitscherlich from May 12, 1946, Mitscherlich estate, UA Frankfurt am Main.

[577] Cf. Jaspers, manuscript of *Über die Errichtung eines Instituts für Psychotherapie*, JLE-GLA.

[578] Jaspers, manuscript of *Über die Errichtung eines Instituts für Psychotherapie*, JLE-GLA, pg. 1.

[579] Jaspers, manuscript of *Über die Errichtung eines Instituts für Psychotherapie*, JLE-GLA, pg. 2.

[580] Cf. this study, pg. 34f..

[581] Jaspers, manuscript of *Über die Errichtung eines Instituts für Psychotherapie*, JLE-GLA, pg. 8.

Jaspers contending that he had not been "a scientific or a moral figure" to whom one could entrust an institute. The controversial issue as to how to train the medical layman is interpreted by Jaspers as an alarming indication that psychoanalytic philosophy was in danger of becoming popularized. We read:

> As soon as psychoanalysis becomes a discipline in its own right as it stands now, represented by psychoanalysts who are, medically speaking, no more than this, the floodgates will open up for all the nonsense which could enter by way of popular writings on psychoanalysis.[582]

As Jaspers contends, the demand for "layman psychotherapists" harbors the intention to import psychoanalytic thought into society at large via areas of application which lie outside the area of medicine.[583] In the period immediately after World War II, this vision appears particularly threatening. As Jaspers writes:

> The phenomenon in itself poses the dangers which, once they have become real, will be hard to subdue because all that is abysmal, enchanting and uncritical will have an easy time of it in light of the reduced capacity to think on the part of young people after twelve years of our failing to educate them.[584]

These polemical verdicts do not imply the total rejection of psychoanalysis one might presume them to be expressing. What Jaspers in fact means is that this "questionable affair" could be promoted if one had reason to hope for its "transformation into a tenable, generally acknowledged procedure with tenable, generally acknowledged results".[585] As guarantor of a brand of psychoanalysis which could be refined into a scientifically tenable form of psychotherapy, the expertise once again names Mitscherlich. "Not in relation to this phenomenon [psychoanalysis], but rather in relation to Mr. Mitscherlich, a founding is justifiable", Jaspers writes[586]. Jaspers revises his trustful judgment concerning Mitscherlich's capacity to keep psychoanalysis within the limits of traditional medicine as early as 1950, however, now arguing his clear-sighted judgment concerning the societal role which psychoanalysis ascribes to itself without mitigative reservations in public. Mitscherlich's first clearly articulated demand that obligatory training analysis be introduced, made in 1949, had been read by Jaspers as an indication of far-reaching intentions, as will be elucidated in the further course of this study.[587]

That Jaspers deems the "framework of the psychiatric clinic" to be indispensible for a possible reform of psychoanalysis led by Mitscherlich corresponds to the

---

[582] Jaspers, manuscript of *Über die Errichtung eines Instituts für Psychotherapie*, JLE-GLA, pg. 5.

[583] Jaspers, manuscript of *Über die Errichtung eines Instituts für Psychotherapie*, JLE-GLA, pg. 7.

[584] Structurally speaking, Jaspers had used the same argument some months earlier in an expertise on Martin Heidegger which primarily cited pedagogical reasons for temporarily rejecting the reinstatement of the philosopher's academic privileges. Cf. Jaspers/Heidegger (1990), pp. 269-274.

[585] Jaspers, manuscript of *Über die Errichtung eines Instituts für Psychotherapie*, JLE-GLA, pg. 4f..

[586] Jaspers, manuscript of *Über die Errichtung eines Instituts für Psychotherapie*, JLE-GLA, pg. 5.

[587] Cf. this study, pp. 111f..

reservation which had already been expressed in 1941/42 concerning the institutionalization in Berlin. As Jaspers had written,

> [t]he main deficiency of this initial institution is that it functions apart from any psychiatric clinic. Psychotherapists who have no sound knowledge of the psychoses gained from their own experience and no contact with them in institutional practice can easily make fatal mistakes of diganosis; they also fall victims to the fantastic nonsense which occupies so much space in the psychotherapeutic literature.[588]

Training analysis, which Jaspers had already viewed critically in 1941/42 and which Mitscherlich wisely failed to mention in his application from 1946, is indirectly excluded from the expertise as an issue to be addressed, for what is defined as qualifying the "medical specialist" are several years of clinical experience alone.[589]

ESTABLISHMENT OF A DEPARTMENT FOR GENERAL THERAPY

Mitscherlich did not mention the controversial training analysis in his dealings with the academic committees although he had already set his sights on it as a training goal, as his correspondence with the psychoanalyst Felix Schottländer documents. In May of 1946 Schottländer had been asked by Mitscherlich to take over training analyses, "collaborating with the institute on an entirely free-lance basis".[590] Mitscherlich indicated to Schottländer how little enthusiasm he had for von Weizsäcker's idea of, as it were, throwing a "first anchor" in the process of institutionalizing psychotherapy by means of an "institute for psychic treatment of inner diseases". As he said, his interests lay much more in institutional collaboration with physicians and psychologists, which would make it possible to focus on treating neurotic disorders while remaining relatively independent of the other clinical disciplines.[591]

Thus Mitscherlich was not at all pleased that Jaspers' expertise definitively demanded an institutional connection between psychiatry and psychotherapy.[592] Kurt Schneider was not taken with the idea either and recommended to the Dean a variation on the idea of setting up a department which would be limited to psychosomatics and not bring Mitscherlich into connection with psychiatry or neurology.[593] Apparently both adversaries put no store by the symbiosis of psychiatry and psychotherapy apostrophized by Jaspers.

Vis-a-vis Jaspers, Mitscherlich candidly labelled his elder's expertise as "clearly hostile", "unobjective" and "one-sided". More than anything else, Mitscherlich was

---

[588] GP 4, pg. 811; cf. AP 4, pg. 678.

[589] Jaspers' manuscript of *Über die Errichtung eines Instituts für Psychotherapie*, JLE-GLA.

[590] Copy of letter from Alexander Mitscherlich to Felix Schottländer from May 29, 1946, Mitscherlich estate, UA Frankfurt am Main.

[591] Copy of letter from Alexander Mitscherlich to Felix Schottländer from May 15, 1946, Mitscherlich estate, UA Frankfurt am Main.

[592] Copy of letter from Alexander Mitscherlich to Felix Schottländer from May 15, 1946, Mitscherlich estate, UA Frankfurt am Main.

[593] Letter from Kurt Schneider to Dean Engelking from August 30, 1946, PA Mitscherlich, UA Heidelberg.

provoked by the thesis that the foundation of the institute ultimately pursued politico-societal goals; he foregrounded the "therapeutic", not the "philosophical" necessity of psychotherapeutic institutionalization and in doing so refused to recognize
Jaspers' capacity to pass judgment as regarded "dealings with patients who were
treated psychoanalytically". Mitscherlich speaks of "tendentious illumination".[594]

In September 1946, the Faculty voted in favor of the compromise suggested by
Richard Siebeck, professor of internal medicine, as the following minutes of the
meeting document:

> For the time being, no decision will be made to establish an independent institute for
> psychotherapy; instead, a work field will be created for Mr. Mitscherlich in which he
> can apply his method. We recommend that this psychotherapeutic position be subordi-
> nated to the Chair for General Clinical Medicine, which is held by Prof. Dr. von
> Weizsäcker.[595]

And yet almost two years pass before the university supplies the funds for the institute, after the American Rockefeller Foundation offers to provide assistance. This
only takes place under the political pressure of the Minister of Justice, Carlo
Schmid, however, who accentuates the key role played by Mitscherlich as one of the
few academics to have acted in an exemplary manner during National Socialism.[596]
In the Summer Semester of 1949, Mitscherlich can begin setting up the Department
for General Therapy, which officially opens its doors in 1950. For all extensive
purposes he works independently of von Weizsäcker's Chair and after von
Weizsäcker's retirement in the 1950's , the department achieves the independent
status of a psychosomatic clinic.[597]

---

[594] Letter from Alexander Mitscherlich to Karl Jaspers from July 16, 1946, JLE-GLA.

[595] Minutes of the meeting at the Dean's office on September 25, 1946 in Heidelberg.
The following persons were present: Richard Siebeck, Curt Oehme, Paul Vogel and
Ernst Engelking. Files of the Department of Psychosomatics, UA Heidelberg, cited in
Henkelmann (1986), pg. 172.

[596] Cf. letter from Carlo Schmid to Rector Geiler from January 6, 1949, PA K.H. Bauer,
UA Heidelberg, citied in Henkelmann (1992), pg. 181.

[597] Cf. Mitscherlich (1980), pg. 193.

CHAPTER SEVEN

CRITIQUE OF PSYCHOANALYTIC
PSYCHOSOMATICS 1949-1953

> Truth indeed lies between two extremes, but not in the middle.
>
> Moritz Heimann[598]

Despite the differences of opinion which emerged between Jaspers and Mitscherlich during the process of applying for the "Institute for Psychotherapy", they remained in contact after 1946. Most significantly, Mitscherlich informed Jaspers of the foundation of the journal *Psyche*.[599] He had edited this journal together with Felix Schottländer and Hans Kunz, a Swiss philosopher and psychologist, since July 1947 under the name *Zeitschrift für Tiefenpsychologie und Menschenkunde in Forschung und Praxis (Journal for Deep Psychology and Anthropology in Research and Practice)*. The monthly periodical, whose spiritus rector was clearly Mitscherlich himself, had made it its goal to reflect on psychotherapy within the framework of international research contributions from all relevant disciplines.[600] In the summer of 1949 Jaspers receives an issue of *Psyche*, but one which had not been sent by Mitscherlich, but rather by Kurt Kolle, a student of psychiatry.[601] Kolle had contributed an article on psychosomatics, which had been treated as an independent topic for the first time at the Internists' conference in Wiesbaden in 1949.[602] But Jaspers was less interested in the contribution by Kolle which had been dedicated to him than the ones which von Weizsäcker and Mitscherlich had presented at the conference

---

[598] Heimann (1966), pg. 5.

[599] Cf. letter from Alexander Mitscherlich to Karl Jaspers from January 30, 1948, JLE-GLA: "After our telephone conversation yesterday I have found no peace realizing that you possess neither the journal nor my book on thirst. Please allow me to send both of these to you – as basis for discussion. The contributions of *Psyche* are for example proof (in my view in any case) of the fact that psychoanalysis has continued to develop – albeit still far from what I myself continue to expect of it. It was good to be able to talk to you for so long yesterday."

[600] Lockot (1994) treats the history of the periodical; cf. pp. 150-166.

[601] Jaspers was viewed as an "inwardly independent psychotherapist". Cf. this study, pg. 120.

[602] Cf. Kolle (1949). The volume is to be found in Jaspers' library, Dr. Hans Saner, Basle. On pg 377 stands: "With sincere regards, the author".

in Wiesbaden; these dominated the issue of the periodical.[603] This coincidental reading provoked Jaspers to such a degree that he formulated two acerbic critiques of psychoanalytic psychosomatics in Basle, where he had accepted a professorship for philosophy in the spring of 1948. In 1950 he published his "Critique of Psycho-analysis" ("Zur Kritik der Psychoanalyse") in *Nervenarzt* and in 1953 "Physician and Patient" ("Arzt und Patient") in *Studium Generale*.[604] These writings were a reaction to the claims made on aetiology by psychoanalytic psychosomatics and the recommendations in favor of training analysis as part of the training program at the University of Heidelberg.

PSYCHOSOMATIC PROVOCATIONS

Viktor von Weizsäcker's Apology of "Unlived Life"

At the conference in Wiesbaden, von Weizsäcker began his lecture entitled "Psychosomatic Medicine" ("Psychosomatische Medizin") with an attack on the customary view of objective science.[605] In allusion to crimes committed by the medical profession during the Third Reich he asks, "how does it happen to be that such undesired things can be done in practice?"[606] By discrediting all medicine with a sole orientation to the exact sciences, he attempts to do what he had already done in his *Denkschrift* concerning the establishment of the institute in Heidelberg, namely to emphasize the urgency of "reforming medicine" by means of psychosomatic medicine.[607] In advocating this view, he speaks of "anthropological psycho-somatics", which, as he expressly states, should be approached from a psychoana-lytically substantiated perspective.[608] "Psychosomatic medicine must be based on deep psychology or it will not be at all," he writes. In avowing to the "psychoanaly-sis of Sigmund Freud" he alludes to the most recent history of "psychiatry in the Reich", which had been, as he says, a "fatality" for all.[609] Depth-psychological psy-chosomatics was to judge human beings from the perspective of anthropological "perfection". The text is very unclear about just what characteristics the perfected human being was to possess, although this ideal took on a normatively eminent significance for psychosomatic therapy. According to von Weizsäcker, the perfected human being was to be understood most clearly *ex negativo*, his opposite constituting the modern, entirely functionalized individual who has been completely integrated

---

[603] Cf. the excerpt by Jaspers, which reads "von Weizsäcker at the Internists' Conference in Wiesbaden,", Psyche III, 331ff., in the folder labelled "Psychoanalysis", JLE-GLA. In this issue of *Psyche,* the following contributions have markings all the way through: von Weizsäcker (pp. 331-341), Mitscherlich's concluding remarks (pp. 391-398) and the Argentinian "Regulations on Training for Psychoanalysts" (pg. 399).

[604] Cf. Jaspers (1950d) and Jaspers (1953a)

[605] Cf. von Weizsäcker (1949), pp. 451-464.

[606] Von Weizsäcker (1949), pg. 453.

[607] Von Weizsäcker (1949), pg. 453.

[608] Cf. von Weizsäcker (1949), pg. 454.

[609] Von Weizsäcker (1949), pg. 455.

into civilization's "operational State".[610] Furthermore, von Weizsäcker outrightly speaks of therapeutic "spiritualization", which in his view leads to unavoidable and valuable conflicts with societal conventions, maintaining that any "successful psychotherapy for organic diseases" goes hand in hand with the "production of a new conflict" on the societal level. "Whether it is a divorce, a political overthrow or a religious revolution, in any case the patient who has been healed in this way will become an adversary of the established order and his physician will be looked upon with disapproval by friends and beneficiaries of the previous order,"[611] von Weizsäcker writes provocatively.

Thus von Weizsäcker's psychosomatic approach is characterized by its unrestrained incorporation of the physician's value judgments concerning what form the patient's life should ideally take on into the treatment process. "Therapy means taking action on the part of the physician, becoming involved in the disease process, accompanying it, intermingling with it, affecting its course."[612] In taking this position, von Weizsäcker devalues the search for objectifiable diagnostic findings which have no connection to personal behavior as an attempt to ignore the decisive subjective roots of disease. As he writes,

> [w]e finally became accustomed to talking of mental disorders rather than moral sins, and ultimately of disease rather than human evil. All of these new labels – nervosity, neurodystonia, psychoneurosis and the moral disease are fig leaves in regard to the human disposition.[613]

Von Weizsäcker accuses scientific medicine of having "fundamentally" lost sight of personal frameworks of meaning by foregrounding objective and value-free aetiologies.[614] Von Weizsäcker believes he is capable of identifying "sin" and "evil" as pathogenically important factors of psychosomatic diseases by "deciphering organ language".[615] As he argued, for the very reason that aetiological correspondences between the psyche and the soma could not be easily determined, an intensification of psychosomatic research was necessary.[616] He suggestively speaks of the ongoing discovery of "unlived" and "abbreviated" life which psychosomatic therapy could perfect and invest with meaning.[617]

The medical question as to whether the patient even wished to adopt the recommended normative patterns of life invested with meaning is left unasked by von Weizsäcker, for he considers this to be a part of medicine. His aim is to use the disease to lead the patient – with the help of the physician – to the "meaning of his life", inevitably turning the latter into a philosophical and religious authority.[618] For the patient is compelled to adopt the physician's values, which are presented to him as part of the medicine. The prerequisite for a well-applied form of value freedom

---

[610] Cf. von Weizsäcker (1949), pg. 458.
[611] Von Weizsäcker (1949), pg. 461.
[612] Von Weizsäcker (1949), pg. 462.
[613] Von Weizsäcker (1949), pg. 459.
[614] Von Weizsäcker (1949), pg. 464.
[615] Von Weizsäcker (1949), pg. 458.
[616] Von Weizsäcker (1949), pg. 548 and 460.
[617] Cf. von Weizsäcker (1949), pg. 460.
[618] Von Weizsäcker (1949), pg. 464.

would be to enlighten the patient about the ultimate scope of the treatment – and von Weizsäcker's model, which defines "the meaning of life" as its defining parameter, has an enormously wide scope – in the sense of informed consent before any kind of therapeutic interaction began to take its course. Apparently von Weizsäcker's psychosomatic approach is founded on a paternalistic physician-patient relationship.

Alexander Mitscherlich: Regarding the "Self-Concealment of Meaning"

Mitscherlich's lecture entitled "The Scope of Psychosomatic Thought in Medicine" orients itself towards von Weizsäcker's high normative aims in that he also attempts to trace the path "from the manifest disease" back to the "meaning of the event".[619] Mitscherlich counters any reservations about psychosomatic interpretations of disease with the impetus of intensified research. As he asks, "what are the limits of this doctrine of diseases? [...] We do not know. [...] Who is better suited to produce the proof than the clinic?"[620]

According to Mitscherlich, every disease involves a "split personality" in the sense that the person in question is incapable of expressing deep wishes spontaneously and is thus unconsciously forced to express their "enciphered symbolization" in the "symptom" as a kind of compromise. Thus the patient 'pays' with the "self-concealment of meaning" whenever the "unconscious part of his personality" is not capable of direct articulation.[621] Thus for Mitscherlich any "successful healing" means helping the "personality to effect a more complete integration, a more successful realization of his or her nature".[622]

This psychosomatic anthropology operates on the premise that the "identity" of the personality exists at birth and gets lost as a result of the repression of civilization.[623] This approach interprets "disease processes" within a biographical framework[624] and connects the idea of unconscious childlike drives with biographical conflicts which lead to a conflict-ridden interplay of "conscious and unconscious strivings".[625] Apart from ideas put forth by Freud and von Weizsäcker, marked by such terms as "unconscious", "biographical" and "personal", existence-philosophical and existence-analytical interpretations are incorporated into this doctrine of disease as well, with Mitscherlich formulating the idea of disease as a kind of existential crisis around 1945. Moreover, he seizes upon a romantically colored body of thought in emphasizing the development of the individual personality and positing a correspondence between conscious intellectual activity and the unconscious emotional depths of the psyche. It is no coincidence that he adopted the title of Carl Gustav Carus' monograph *Psyche* as the programmatic name for his journal.

---

[619] Mitscherlich (1949a).
[620] Mitscherlich (1949a), pg. 42f..
[621] Mitscherlich (1949a), pg. 39.
[622] Mitscherlich (1949a), pg. 51.
[623] Mitscherlich (1949a), pg. 48.
[624] Mitscherlich (1949a), pg. 44.
[625] Mitscherlich (1949a), pg. 47.

Mitscherlich stylizes depth-psychological psychosomatics as an island of "human impartiality" amidst a misanthropic industrial society. Thus he is not solely interested in "treating symptoms" and restoring his patients' "capacity to work and enjoy life", for as he sees it, these therapeutic goals only benefit de-individualized societal tendencies.[626] Instead, citing the "anthropological responsibility" of the psychosomaticist, Mitscherlich attempts to aid the individual in furthering the "maturation of his personality".[627] The guiding idea behind this enterprise is the harmonious correspondence between the unconscious and the conscious, with the latter being identified as decisive for the development of the personality. In Mitscherlich's view, this makes a depth-psychological approach absolutely necessary. As he writes,

> [u]nconscious psychic activity and unconscious bodily performance are much more closely connected than consciousness and artificially isolating physiological experimentation. This rediscovery of the identity of what is essentially separate, the mysterious interpenetration in the enactment of a person's life calls for new forms of research.[628]

By defining the "maturation of the personality" as the ultimate goal of treatment rather than the purely pragmatic and instrumental goal of "healing the symptoms", Mitscherlich lays the basis for his argument in favor of a time-intensive, "financially costly depth-psychological therapy" which greatly impacts the personality. At the conference no mention is made of what form this kind of therapy is to take, but the conference issue of *Psyche* makes it unmistakably clear that the modus which Mitscherlich has in mind is psychoanalytic training analysis, for his closing words are accompanied by the Argentinian *Training Regulations for Psychoanalysts* to which the following editorial comment is added: "In light of our current discussion of the same problems, these demanding regulations for basic psychoanalytic training appear to us to be valuable enough to present them to our readers."[629]

JASPERS' REACTIONS 1950-1953

American Circumstances – Hannah Arendt on Psychoanalysis (1)

Until the conference issue of *Psyche* came out, Jaspers believed Mitscherlich to be capable of assessing psychoanalytic ideas and identifying scientifically sound aspects which could be put to good use for doctrine-free academic psychotherapy without any special training analysis. After the department was established in 1949, Jaspers was forced to recognize, on the basis of the two articles on psychoanalysis and the accompanying psychoanalytic training regulations, that he had been mistaken. Indeed, during the years to come, training analysis was to become a central component of advanced academic training for psychotherapists, albeit without

---

[626] Mitscherlich (1949a), pg. 50f..
[627] Mitscherlich (1949a), pg. 50.
[628] Mitscherlich (1949b), pg. 397.
[629] Argentinian Psychoanalytic Society (1949), pg. 399.

becoming mandatory, as Jaspers had feared. In 1950 he reacts first of all by publishing his article entitled "Critique of Psychoanalysis", and in 1953 he publishes "Physician and Patient" as a contribution to a special issue of *Studium Generale* whose publication he had personally suggested;[630] as Jaspers remarks, the "curious position" which von Weizsäcker had taken occasioned the choice of a medical topic.[631]

Jaspers was surprised that the psychoanalytically oriented psychosomaticists received so much attention at the Conference for Internal Medicine in 1949. "The degree of recognition in the discussion conducted by non-analysts" and the "caution which implied that perhaps there was something to it after all" are viewed by Jaspers as indications that this "faith" had already impacted scientifically based medicine to a strong degree.[632] In response to the internist Curt Oehme, who attempted to defend psychoanalysis as an innovation which was worthy of being protected, [633] Jaspers responds:

> The enterprises which I am referring to have been so successful and have become so well-known all over the world, where they enjoy so much propaganda, that I deem a clear and decisive word from me to be valuable in this situation. [...] What I put forth in the short aticle is no momentary, incidental annoyance but rather the attempt to, as it were, drop a little bomb to draw attention.[634]

Later Jaspers wrote to Oskar Pfister, a psychoanalyst who had published a critical reply to Jaspers in *Psyche*[635], saying that "reliable information on the development of psychoanalysis within institutional frameworks, particularly in America" had motivated him to formulate his critique of psychoanalysis once more.[636] Most probably this information came from Jaspers' emigrated student Hannah Arendt, who had paid almost annual visits to him since 1949 and like hardly anyone else from the younger generation provided him with "concrete knowledge of the world".[637]

As an institutionally independent representative of the Horkheimer Institute for Social Research, which had been moved to the USA, Siegfried Kracauer articulates apprehensions similar to those of Jaspers in 1948, observing:

> Psychiatry and in particular psychoanalysis currently enjoy incredible popularity in this country. In the decades before the war they were only fashionable among intellectuals; today the fashion has become a mass phenomenon.[638]

Ellenberger reports that the forced emigration of European psychoanalysts to England and in even larger numbers to the USA from 1933 on had caused psychoanalysis to flourish there beginning in the war years. As he writes, psychoanalysts were appointed to leading positions in psychiatric departments of universities and

[630] Cf. Jaspers (1953a).
[631] Copy of letter from Karl Jaspers to Manfred Thiel from April 12, 1952, JLE-GLA.
[632] Jaspers (1950c), pg. 66f.
[633] Cf. letter from Curt Oehme to Karl Jaspers from February 25, 1951, JLE-GLA.
[634] Copy of letter from Karl Jaspers to Curt Oehme from March 3, 1951, JLE-GLA.
[635] Pfister (1952).
[636] Copy of letter from Karl Jaspers to Oskar Pfister from September 20, 1952, JLE-GLA:
[637] Cf. AJC, pg. 33.
[638] Kracauer (1948), pg. 319.

their body of thought penetrated the cultural life of intellectuals.[639] Arendt will have informed Jaspers of these developments, particularly since she did not favor the dominant role which psychoanalysis played for the intellectual self-understanding of Americans.[640]

Jaspers took this information about the much more advanced influence of psychoanalysis on American intellectuals as an indication that a similar development would occur in post-war Germany if one did not prevent psychoanalysis from exerting an influence on academic training. Only within this context is the polemical acerbity of the two articles "Critique of Psychoanalysis" and "Physician and Patient" understandable. For the large part, they address purely medical issues such as the classic question as to the aetiological and therapeutic scope of psychosomatic hermeneutics. But the focus on regulations concerning training analysis, which are viewed very critically in "Critique of Psychoanalysis" in 1950 as a questionable form of training indicates the politico-societal dimension of Jaspers' attack. He wanted no university-trained psychoanalysts who, like the academic elite in the USA, would exert a formative influence on cultural life. His critique of psychoanalysis is also motivated by the "antiauthoritarian" position which Jaspers shared with other European intellectuals who had joined forces since 1950 around the time of the Conference for Cultural Freedom in Berlin. He viewed psychoanalysis as he did marxism, namely as a politically relevant ideology, taking the view that for this reason it was important to take a stand against it outside of the medical context as well. "It is unavoidable that even today, what is true must clothe itself in propaganda in order to reach the ears of the people,"[641] Jaspers reluctantly observes. The 1950 guest lectures in Heidelberg entitled *The Perennial Scope of Philosophy* (*Vernunft und Widervernunft*),[642] which were soon published in book form, and the article entitled "Freud and Marx" published in *Monat*,[643] both of which formulated almost the identical message, acted on this insight, in particular the lectures. The political aspects of Jaspers' critique and the way in which they manifest themselves in the intellectual context of this period will be examined in the next chapter. The purely medical debate which Jaspers' late critique of psychoanalysis took up again will form the initial focus of inquiry.

---

[639] Cf. Ellenberger (1970), pp. 1163 and 1172.

[640] Cf. Arendt (1979), pg. 117. Here she rejects psychoanalysis in particular due to its excessive and suggestive use of metaphors. In 1966 Arendt reports the self-evident fact that around 1933, the discussions conducted among intellectuals had been saturated with psychoanalytic terminology and that Jaspers' opposition had been as unpopular as had been the critique during the 1940's in the USA. Cf. letter from Hannah Arendt to Mrs. Decker from May 18, 1966; copy from the Arendt estate (Library of Congress, Washington, D.C.), in the possession of Prof. Bernd Neumann (University of Trondheim).

[641] Jaspers (1954a), pg. 20.

[642] Jaspers (1950b), pp.18-22. Jaspers criticizes psychoanalysis as a movement defined by a "world view" which had led to a "neglect" of science, commenting in addition on some medical aspects of the issue.

[643] *Der Monat* was an international journal founded in Berlin in 1948 by the American journalist Melvin J. Lasky which served as a forum for anti-totalitarian intellectuals who emerged from the Conference for Cultural Freedom until the mid-1960's. Cf. Martin (1999).

Mitscherlich, who admitted to having skirted Jaspers' "Critique of Psychoanalysis", maintaining that he had only read it for "editorial reasons", responds to Jaspers shortly before the "Critique" appears. He writes, "the trenchancy of your attack governed my response."[644] In the following, Mitscherlich's reply – "Critique or Politics?" ("Kritik oder Politik?") – will be read as an oppositional view of psychoanalysis in the context of my interpretation of Jaspers' two articles "Critique of Psychoanalysis" and "Physician and Patient".[645]

"Biological" Limits of Psychosomatic "Salvific Doctrines"

Jaspers decidedly opposes the holistic claim made by psychosomatics and its belief that in emphasizing the scientifically limited perspective of medicine it could make individual, cultural and social connections by "deciphering the organ language."[646] In doing so, he emphasizes the scientifically limited perspective of medicine, writing, "I am a physician by virtue of expert knowledge; expert knowledge is based on objectification, and objectification in turn on distancing oneself."[647] For this reason he accentuates the purely somatic foundation of the pathogenesis of neuroses, which, in his view, could be complemented by existential understanding – albeit without any claims being made to scientific objectivity. Thus for Jaspers, existential "understanding of meaning" and causality "devoid of meaning" were two separate phenomena.[648] In his view psychosomatoses, like neuroses and psychoses, are subject to mechanisms devoid of meaning.[649] To be sure, in the sense of a specific vulnerability, Jaspers does not rule out the possibility that there might be certain meaningful, explainable factors which influence the outbreak of a mental disorder. If no specific vulnerability were to exist, individuals could repress and forget things without this causing any serious somatic or psychic disorders to ensue,[650] he posits. As Jaspers sees it, due to causally decisive "unknown extraconscious mechanisms", the search for "meaningful and comprehensible connections" of disorders does not lead to any verifiable results; at best, it is beneficial on a purely human level, but it belongs in the realm of "poetry and philosophy" and does not constitute a task of the physician.[651] With clear ironic undertones, Jaspers remarks on the hermeneutic claims made by psychosomaticists, writing that "everything which happens to and in human beings has some meaning".[652]

Mitscherlich responds to Jaspers' epistemologically skeptical theory of neurosis by writing:

> Efforts made within the field of psychoanalysis have shown that no adequate view of mankind emerges if one distinguishes between causality devoid of meaning, quasi

---

[644] Letter from Alexander Mitscherlich to Karl Jaspers from March 18, 1951, JLE-GLA.
[645] Cf. Mitscherlich (1951).
[646] Cf. Jaspers (1953a), pg. 20 and von Weizsäcker (1949), pg. 458.
[647] Jaspers (1953a), pg. 27.
[648] Jaspers (1950c), pg. 60.
[649] Jaspers (1950c), pg. 61
[650] Jaspers (1950c), pg. 61.
[651] Cf. Jaspers (1953a), pg. 30f..
[652] Jaspers (1950c), pg. 61.

free-floating notions of meaningfulness and meaningful decision-making (by the ethical personality, for example).[653]

In opposition to Jaspers, Mitscherlich calls for the "psychosomatic unity of the personality" in which the "biological" element is subject to a meaningful "expressive event" so that in favorable cases "insights" into this pathology could effect an extinction of symptoms.[654] In terms of psychosomatics, Mitscherlich makes the same connections which Freud had made in regard to the treatment of neuroses, positing that correct insights into the empirical connections of symptoms can cause them to vanish. Jaspers deems this correlation between insightful understanding and an improvement of symptoms "questionable", claiming that the positive effects could not be traced back to specific insights, but were primarily produced by the suggestive influence of the physician's personal and methodological aura. As he writes,

[i]t has been a known fact that for centuries, all psychotherapeutic methods have been successful when used by effective personalities. One can see that psychoanalytic methods yield just as many successes and failures as do other methods.[655]

Jaspers refers to psychoanalytic psychosomatics as a "salvific doctrine" which succeeded theology and philosophy in so far as it aimed to effect a transformational "rebirth" of the personality instead of a restoration of the "biological health of the body".[656] In terms of their comprehensive goals, Mitscherlich's notion of psychoanalytic "maturation of the personality" and von Weizsäcker's concept, which sees in psychosomatic treatment the potential for coming closer to the "meaning of life", can be compared with the model of existence-philosophical self-reflection, the difference being that Jaspers does not attempt to legitimize philosophical self-reflection scientifically.

In order to sketch the further extent of the medical debate one might add that the ambitious psychosomaticist Paul Christian, the successor to von Weizsäcker's Chair in the Department of General Clinical Medicine, and Walter Bräutigam, who succeeded Mitscherlich as Director of the Psychosomatic Clinic in 1968, held a more conservative view of the scope and conclusiveness of the psychosomatic approach. In particular, in 1961 they criticized psychodynamic models of conflict as they had been presented by von Weizsäcker and Mitscherlich in 1949 as monocausal simplifications of "multi-conditional" aetiologies of disease.[657] For one, in their textbook *Psychosomatic Medicine (Psychosomatische Medizin)*, the authors criticize Mitscherlich for not accompanying his "differentiated psychological hypotheses"

---

[653] Mitscherlich (1951), pg. 167.

[654] Mitscherlich (1951). pg. 167.

[655] Jaspers (1950c), pg. 60.

[656] Cf. Jaspers (1953a), pp. 32-34.

[657] Bräutigam/Christian (1961), pg. 354. In more concrete terms, the authors relativize Mitscherlich's postulate on "simultaneous psychophysical events", which, as his critics point out, correlated verbal expressions like "to stand under pressure", as descriptions of psychic conditions, suggestively with the bodily phenomenon of blood pressure. Cf. Bräutigam/Christian (1961), pg. 351f..

with "equally differentiated observations on physiological and pathological bodily processes".[658]

Jaspers solves the normative dilemma of holistic approaches by orienting himself in the direction of "objectivistic" theories of aetiology. For him, existential communication alone might result in a "word of the genuinely present physician uttered at the right moment" completely "incalculably coinciding with the freedom of the patient" and leading him to reflect upon his life situation more carefully. But as a participating "subject", the physician must not make any remarks of a "precisely objective nature" concerning the patient's biography, Jaspers adds.[659] If he does, which is to say, if he attemps to decipher the patient's organ language unequivocally, he oversteps the boundaries of his profession. In regard to von Weizsäcker – who had stylized the patient in psychotherapeutic treatment on his way to recovery as an "opponent of customary order" – Jaspers speaks of a "concealed, fanatical and destructive tendency" inherent in psychosomatic thought.[660] As early as 1947 he had advised the philosopher Gerhard Krüger against recommending von Weizsäcker as a physician to potential patients, saying that von Weizsäcker was only too quick to speculate on life-environmental causes of disease. As he writes,

> I value Mr. von Weizsäcker as an educated person and on the basis of some ideas he has put forth, but as a physician I would have little trust in him because he is a man who murmurs, almost with more philosophy in his head than medicine, but bad philosophy. As a physician, he appears to me to be immodest as regards his basic attitude, making the human being much too much the object of treatment by virtue of putative insights. But he has a name. He is a controversial figure among colleagues, but no one doubts that he is very intelligent, and right they are.[661]

Mitscherlich attempts to defend the highly normative remarks made by von Weizsäcker about the pathogenetic connections between "disease", "culpability" and "evil" against Jaspers' vehement criticism.[662] He interprets the theological concept of "guilt" within a new, psychological framework after Jaspers pointed to it as characteristic of the moralistic tendency of psychosomatics. As Mitscherlich writes,

> [i]t might be that some emphatically Christian-oriented psychoanalysts have been uncareful enough to very simplistically characterize poor decisions made within the realm of human responsibility in terms of culpability. [...] In this case, [this concept] would mean that an individual had culpably neglected a certain path towards self-fulfilment in favor of an abnormal path. When the word is used in this way, no moral reproach would be attached to it, however.[663]

For Mitscherlich, psychoanalysis functioned as a therapeutic instrument used to overcome the "malposition" which the patient had adopted to escape from "genuine demands". This therapeutic correction of an individual's personal "malposition", which von Weizsäcker calls "Schuld" (culpability), is interpreted by Mitscherlich with an existentialist gesture as the challenge of viewing oneself in the condition of

---

[658] Bräutigam/Christian (1985), pp. 43-46.
[659] Cf. Jaspers (1953a), pg. 28.
[660] Jaspers (1950c), pg. 62.
[661] Copy of letter from Karl Jaspers to Gerhard Krüger from April 16, 1947, JLE-GLA.
[662] Jaspers (1950c), pg. 62.
[663] Mitscherlich (1951), pg. 172f..

the disorder as "self-reliant and self-fulfilling".[664] Mitscherlich's psychoanalytic-existentialist interpretation of the concept of culpability harbors the danger of latent moralism and paternalism on the part of the physician, since medico-psychological language does not demonstrate its normativity as explicitly as the religiously connoted concept does.

For Mitscherlich, experiencing such self-fulfillment during the therapeutic process was not only the task of the individual in question, but also of the psychoanalyst, whose task was to liberate the patient from the "dead end street of the disease".[665] The heteronomous feature of psychoanalytically prestructured self-fulfillment is concealed by a lofty description of the physician's influence on the process of self-reflection. "Genuine human solidarity" lies in the fact, we read, that the physician is willing to accompany the patient on his inward "journey to Hades".

In his articles, Jaspers evaluates the new psychosomatics with its lofty reform consciousness in political terms, referring to it as a "total revolution in medicine".[666] In doing so, he cites drastic examples in order to discredit von Weizsäcker's subjective medicine. In 1950 he employs the questionable statement of a psychoanalyst who had embraced National Socialism in 1933 for a wholesale discreditation of psychoanalysis, writing: "What is called therapy in the vagueness of the meaning of healing is revealed by the words of a well-known psychoanalyst uttered in 1933: that the influence of Adolf Hitler constituted the greatest psychotherapeutic act."[667] In 1953 Jaspers, in an effort to underscore "von Weizsäcker's grotesque formulations",[668] relates an event which had occurred in Heidelberg in 1951 and had caused quite a stir. He cites newspaper reports covering the case of the general physician Dr. Göring, who had taken a young patient into his home and subjected him to extreme heat and cold for the purpose of administering a kind of shock therapy. This had ultimately led to the death of the young man. Von Weizsäcker had acted as an expert witness in the court case, and is quoted as having said: "He wanted to use his means of helping the boy. [...] I must admit that he took a risk. But who doesn't? In any case, I do not see that any border has been crossed which has been set by the Code of Penal Law."[669] Jaspers interprets the court transcripts of the case, parts of which were published in the local press, in such a way as to make von Weizsäcker appear as a representative of psychoptherapeutic arbitrariness who intentionally discarded substantiated scientific knowledge in order to try out unconventional methods of psychiatric treatment at the cost of the patient. Jaspers turns the blatantly

---

[664] Mitscherlich (1951), pg. 173.

[665] Mitscherlich (1951), pg. 173.

[666] Jaspers (1953a), pg. 36.

[667] Jaspers (1950c), pg. 61. Jaspers explained the circumstances to the psychoanalyst Oskar Pfister. Cf. the copy of a letter from Karl Jaspers to Oskar Pfister from September 20, 1952, JLE-GLA: "Hattingberg's remark to the effect that Hitler's renewal of the German people constituted the greatest psychotherapeutic act and a number of other things increased my apprehensions."

[668] Copy of letter from Karl Jaspers to Oskar Pfister from September 20, 1952, JLE-GLA.

[669] Jaspers (1953a), pg. 22f. In Jaspers' estate, a newspaper clipping from the *Rhein-Neckar-Zeitung* with the caption "Expert witness partially for – partially against Dr. Göring" is to be found (in the file "Physician Patient") which this quote is taken from.

questionable expertise given by von Weizsäcker into a *pars pro toto* in order to discredit the entire psychosomatic research approach as subjectively arbitrary and life-threatening for the patients who were subjected to it.

It is important to note that during these years, Jaspers had observed incomparably more serious cases of psychiatric maltreatment, to which he had reacted with much greater restraint, and that he did not withdraw his trust in psychiatry after the facts of such cases became known. Although he welcomed Mitscherlich's documentation of the crimes which had been committed under the National Socialists, he did not wish to take on the role of the Enlightenist himself in the field of psychiatry, and in personal contacts with Kurt Schneider at least, he expressed understanding for Schneider's concern that publications on activities in the field which reached readers beyond the circle of specialists might hamper efforts on the part of the discipline to build trust.[670] Unfortunately Jaspers applied a double standard when he passed judgment on the activities of academic psychiatrists and psychosomaticists after 1945. Whereas he viewed psychiatric misdeeds as singular events which were attributable to a few inhuman personalities, a very dubious expertise written by von Weizsäcker which was hardly typical of psychosomatic medicine sufficed to disqualify its representatives as irresponsible members of the medical profession.

In ascertaining this, I have no intention to dispute the fact that von Weizsäcker as well as other representatives of psychosomatic medicine in Heidelberg had a tendency to indulge in extremely questionable speculations in their attempts to find the "meaning" of diseases for the lives of the patients who were afflicted with them. After having read Jaspers' "Physician and Patient", Karl Löwith, a philosopher who strived for sober partiality, related his own experiences with the Heidelberg school of psychosomatics to Karl Jaspers, writing:

> It confirms my resistance to the immoderate psychologization which prevails in Heidelberg in the circle surrounding von Weizsäcker. Last semester some physicians asked me to participate in a work group. I was appalled by the uninhibited pseudophilosophy and even anthropological 'theology'. The only thing one can say to their credit is that they are subjected to the depressing experience of a modern, mechanized clinic from day to day.[671]

CONTROVERSY OVER TRAINING ANALYSIS

"Serviceable are Those Who can be Trained"

In 1950 Jaspers no longer describes psychoanalysis as the historical sectarian ideotype but rather portrays its ongoing development as a sectarian institution. As he writes, "psychoanalysts have been founding societies for decades. These strive to acquire the right to issue diplomas on the basis of the organization of training operations. Like sects, they appeal to solidarity." Jaspers indirectly interprets the

---

[670] Cf. copy of letter from Karl Jaspers to Kurt Schneider from March 19, 1947, JLE-GLA.
[671] Letter from Karl Löwith to Karl Jaspers from October 12, 1953, JLE-GLA.

establishment of the institute in Heidelberg and the publication of regulations on psychoanalytic training in *Psyche* as important stages in this development. As he writes,

> the step towards breeding psychoanalytically orthodox psychotherapists is already approaching; it will be implemented by radical differentiation between the prerequisites for obtaining licensure to practice medicine and the planned licensure for practicing psychoanalysts.[672]

Already in 1941/42, while drafting a model for school-integrative psychotherapy, Jaspers tolerated training analysis as a facultative element,[673] but he nevertheless posed the question as to whether "the demand for a training analysis does not sometimes hide what one might call the demand for a declaration of faith and the vindication of something that pertains more to the preservation of a sect than to a public form of therapy".[674] At this time he almost prophetically continued by writing: "It would be a confirmation of my suspicions if there should be a demand for training analyses according to the different psychotherapeutic schools and a separation of one from the other [...]."[675] His critique of Mitscherlich's call for mandatory training analysis is merely the consistent reformulation of Jaspers' earlier reservations. In keeping with these, Jaspers does not oppose facultative training analysis, but he speaks out vehemently against obligatory training analysis. As he contends, the university could "permit training analysis to take place without making it a condition for acquiring diplomas".[676]

Jaspers goes on to call into question the special conditions placed on self-reflection during training analysis, which made the analysand – the future analyst – subject to the training analyst and the theory of neurosis he subscribed to. Jaspers does not view this as a free process of self-determination. He puts forth the argument which he developed in his 1915 manuscript entitled *Solitude,* namely that the "existential process of self-illumination" was not possible unless a symmetrical and personal relationship of responsibility governed the interaction of the partners in communication, for which the "life community of existential communication" served as a model.[677] In contrast, Jaspers looks upon training analysis as a form of direction socialization analogous to religious "exercises" which strived for a certain kind of "truth" through massive consciousness training within a predetermined conceptual framework. The process was viewed as successful if the individual who had been "bred" in this way became a "suitable member in the community of faith of the planned future", such success being guaranteed by a long period of training analysis.[678] Jaspers concludes with the ironic remark: "Serviceable are those who can be trained."[679]

---

[672] Jaspers (1950c), pg. 64.
[673] Cf. AP 4, pg. 680 and this study, pg. 85f..
[674] GP 4, pg. 814; cf. AP 4, pg. 680.
[675] GP 4, pg. 814; cf. AP 4, pg. 680.
[676] Jaspers (1950c), pg. 66.
[677] Jaspers (1950c), pg. 65.
[678] Jaspers (1950c), pg. 64f..
[679] Jaspers (1950c), pg. 64f..

Despite his radical critique of obligatory training analysis, Jaspers suggests the possibility of a compromise in that he speaks of the "inwardly independent psychotherapists" who use "psychoanalytic methods" but do not "organize and technicize" the process of self-reflection, but rather engage with patients in "historical communication".[680] Later on, the psychiatrist Kurt Kolle, whom Jaspers had known since 1926 and whom he had supported in the early 1950's,[681] seizes upon this dictum of the "inwardly independent psychotherapist" in his article entitled *Karl Jaspers as Psychopathologist (Karl Jaspers als Psychopathologe).*[682] He can be considered as one of those independent psychotherapists who enjoyed Jaspers' confidence.

Kolle had already defended the notion of "training analysis" in his earlier dealings with Jaspers, for in his view, "self-illumination without any outside help" was only possible in exceptional cases – as in Freud's – assuming one was convinced that the "dream analysis" which uncovered the unconsious was indispensible.[683] Jaspers had answered him as follows:

> Concerning psychoanalysis, I hope I have not been so derogatory as your words would suggest. In terms of particulars, I have in fact been affirmative to quite a far-reaching extent. I radically reject world views and sects. Here a stupid surrogate philosophy is at work. Freedom is no object for research, but rather a matter for philosophy.[684]

Regarding Kolle's defense of training analysis from 1956, without which, as he says, the "masses of the modern world" – unlike Freud – could not find their way in independent self-reflection,[685] Jaspers replies as apodictically as he had in 1950,[686] contending that the "training and education of the physician" should not be "anticipated or brought about by force through compulsory training regulations and examination requirements".[687] The term "controlled self-observation" is called a "deceptive euphemism", a "deviation from the actual self to an imaginary self, from genuine freedom to illusory freedom, from openness of an individual's nature to delight in intellectual and spiritual violation".[688]

In other words, Jaspers rejected psychoanalytic socialization as a "technicized process" requiring a "so-called expert". He did so primarily in view of the tasks of the university, which, as he felt, should not orient themselves towards any special philosophy or religious imprint, but rather facilitate individual adoption of intellectual and spiritual traditions. As he saw it, the universities should merely offer the opportunity for individuals to inquire of their own free will into various normative or "intellectual" perspectives without being forced to become a member of a specific intellectual denomination.

Thus Jaspers rejected the "revival of the old schools of philosophy from Greek and Roman antiquity" in the academic sphere, which is what, in Ellenberger's eye,

---

[680] Jaspers (1950d), pg. 59f..
[681] Cf. Bormuth (1996).
[682] Kolle (1957a), pg. 461; cf. Kolle (1957), pg. 459.
[683] Letter from Kurt Kolle to Karl Jaspers from September 4, 1947, JLE-GLA.
[684] Letter from Karl Jaspers to Kurt Kolle from June 9, 1947, FA Kolle.
[685] Kolle (1957a), pg. 462; cf. Kolle (1957), pg. 460.
[686] Jaspers (1957a); regarding Kolle cf. pp. 804-810 und Jaspers (1957), pp. 800-805.
[687] Jaspers (1957a), pg. 806; cf. Jaspers (1957), pg. 801.
[688] Jaspers (1957a), pg. 807; cf. Jaspers (1957), pg. 802.

psychoanalysis, as a 'demoninationally organized' movement, had come to success-fully represent. As Ellenberger argues, from the perspective of such a correlation with antique models, it seems wise that psychoanalysis demanded more than an expenditure of time and money, calling for a radical "surrender of the intimate sphere" so that future analysts would be more "indissolvably" bound to the psycho-analytic society than the members of ancient philosophical schools had been to their institutions.[689] To be sure, Jaspers expected universities to convey traditions in a certain way, with the instructors adopting the formative role of normative models in the process of forming personalities in an existence-philosophical sense who were to feel committed to the occidental intellect in their own individual way. The "idea of a university" was insofar not value-free in a value-neutral sense of the word. On the contrary, its perspective was defined by the theoretical value judgment which in-formed Jaspers' philosophy. Universities were not only to be understood as institutes of learning which promoted individual disciplines. As was said before, in light of the crisis of modernity they were also to promote the formation of a moral elite.

"Truthfulness" vis-à-vis One's "Counterpart"

In 1951 Mitscherlich clearly realized that Jaspers was "implicitly" attacking his institute in his "Critique of Psychoanalysis". He alleged that Jaspers aimed for a general proscription of training analysis although Jaspers had merely called its obligatory character into question.[690] In his reply entitled "Critique or Politics?", Mitscherlich does not touch upon the issue regarding requirements for psychothera-peutic training, however. Instead, he undertakes an apologia of training analysis, but one which is formulated completely within the internal perspective of psychoana-lytic self-understanding. He writes:

> As I say, I agree with Jaspers that it would be absurd to make training analysis manda-tory. In taking this view, I see less the danger of a threat to the freedom of the individ-ual. The potential threat would lie in the possible destruction of analysis itself. Whoever subjects himself to training analysis merely to acquire licensure to practice psycho-analysis would be a direful analyst inspite of it.[691]

Mitscherlich goes on to say – in a rather cavalier way and putting forth less than convincing arguments – that "anyone who does not of his own free will desire this educational experience has countless opportunities to receive training in other ways at other places".[692] Furthermore, Mitscherlich attempts to expose the rejection of training analysis in a psychologizing manner by attributing it to a false sense of self-assuredness. "Generally speaking, this kind of self-assuredness is not genuine. Training analysis would be an excellent tool for finding out whether it is or not."[693]

Furthermore, it is interesting to note how Mitscherlich responds to the reproach that training analysis manipulates future psychosomaticists due to the technicized

---

[689] Ellenberger (1970), pg. 765.
[690] Mitscherlich (1951), pg. 181.
[691] Mitscherlich (1951), pg. 181.
[692] Mitscherlich (1951), pg. 181.
[693] Mitscherlich (1951), pg. 182.

socialization which it entails. As so often, when psychoanalysis is attacked for its putative ideological tendency – and Jaspers undoubtedly raises objections of this kind – the attacked camp reacts by claiming that its aim is to effect the opposite, namely to dismantle ideological thought in the sense of "exclusive truth". Mitscherlich does so when he writes:

> During training analysis, there is no rehearsing of any kind of world view or faith. This is exactly what does not happen. On the contrary, every faith and every world view is subjected to more profound and free reflection than that which human beings are in possession of in their active, daily lives.[694]

In a philosophizing, moralistic tone Mitscherlich justifies the analyst as a confidant of the inner life. He writes:

> It does not only involve the moral demand of being honest towards oneself. Honesty of this kind still always stands in a deep relationship to the reality of others. Whatever a human being has to say to himself he must at the same time take responsibility for as an act of ultimate truthfulness vis-a-vis his fellow human beings. [...] If we want to speak of something being thrusted upon someone, what I can say is that what is instilled into the analyst is nothing more than the expectation that self-recognition should not be an act performed in isolation but that one remains answerable to others as well.[695]

Mitscherlich explains the "adoption of truthfulness vis-a-vis one's counterpart" as a genuine human need.[696] As he contends, anyone who is interested in psychotherapeutic training but does not wish to undergo psychoanalysis himself must seriously ask himself, after reading this, whether he conforms to the anthropological norms of human social life in the first place. Thus the aspiration to share one's inner life only with those individuals whom one feels trustingly connected to personally – this being an aspiration affirmed by Jaspers in different cultural terms – is indirectly depicted as being morally questionable.

In order to refute Jaspers' reproach that psychoanalytic socialization manifested tendencies towards technicization, Mitscherlich draws the picture of a form of communication based on human understanding which he expressly orients towards the ideal of the "life community based on existential communication".[697] In doing so he implicitly turns to the dialogic philosophy of Martin Buber, who had stood in close relations to von Weizsäcker since the 1920's, speaking of the "cultivation of the I-Thou-relationship in the human world".[698] As is to be expected, this "existential encounter" within the framework of psychoanalysis is distinguished from scientific medicine in positive moralistic terms in that the aetiological credo that disease is to be viewed as a "meaningless causal event involving organic processes" is automatically associated with a less understanding relationship between physician and patient.[699] Adopting the gesture of the puzzled philanthropist, Mitscherlich writes:

---

[694] Mitscherlich (1951), pg. 177.
[695] Mitscherlich (1951), pg. 177.
[696] Mitscherlich (1951), pg. 177.
[697] Mitscherlich (1951), pg. 178.
[698] Mitscherlich (1951), pg. 179.
[699] Mitscherlich (1951), pg. 178.

There is still no explanation for why Jaspers, who affirms the existential significance of life communities (as I assume, in the sense of marriage and great friendships) should resist so decidedly the new foundation of a truly interpersonal, supportive relationship between patient and physician in a time of completely unexistential communication between human beings (in the sense of purely functional, mutual allocation).[700]

Mitscherlich goes on to accuse existential communication of cultivating an elite attitude because as he claims, it expected those who engaged in it to draw upon the philosophical tradition in doing so, and this simply asked too much of many individuals. Rather than fulfilling their direct need for human understanding, Jaspers' dictum referred such persons, drained by our achievement-oriented society, to quite remote and demanding philosophies, Mitscherlich contends, writing:

And what should become of all of those who, overtaxed by their lot in life, lost in our times, helpless in light of self-alienation finally find themselves again in illness? Will Nietzsche, the wise men and the poets be able to give more to the carpenter, the packer, the housewife, the sailor, the bankteller, the financial consultant and the locomotive driver than the great religions of their day have been able to? Can they replace what these people thirst after, the basic prerequisite for genuine human existence which they lack, namely genuine acceptance by a Thou, by another who understands them without making demands or accusations?[701]

Despite all the rhetoric, Mitscherlich's critique contains a question which has been raised time and again concerning the concept of existence philosophy, namely the question as to whether its conscious abandonment of culturally unequivocal signifiers does not overstrain humankind's capacity. Even a student close to Jaspers like Jeanne Hersch criticizes Jaspers' existence philosophy for not having solved the modern dilemma of orientation because, as she contends, it does not convey any clear cultural identity which individuals could adopt without further reflection.[702] Jaspers points to the possibility that when the human conscience is confronted with exceptional situations like National Socialism, some individuals might be guided "directly by the godhead" in their capacity to offer resistance without "worldly or churchly authority". Consequently, such individual life testimonies could act as clear cultural signs to the same degree as in former times, even though this was difficult in light of the "glare of public flaunting".[703]

The need for clear cultural identity is exactly what Mitscherlich means when, in this context, he mentions those religions which were wise enough to relieve human beings of the burden of freedom. He speaks of the "interpersonally unconditional intimacy" of training analysis and warns with a moralizing gesture of the consequences of cultural deprivation which would result if there were to be no "face-to-face" encounter between human beings which gave them the chance to verify their "truthfulness".[704] In light of Mitscherlich's great hymn to psychoanalytical interpersonality, who would want to scrutinize the therapeutic situation more

---

[700] Mitscherlich (1951), pg. 179.

[701] Mitscherlich (1951), pg. 180.

[702] Cf. Hersch (1957a), pg. 609f.; Hersch (1957), pg. 602.

[703] Cf. Jaspers (1957a), pg. 771; Jaspers (1957), pg. 769. This line of argumentation addresses the consequences of existence-philosophical life conduct as it was developed in *Man in Modern Times*. Cf. this study, pp. 48-53.

[704] Mitscherlich (1951), pg. 180.

closely? The rhetoric of humanity clouds the view of the quite heteronomous set of conditions required of the situation in which training analysis was to take place.

Mitscherlich makes somewhat more concrete statements when he attempts to dispel the reproach of psychoanalytic "indoctrination". What he brings forth in order to justify the personal examinary role of training analysis is not much. In case a candidate "fails", this lies solely in his or her personal immaturity and a lack of professional capacity and not in the alleged "disobedience" towards an "orthodox dogma",[705] Mitscherlich says. Once again he evokes the humanity in whose service the psychoanalyst examined the "basic human talent" of the candidate in order to guarantee effective "solidarity between the physician and the patient" in a rationalized world.[706] In no way does he problematize the criteria which are applied to assess the reliability of the examination process.

Mitscherlich ultimately stylizes psychoanalysts and the training analysis which shapes them as being engaged in a kind of anti-conformist enterprise within a conventionalized society. As opposed to Jaspers' view that only a few, organically predisposed persons developed neuroses, Mitscherlich looks upon such persons as particularly sensitive seismographs who react to society's ill conditions in a particularly subtle and exacting way. As Mitscherlich writes,

> [a]nalysis is not life. But for very many people – including 'healthy' ones – there is no life in our times without this initial experience of self-encounter. Whoever adopts the psychoanalytic profession will not be dealing with healthy human beings in the customary sense of the word, i.e. with those who succeed in repressing, with those who suffer in silence, but rather with those who live in a state of uprise, in uprise against themselves and the world.[707]

Critique or Politics?

Mitscherlich's reply, entitled "Critique or Politics?", attacks both poles of Jaspers' critique of psychoanalysis with rhetorical shrewdness. Jaspers is not only interested in a science-theoretical assessment of psychoanalysis, but also in a publicly effective depiction of existence-philosophical reservations against the imminent anchorage of psychoanalysis in the state university system. Thus Mitscherlich reproaches Jaspers for having "propagated his world of values by discriminating against that of his opponents",[708] portraying psychoanalysis as a societally destructive "secret doctrine".[709] "Critique of Psychoanalysis" contains what is not exactly a mild reproach of totalitarianism which places psychoanalysis in structural analogy to the "historico-sociological ideas" of marxism, thus judging it as a dictatorship from within.[710] Mitscherlich replies to this anti-totalitarianist critique with complete self-assurance by confronting Jaspers with the same argument, writing:

---

[705] Mitscherlich (1951), pg. 178.
[706] Mitscherlich (1951), pg. 178.
[707] Mitscherlich (1951), pg. 179.
[708] Mitscherlich (1951), pg. 175.
[709] Mitscherlich (1951), pg. 173.
[710] Jaspers (1950d), pg. 62.

> Is it the totalitarian claim of the philosopher which desires to hold sole, rigorous watch over all that is essential and meaningful in human life, who only acknowledges his own authority in the realm in which we begin to look for meaning? This would seem to reveal a motive of political (rather than critical) reaction.[711]

In responding in this way, he points out the important role which Jaspers played as an intellectual in post-war German society[712] even though his role as a moral authority was controversial. Mitscherlich speaks of the Germans and their "addiction to authority", which had made them believe Jaspers' critique of psychoanalysis uncritically and had in turn compelled Mitscherlich to oppose Jaspers so resolutely.[713] As was already mentioned, Jaspers intensified his critique of psychoanalysis during this time through two publications, *Marx and Freud*[714] and *Reason and Anti-Reason in Our Time,*[715] politicizing it to an ever increasing degree. Mitscherlich demonstrated a keen awareness of Jaspers' farther-reaching intention, which was to prevent psychoanalysis, as a culturally and thus also politically effective phenomenon, from becoming a philosophical authority in the young Federal Republic.

The last reactions to his "Critique of Psychoanalysis" reach Jaspers in the fall of 1952, when Mitscherlich sends him a copy of *Psyche* including a contribution by the Swiss psychoanalyst Oskar Pfister entitled "Karl Jaspers as Sigmund Freud's Adversary" ("Karl Jaspers als Sigmund Freuds Widersacher").[716] Jaspers answers: "Unfortunately I can offer no public reply to you or Pfister as I have no time to do so, at least for the time being. My word must suffice."[717] It is unclear whether a meeting ever took place between Mitscherlich and Jaspers in the time thereafter despite the wish for an interchange on both sides. In contrast to his psychologizing balancing of accounts rendered in *A Life for Psychoanalysis* decades later,[718] one of Mitscherlich's last letters to Jaspers evidences the high level of dispute which they engaged in during this time. Mitscherlich writes:

> My memories of Plöck 66 during the war are vivid – and I continue to be very grateful to you for these quite hours. Nothing has changed as far as that goes, even though we now appear in public as decided adversaries. I am sure that you will not read this as a private softening of my antagonism in print but rather as it is intended – as a sign of affection despite differences of opinion on many issues. And since I have no fear of authority, particularly when it errs in such a strange way, I say this so as not to spoil the relationship which matters to me, namely its human aspect.[719]

---

[711] Mitscherlich (1951), pg. 179.
[712] Mitscherlich (1951), pg. 182f..
[713] Mitscherlich (1951), pg. 183.
[714] Jaspers (1950b). The content is in part identical with the Heidelberg Lectures, but is expanded to included some drastic examples and polemical commentary.
[715] Jaspers, *Reason and Anti-Reason in Our Time*, pp. 18-22.
[716] Cf. Pfister (1952) and letter from Alexander Mitscherlich to Karl Jaspers from Sept. 9, 1952, JLE-GLA.
[717] Draft of letter from Karl Jaspers to Alexander Mitscherlich from Sept. 20, 1952, JLE-GLA.
[718] Mitscherlich (1980), pg. 125.
[719] Letter from Alexander Mitscherlich to Karl Jaspers from March 18, 1951, JLE-GLA.

CHAPTER 8

ON THE CRITIQUE OF PSYCHOANALYSIS
AND SOCIETY 1950-1968

> Criticism of conformance begins to serve new conformance.
>
> Ivan Nagel[720]

The politico-societal aspects of Jaspers' critique of psychoanalysis cannot be understood without knowing something about the intellectual anti-authoritarianism which led to an intensification of his reservations from 1950 on. The correspondence between Jaspers and Carl Friedrich von Weizsäcker from the year 1953, which addressed the "'totalitarian' trait" of psychoanalysis, shows evidence of this development.[721] Moreover, *The Perennial Scope of Philosophy* and *Marx and Freud*, both published during these years, are shaped to a considerable degree by the anti-authoritarian approach.[722] Jaspers last criticized Freud's thought publicly in 1964 in the form of two television lectures on psychoanalysis and scientific value-freedom.[723] Once again, his aim was to counteract the dreaded influence of psychoanalysis on the life conduct of the bourgeois elite; here the existence-philosophical motivation conspicuously permeates the medical line of argumentation and overshadows it, however. From the perspective of a history of mentality, his position is diametrically opposed to the societal role of psychoanalysis as defined by Alexander Mitscherlich and Jürgen Habermas during these years. Mitscherlich's socio-psychological study *Society without a Father (Auf dem Weg zur vaterlosen Gesellschaft)*[724] and Habermas' *Knowledge and Human Interests (Erkenntnis und Interesse)*[725] express confidence in the prospect that as a socio-psychological theory, psychoanalysis could help to effect a scientifically legitimized change of societal conditions which would provide room for individual self-realization. An examination of these texts will yield insights into the foundations of the argument which heightened the politico-societal importance of psychoanalysis from the 1960's on, this being a development which Jaspers tried in vain to avert.

---

[720] Nagel (2001), pg. 66.
[721] Letter from Carl Friedrich von Weizsäcker to Karl Jaspers from September 3, 1953, JLE-GLA.
[722] Cf. von Weizsäcker and Jaspers (1950b).
[723] Cf. KSA, pp. 93-117.
[724] Cf. Mitscherlich (1963).
[725] Habermas (1968).

TOTALITARIANISM AND "COUNTER-PROPAGANDA" 1950-1954

Psychoanalysis and "Secularization" – Carl Friedrich von Weizsäcker Contra Jaspers

Before "Physician and Patient" appeared in the *Studium generale* in the autumn of 1953, Carl Friedrich von Weizsäcker, as co-editor of the journal, prompted Jaspers to tone down the critical passages on the kind of psychosomatic treatment propagated by his uncle.[726] After Jaspers refused to do so despite long discussions and exchanges of letters, Carl Friedrich von Weizsäcker relinquished his office out of family loyalty. One strong motivation to do so was the disease which Viktor von Weizsäcker had been afflicted with since 1951 – Morbus Parkinson –, which occasioned the nephew to justify his move by citing the "Strauß-Nietzsche example".[727] Like his uncle, Carl Friedrich von Weizsäcker defended psychoanalytic thought against Jaspers' critique even though he clearly identified certain aspects of arbitrariness, one-sidedness and absolutization as dangers. To underscore the danger he sees as emerging from psychoanalysis, Jaspers draws an extremely questionable historical parallel to the political situation during the National Socialist dictatorship, writing:

> It is analogous to the discussions on National Socialism in 1933. 'It has some good aspects, it succeeded in eliminating unemployment, [...] it effected national restoration. [...]' etc. As the opposing view goes, it is of the devil, and for this reason it must be rejected completely, and the appeal to the individual must be: be aware that you are dealing with the devil; you are ending up in realms in which you do not want to be.[728]

Jaspers' rejection of psychoanalysis is radical. As he writes, "I look upon every physician who takes this path as lost if he does not use the substance left in him to one day see clearly." Just how grave Jaspers thought psychoanalysis' influence on society was can be inferred from the fact that he not only drew the aforementioned analogy, but that he also illustrated his monition to Carl-Friedrich von Weizsäcker by citing his own concrete experiences with the dictatorship, saying, "as Germans we have learned from what we experienced and have become sensitive to such possibilities, like seismographs".[729] Without a doubt, Dolf Sternberger's observation that Jaspers' experience with "Hitler's dictatorship" had turned him into a "political philosopher"[730] is also apt in regard to his critique of psychoanalysis after 1945.

---

[726] Cf. letter from Carl Friedrich von Weizsäcker to Karl Jaspers from July 28, 1953, JLE-GLA.

[727] In his first *Untimely Meditation* (*Unzeitgemäße Betrachtung*) – *David Strauss: The Confessor and the Writer* (*David Strauss Der Bekenner und Schriftsteller*), written in 1873 – Friedrich Nietzsche had acerbically attacked the critical theologian shortly before his death, calling him a "typical *Bildungsphilister*". This brought reproaches of ruthlessness from various sides. Cf. Nietzsche (1980), vol. 1, pp. 157-242.

[728] Copy of letter from Karl Jaspers to Carl Friedich von Weizsäcker, August 8, 1953, JLE-GLA.

[729] Copy of letter from Karl Jaspers to Carl Friedrich von Weizsäcker, August 8, 1953, JLE-GLA.

[730] Sternberger (1963), pg. 133.

In his rebuttal of Jaspers' objections, Carl Friedrich von Weizsäcker attempts to diminish the polemics by placing psychoanalysis within the wider horizon of the "philosophical understanding of modernity". He determines the modern "turn towards the reality of the world" in the customary way by calling it "secularization",[731] but his interpretation consciously distances itself from the predominant notion of modernity.[732] For reasons of Christian faith, Carl Friedrich von Weizsäcker does not want to dispense with the dualism of time and eternity or immanence and transcendence as the traditional coordinates of thought and action. In the form of a "mythological allegory", he speaks of modernity as having elevated "one of the many partial godheads" to the "level of a god" because since the advent of Christianity it had not been possible to exist in any value systems which were not monistic.[733] The traditional interpretation of modernity, which Jaspers and Carl Friedrich von Weizsäcker absolutely share, assumes the possibility of a transcendent relationship. This allows them to hierarchize the plurality of immanent value patterns through the superordinated authority of the transcendental. As von Weizsäcker contends, only by employing this kind of hierarchization can the danger of an inflated, purely immanent – for example scientific – reference of value be averted which would otherwise result in "totalitarianism" and the "false secularization of the Christian experience of God".[734] Modern "secularization" is "false" because while dispensing with the claim of Christianity to a transcendent realm it adopts salvific thought.[735] This view rests on Karl Löwith's analysis of the history of ideas, which draws parallels between the modern myth of progress and its notion that life should be subordinated to a certain point of reference in the interests of future optimization and the "eschatalogical expectation of a new earth and a new heaven" which informed the Christian tradition.[736]

Carl Friedrich von Weizsäcker sees his dispute with Jaspers as being grounded in their various notions as to whether – as von Weizsäcker holds – the phenomena of "false secularization" and potential "totalitarianism" are a "trait of the modern history movement" as a whole, or whether only marxism, psychoanalysis and race hygiene had the tendency to design salvific utopias according to the Christian paradigm, as von Weizsäcker aptly interprets Jaspers as contending. In any case, von Weizsäcker indirectly concedes to Jaspers that psychoanalysis, by virtue of its interest in inner self-understanding, evidenced a more pronounced permeation of value judgments than the natural sciences did and that its application could result in very

---

[731] Copy of letter from Carl Friedrich von Weizsäcker to Karl Jaspers from Sept. 2, 1953, JLE-GLA.

[732] Cf. Koselleck (1985), pg. 184: "From 1800 on secularization becomes a historico-philosophical dimension. The two-world doctrine as ultimate legitimization for political action and social behavior is replaced by history and historical times, which are now evoked and mobilized as the ultimate legitimizing authority for political planning and social organization."

[733] Letter from Carl Friedrich von Weizsäcker to Karl Jaspers from September 2, 1953, JLE-GLA.

[734] Letter from Carl Friedrich to Karl Jaspers from Sept. 2, 1953, JLE-GLA.

[735] Letter from Carl Friedrich von Weizsäcker to Karl Jaspers from Sept. 2, 1953, JLE-GLA.

[736] Cf. Löwith (1953) and (1949).

serious consequences for individual self-understanding. He differentiates two kinds of psychoanalysts, however, for as he claims, not all of them courted "narrow-minded totalitarianism". He views his uncle Viktor von Weizsäcker as one of the trustworthy representatives of the field who had not succumbed to the scientific expectation of redemption which in Löwith's eyes had emerged from the Christian pre-history of modernity. As he claims, his uncle had been immune against this kind of scientific totalitarianism by virtue of the fact that he had already expressly connected the psychoanalytic aspect of his psychosomatics with the "realm of religion".[737]

Carl Friedrich von Weizsäcker justifies this conscious integration of religious ideas into scientific thought by claiming that the Christian framework incorporated a "turn to the reality of the world" and that therefore secularization could be effected "falsely" or "demonically" but also "properly". In the terms of value freedom, Viktor von Weizsäcker was therefore justified in using religious value judgments to guide psychosomatics whenever it was necessary to clarify the personal self-understanding of human beings scientifically, for from this perspective of secularization, "demonic totalitarianism", as a "specific temptation of our times", posed itself as a danger, – for example if unreflected scientific notions of redemption penetrated psychoanalysis. In contrast, Carl Friedrich von Weizsäcker criticizes the demand which Jaspers had made on his uncle to keep the sciences value-neutral, contending that this constituted an evasion of the unavoidable normativity of every discipline in science-theoretical terms. Von Weizsäcker writes:

> I believe that by applying the apt insight that the devil is at work here one can distance oneself from psychoanalysis as well as from every other decisive step which has been taken in modern times, as has indeed been done time and again. But I believe that by distancing oneself in this way one evades the very decision which can only be made if one treads on the burning floor with the awareness that it is indeed burning. To me it seems illusionary to believe that it would be possible to single out an area in which reason is safeguarded against the demonic temptations of our time.[738]

Thus in light of modernity with its lack of orientation, Carl Friedrich von Weizsäcker champions a kind of psychotherapeutic medicine which fostered religiously derived ideas unbashedly, – even if the pioneers of this discipline ran the risk of having to make sacrifices like those lamented in the course of the purification of the sciences. He views these losses as unavoidable, however, because as he sees it, "demonic" forces would otherwise assert their unreflected scientific notions of redemption. The patient can be fortunate enough to encounter a "properly" secularized psychoanalyst or have the bad fortune of engaging with a "falsely" secularized one, he says. According to this, the 'right' physician is the one who is conscious of the transcendental realm and allows his religious mindset to influence his therapeutic work.

---

[737] Letter from Carl Friedrich von Weizsäcker to Karl Jaspers from Sept. 2, 1953, JLE-GLA.

[738] Letter from Carl Friederich von Weizsäcker to Karl Jaspers from Sept. 2, 1953, JLE-GLA.

Apparently this notion of secularization is more conservative than Jaspers' is, since it seamlessly connects medico-scientific authority to the Christian tradition. Von Weizsäcker does not take the epistemological position of modernity seriously, but instead adheres to the Christian tradition as the unquestioned authority for society at large. In contrast, Jaspers' view of modernity can be referred to as para-conservative. On the basis of his Kantian epistemological skepsis, Jaspers deems the traditional framework to be applicable solely in terms of individualized certainty and clearly speaks out against advising the individual to adopt religious value patterns within the framework of medico-scientific treatment while appealing to the authority of the physician in the process.

Carl Friedrich von Weizsäcker concludes his remarks by quoting Schiller: "Let there be enmity between you. The alliance is premature. Part ways in your search and truth will be found."[739] Jaspers never replied to this substantial letter. Many years passed before the contact between the two was reestablished.

"Loss of Authority" as the Cause of Totalitarian Dominion

From the perspective of a history of ideas, the notion of authority which Jaspers makes public after 1945 in his book entitled *On Truth* (*Von der Wahrheit*) is assigned to the conservative camp.[740] And yet in the chapter entitled "Decline of Authority", Jaspers develops a concept of authority which does anything but justify itself by appealing to typical traditionalism. He distances himself from attempts to preserve "obsolete authority" by erecting a clear hierarchy of values.[741]

The special feature of Jaspers' concept of authority is that he leaves all the burden of justification up to the individual. For the postulated "concealment" of transcendence, as he calls it in *Man in the Modern Age*,[742] or the "ungraspable goal" of "the One", as he writes in *On Truth*,[743] only allows for authority to be asserted on a basis of personal faith. No societal norms which are valid per se exist any more. In accordance with this view, Jaspers connects the "faith in authority" with "lasting uncertainty" about its legitimization.[744] Thus the individual process of adopting the metaphysical tradition determines the subjectivity of all relationships to authority and their social equivocality; in this view, it is only possible to speak of para-conservative variants of authority. For what Jaspers' philosophy shares with the "conservatism" which manifested itself after 1789 is the Christian tradition of thinking in terms of immanence and transcendence[745] but without any striving for a normatively graspable restoration of value judgments previously invested with transcendental justification. Thus existence philosophy met conservative forces with a clear portion of sympathy but it did not allow its language of ciphers to be spelled out clearly. In

---

[739] Schiller (1962), vol. 1, pg. 257.
[740] Cf. Greiffenhagen (1986), pg. 173f..
[741] W, pg. 820f..
[742] MMA, pg. 194; cf. GS, pg. 200.
[743] On Truth, pg. 829.
[744] On Truth, pg. 829.
[745] Cf. Greiffenhagen (1986), pg. 43f.

contrast, Jaspers rejected those Enlightenist strains which dispensed with the transcendental dimension after 1789. For this reason his concept of authorities takes an intermediate position between modern individualism and conservative transcendental thought and as such it must appear "ambiguous". In my eye, Jaspers' affinity to tradition constitutes the more pronounced aspect, however, as the last lines of *Man in the Modern Age* would seem to suggest. We read:

> Apart from the religion embodied in ecclesiastical conditions, there is in the world no philosophical selfhood, no genuine religion, which does not regard any other possibility than that of true selfhood as an adversary and a spur. [...] In the contemporary forecast, these adversaries whose tension as authority and freedom is the life of that spirit which is never completed, must solidarise themselves against the possibility of Nothingness.[746]

According to Jaspers in his orientation towards Weber's concept of "life conduct", the decline of authority manifests itself in the fact that customary action is no longer accompanied by a "keen awareness" of justifying authority, but rather is taken in conventional terms as a "dilution of the traditional framework".[747] Jaspers' concept of authority, which is per se capable of dispensing with a form of ultimate, pan-societal certainty, is poised equidistant from the two poles of absolute certainty as it is provided by traditionally avouched authority and the equally absolute uncertainty generated by the modern decline of authority. As Jaspers writes: "Faith in authority accepts lasting uncertainty."[748]

In 1955 Hannah Arendt attributed the problem of modern totalitarianism in a similar way to the vanishing of the occidental concept of authority which had been unquestioned into the Age of Enlightenment. She posits:

> Politically speaking, the most evident indication of the modern decline of authority is of course the emergence of totalitarian apparatuses of dominion which, in terms of ideological as well as practical morality, presuppose the breakdown of all traditionally safeguarded authorities in political as well as societal life.[749]

Like Jaspers, Arendt declares the modern lack of orientation to be a psychological weak point which the totalitarian lever of domination could latch onto.[750] But unlike Jaspers she not only rejects the scientific utopias of progress as new surrogate authorities, but also all attempts to reinstate traditions.[751] She speaks out in favor of the authority of a legal order in the sense of the American constitution, however, which treats the transcendental realm as a matter of private life which is to be respected but which it does not represent.[752] With his para-conservative position, Jaspers was not in agreement with this idea, responding to Arendt as follow:

---

[746] MMA, pg. 205; cf. GS, pg. 211.
[747] Cf. *On Truth*, pp. 825-827.
[748] On Truth, pg. 827.
[749] Arendt (1957), pg. 121f..
[750] Arendt (1957), pg. 122.
[751] Arendt (1957), pg. 125.
[752] Arendt (1957), pg. 167f..

Perhaps there is still much more authority in the world than there seems to you to be. [...] A holding onto and a growing affirmation of all the authority we can find is to be desired. Your view is almost entirely bleak.[753]

Reason and Anti-Reason in Our Time

The anti-authoritarian turn of the critique of psychoanalysis is closely connected to the problem of authority in modernity sketched above. Jaspers speaks of the modern lack of orientation which understandably searches for a "world order" as a "valid answer" and which did not satisfy itself with time-related "processes of self-deception".[754] The "evasion of the freedom" to make decisions after the "disenchantment of the world" is quasi the 'bad' solution of the "border situation" which modernity constitutes for Jaspers.[755] Jaspers fundamentally deems modern "rationalizations" of various kinds as capable of supplying corresponding surrogate authorities whose value patterns succeed in orienting and regulating life conduct in light of the "new complexity" by providing completed world views and enclosures.[756]

But *Reason and Anti-Reason in Our Time* makes it unmistakably clear which disciplines Jaspers is most apprehensive of. Marxism and psychoanalysis are accused to an equal degree of preventing, through their "false total Knowledge", the "possibility of authentic personal being", i.e. the unfolding of individuality and of "liberating" the individual from "his freedom". According to Jaspers, both scientific theories, as surrogate authorities, impose normative patterns upon the individual, thus taking away his hold on existence and making him incapable of determining his own life conduct in a considerably self-reliant fashion.[757]

In 1951 Jaspers writes to Arendt regarding these theses. "There's nothing new in them," he notes, "just old material presented 'pedagogically' for my German students."[758] In the volume entitled *World Orientation (Weltorientierung)* of the *Philosophy* of 1932, Jaspers had already written:

If philosophy and sociology are viewed as knowledge of the actual existence of human beings then they have relinquished their character as empirical sciences. [...] It is the expression of the evasion of possible freedom and a misconception of what is scientifically possible if ultimate truth about existence is alleged to have been found in formulas, the psychoanalytic and the marxist ones having proven to be most suited for exterminating human dignity.[759]

And yet the critical remarks directed towards both disciplines become even more polemical after 1945 since Jaspers now judges them to pose a real threat to the young democratic project.

---

[753] Letter from Karl Jaspers to Hannah Arendt from April 12, 1956, in: AJC, pg. 284.

[754] RAR, pg. 27; cf. VW, pg. 22.

[755] Cf. PW, pg. 229.

[756] PW, pg. 306.

[757] RAR, pg. 35f and Jaspers (1950b), pg. 150.

[758] Letter from Karl Jaspers to Hannah Arendt from January 7, 1951, in: AJC, pg. 162.

[759] Ph 1, pg. 205.

Based on his experience of dictatorship, Jaspers sees psychoanalysis in particular as endangering the as yet unstable mentality of the leading educational elite. In *Reason and Anti-Reason in our Time* he treats it as an "illusory solution" to the question of authority in that it presents itself as a contemporary, scientific form of life conduct but one which integrates speculative and as such questionable notions like that of a "total biography as life drama", an "Indian doctrine of karma envisioning a prehistoric deed of freedom" or "culpability from earlier lives". Without a doubt all of these topoi allude to the way psychoanalysis presented itself in Heidelberg after 1945. Here Jaspers is extrapolating on the basis of the climate in America, where psychoanalysis was enjoying widespread public recognition accompanied by "jubilation and competence in ultimate victory" on the part of its representatives.[760]

Unquestionably Jaspers has psychoanalysis in mind when, in criticizing the to-talitarian age he speaks of "societies" which asserted the "power to impose their faith" and engaged in "formation of sects", noting that the "unconditional requirement of the so-called training analysis" took on a special function.[761] He refers to the "absolute knowledge" which binds the client authoritatively in the process of being psychoanalyzed.[762] It almost seems as if when putting forth his critique of totalitarianism, Jaspers viewed psychoanalysis from the perspective which Hannah Arendt developed in her book on modern totalitarianism in respect to secret societies. In such "secret societies", she claims, preliminary phases of the typical "totalitarian demand for the creation of a 'life totality'" exist which rob the individual of all liberties.[763] As Arendt argues, the necessary integration of the intellectual elite into totalitarian movements was not attributable to a modern lack of orientation; it resulted from special socialization efforts made in specific institutions whose clandestine strategies enhanced their effectiveness. As Arendt writes:

> Without the elite and its artificially induced inability to understand facts as facts, to dis-tinguish between truth and falsehood, the movement could never move in the direction of realizing its fiction.[764]

Jaspers fears that psychoanalysis will exert a devastating influence on society's elite. His dread is primarily fed by reports by Hannah Arendt on its wide dissemina-tion in North America. In particular, information on the dubious role played by compulsory psychological consultancy during the McCarthy Age, which evidenced totalitarian traits, heightened Jaspers' apprehensiveness, as the following section will show.

Jaspers' *Battle against Totalitarian* (*Kampf mit dem Totalitarismus*) concerns it-self with how to preserve individual freedom in Western nations. His "battle for freedom within the free countries" is an attempt – to quote Isaiah Berlin – to pre-serve the "negative liberties" for the politically mature citizen, i.e. to prevent the State or science from patronizing the members of society when it came to shaping

---

[760] RAR, pg. 25.
[761] RAR, pg. 24f.
[762] Von Weizsäcker, pg. 20.
[763] Arendt (1955), pg. 568.
[764] Arendt (1955), pg. 372f..

their personal sphere of life.[765] Jaspers designates this striving in terms of the international anti-totalitarian circle of intellectuals itself as a "battle for cultural freedom".[766]

"Cultural Freedom" or "Compulsory Analysis"?– Hannah Arendt on Psychoanalysis (2)

At the end of the 1940's, a network of anti-totalitarian intellectuals formed in Europe. The American journalist Malvin J. Lasky was most instrumental in initiating this development. With his impassioned appearance in 1947 at the "First German Writers' Congress" in Berlin he had heralded the Cold War among intellectuals by publicly decrying not only American, but also Soviet repression against them.[767] After the end of the war, Lasky served as a military journalist in Heidelberg until the Spring of 1946. Here he met Jaspers, winning his trust; surely his friendly relations with Hannah Arendt contributed in no small measure to this development. During the Berlin Blockade in 1948, Lasky joined forces with Francois Bondy and established the journal *Der Monat,* which provided a forum for European and North-American intellectuals well into the 1960's.[768] Jaspers was elected as a member of the five-person honorary chairmanship of the 1950 "Congress for Cultural Freedom" in Berlin. As an event with 1,800 participants – an exceptional number in those times – the congress drew the attention of the media. Staged shortly after the Korean War had broken out, the "single-minded community" wanted to demonstrate the "acute moral and political endangerment of all kinds of freedom by the totalitarian State".[769] A 14-point "manifest" was drawn up with the proclamation of an "axiomatic truth", namely that "intellectual freedom is an unalienable human right".[770] Jaspers sympathized with the agenda of the association focussed on intellectual freedom, and he wrote emphatically affirmative prefaces to Czeslaw Milosz' 1953 book entitled *Mislead Thinking*[771] as well as Lasky's *White Book*[772], published in 1956, which concerned itself with the defeated uprising in Hungary.

Jaspers' commitment to the anti-totalitarian cause among Germany's intellectuals was based in no small measure on the conviction that the socialization of the academic elite was crucial due to the key role they played in a modern society, this being a view he had already aired in *Man in the Modern Age.*[773] He envisions a *de facto* oligarchic democracy in which "a few individuals" ultimately determine political

---

[765] Cf. Berlin (1995b).

[766] Jaspers (1954b), pg. 96.

[767] Cf. Ackermann (2000), pg. 56f..

[768] Cf. Ackermann (2000), pg. 60f. Besides Jaspers, contributors were Arnold Toynee, Bertrand Russell, George Orwell, Albert Camus, Ignacio Silone and Alexander Mitscherlich.

[769] This was the way the proceedings of the congress summed up the event. Cf. *Der Monat* 2 (1949), pg. 339.

[770] The "manifest" in its entirety is printed in Ackermann (2000), pp. 74-76.

[771] Cf. Jaspers (1953b).

[772] Cf. Jaspers (1958c)

[773] Cf. this study, pg. 53f..

policy.[774] This was not to be an "elite in the sense of class distinctions", however. Jaspers is indeed consciously vague in characterizing it as an "anonymous" nobility[775] consisting of a "sociologically indeterminate selection of individuals".[776] This "minority" was to serve as models for "mass society" by virtue of the "higher order of their norms", which is to say, their arcanely cultivated individuality was to be utilized for the "reformation of community in the true sense of the word".[777] In 1958 we read: "The implementation of democracy is dependent upon the selection of the best in all realms of life."[778] Jaspers had not given up this idea of a socially independent elite whose socialization in mass society was to derive from academic and private impeti, this being an idea which he had entertained during the years of 'inner emigration' under the National Socialists. During this time, he had survived by withdrawing into the only still existing retreats – into the private sphere of friends and family.

This elitist political model was connected to the hope for the establishment of a "right-minded" democracy, but Jaspers also saw the danger of an ideologization of the intellectual elite. Due to its function as a mediator, it would then induce a totalitarian turn of society, he argues. Long-term, it would eliminate all forms of socialization which were not totalitarian. Jaspers suspected psychoanalytic socialization, as a process which consciously foregrounded anti-traditional and rationalizing tendencies, of forming the pre-stage of a totalitarian form of education. As he writes, "the totalitarians know how they want to do it. They organize education like a mechanical apparatus according to scientifico-technical, and in particular psychological considerations."[779] Jaspers viewed efforts to establish psychology as an "instance" of education as a "calamitous modern mistake".[780] "As a science, psychology is not decisive for education; without it, education would retain all of its essential aspects although incidental contributions under the guidance of the educator could be useful,"[781] Jaspers contends. Psychologically, and in particular psychoanalytically oriented socialization is described as a kind of functionalized "drill" which caused individual self-education to "collapse" because it only truly fulfilled itself within a "totalitarian" framework, he argues.[782]

Jaspers' pronounced sensitivity towards psychologically manipulative forms of socialization in regard to potentially totalitarian developments was aggravated by Hannah Arendt. In 1953 she believed for some time at least that the fanatical anticommunism which she was witness to in the USA might escalate in the direction of a dictatorship. She reports:

> The republic, which should define the framework and the limits of democracy, is being dissolved from within by democracy. Or one could say: The society is overwhelming

---

[774] Jaspers (1956), pg. 73.
[775] Cf. this study, pg. 52f and GS, pg. 195.
[776] Jaspers (1956), pg. 73.
[777] Jaspers (1956), pg. 74.
[778] AZM, pg. 443.
[779] Jaspers (1952), pg. 29.
[780] Jaspers (1952), pg. 32.
[781] Jaspers (1952), pg. 33.
[782] Jaspers (1952), pg. 38.

the republic. This process is underway, and whether it can be stopped is very, very questionable, even if McCarthy is defeated.[783]

During the McCarthy era, so-called "psychiatrists" and "social workers" adopted suspicious roles, Arendt felt, in that they supported an effective and paranoid witch hunt which targeted non-conformist intellectuals by providing compulsory "psychological guidance" and "obligatory psychoanalysis".[784] In a letter to Karl Jaspers she observes:

> "All that is 'very interesting,', especially the fact that public opinion can remain unorganized, that it needs no 'movement,' that everything proceeds almost automatically. [...] And there is much more, all of it brought about without violence and only through pressure. Concentration camps are highly unlikely, even if the present course continues to be pursued. Much more dangerous is the role of the so-called psychiatrists and the social workers, all of whom have psychoanalytical training and who give their clients only 'psychological guidance', not material aid. (The material aid is regulated by law; one has a right to it. But anyone who makes use of this right has to accept psychological guidance!! In other words, there is already obligatory psychoanalysis for anyone who is in financial need. [...])."

Jaspers is most probably referring to Arendt's observations when he makes the following statement:

> This battle against communism, indispensible in the face of all tangible forces of this enemy, has reached a point – in part with unquieting rapidity – at which it begins to use totalitarian methods itself. This happens as a result of the described generation of fear, mutual mistrust, and inquistory and denunciatory procedures. [...] If one resorts to totalitarian methods to combat totalitarianism, one's own cause is transformed unexpectedly. In battling against the dragon, one becomes a dragon oneself.[785]

Arendt ascribes an extremely dubious role to academic theory formation, writing:

> The confusion over these matters among intellectuals is immense. The blame lies with the sociologists and psychologists in whose conceptual swamps everything founders and sinks. They, too, of course, are only a symptom of the mass society, but they play an independent role as well.[786]

On the one hand it is difficult to say whether Arendt intensified Jaspers' verdicts on psychoanalysis or merely confirmed them. On the other hand is it quite possible that Jaspers shaped his student's perception of American society. However one is inclined to assess the situation, Arendt's influence on Jaspers' political perspective was considerable, for she supplied him with much of the information on the world which he had become quite out of tune with while leading a withdrawn existence in Basle.

---

[783] Letter from Hannah Arendt to Karl Jaspers from December 21, 1953, in: AJC, pg. 235f..

[784] Cf. Letter from Hannah Arendt to Karl Jaspers from May 13, 1953, in: AJC, pg. 213f..

[785] Cf. Jaspers (1954b), pg. 96.

[786] Letter from Hannah Arendt to Karl Jaspers from December 21, 1953, in: AJC, pg. 236.

Siegfried Kracauer, who acted as an independent cultural critic during the years of American emigration for the Frankfurt School and was close to its guiding figures Horkheimer and Adorno, viewed psychoanalysis critically as an influencial surrogate for meaning in a culturally crumbling industrial society.[787] He described the psychological strain put on the young North-American civilization in particular by modern "intellectual homelessness", contending that psychoanalysts were trying to fill the "societal void" authoritatively through psychotherapeutic "re-education" as a kind of normative cultural substitute.[788]

Although Jaspers emphasized the necessity of "propaganda" in counteracting "totalitarian forces" which were virulent in the 1950's, he distanced himself increasingly from the direct political ambitions of the Congress for the Freedom of Culture because he had grave doubts about its integrity in the extremely anti-communist climate of the McCarthy years. In this case, his judgment was clearly shaped by Arendt, who reproached influential representatives of the congress for their affirmative view of McCarthy.[789] Jaspers agreed and demanded of the European representatives of the congress that they forcefully demonstrate "in public against the repercussions of McCarthy's campaigns".[790] Despite the assurances of the congress headquarters that they had not remained silent on the issue of McCarthy's politics, Jaspers never directed words of greeting to any of the congresses after this time, as he had done in 1950.[791]

In retrospect, the plan to organize an intellectual movement of "individualistic personalities" informed by the idea of "anti-totalitarian anti-communism" appears ambivalent, particularly in view of the indirect support of the CIA which later came to light.[792] And yet – notwithstanding certain international distinctions – the protagonists appeared to facilitate a coherent form of social liberalism and to relativize the anti-totalitarian ideology which had begun to become repressive in the shadows of McCarthyism. This self-critical tendency documented itself in contributions to the pluralistic journal *Der Monat*.[793] It is important to emphasize this fact in this context. For although when using the concept 'totalitarian' Jaspers inevitably implied the ideological anti-communist interpretation, what he had in mind was in fact the brand of liberal self-understanding which aimed to preserve the "negative liberties" of cultural and political self-determination.

During the age of the Cold War the notion of 'totalitarianism' increasingly took on a "normative" and often "ideological" meaning which gave it rhetorical punch in intellectual debates – irrespective of the liberal motives of many anti-totalitarian

---

[787] Cf. Kracauer (1948).
[788] Kracauer (1948), pp. 323 and 330.
[789] Letter from Hannah Arendt to Karl Jaspers from May 13, 1953, in: AJC, pp. 245-253; pp. 249 and 251.
[790] Copy of letter from Karl Jaspers to the Congress for the Freedom of Culture, June 12, 1953, JLE-GLA.
[791] Letter from the Berlin Office of the Congress for Freedom of Culture to Karl Jaspers from March 15, 1953, JLE-GLA; cf. Jaspers (1949/50).
[792] Hochgeschwender (1998), pp. 588 and 591.
[793] Hochgeschwender (1998), pp. 587-589 and Martin (2000).

intellectuals.[794] Just how quick Jaspers was to scent out totalitarian thinking – even where psychoanalysis and marxism were not involved – as soon as any value-orienting statements were made which showed no affinity to the existence-philosophical perspective[795] is shown by the following. As Jaspers contends:

> [i]n the world of freedom there are all those intellectual forces, however, which want to willfully or unwillfully destroy freedom. There are many who decry totalitarianism but who promote it through their own way of thinking because their own intellectual perspective is not rooted in the truth of its reliable existence but instead clandestinely urges violence and obedience.[796]

Unquestionably, Jaspers was not immune against the tendency to erect ideological walls himself in the course of the debate on totalitarianism, – walls which were intended to protect him against influences contrary to his existence-philosophical project.

LIFE CONDUCT IN THE FEDERAL REPUBLIC 1964-1968

"Television University" on Psychoanalysis and "Value Freedom"

Jaspers' last remarks on psychoanalysis were made in 1964, when he devoted a chapter of his television lectures entitled *Small School of Philosophical Thought* (*Kleine Schule des philosophischen Denkens*)[797] to psychoanalysis and marxism. In the framework of this "television university", which he found quite appealing, he hoped to reach the "masses",[798] or, as he puts it more precisely in another passage, "individuals in the masses".[799] Like the *Philosophy* of 1932, this condensed essence of existence philosophy introduces psychoanalysis and marxism as "universal sciences" which competed with philosophy by formulating comprehensive anthropologies.[800]

Jaspers presents his remarks on marxism and psychoanalysis in the form of dialogues which he sets in the 1920's.[801] Mitscherlich, as the psychoanalyst who had written *Critique or Politics?*, is in part prevailed upon to act as interlocutor. Jaspers' criticism focusses on training analysis. For him it constitutes the decisive vehicle for "indoctrination" in "areas of total dominion".[802] In contrast, the lecture emphasizes the limited, value-neutral orientation of the psychology of understanding which, in Jaspers' scheme, is augmented by an existence-philosophical perspective. According to this, any far-reaching questions of meaning and values concerning life conduct

---

[794] Cf. Ackermann (2000), pg. 14.

[795] Jaspers (1954a), pg. 18f..

[796] Jaspers (1954a), pg. 14.

[797] Cf. KSP.

[798] Letter from Karl Jaspers to Hannah Arendt from November 16, 1963, in: AJC, pg. 533.

[799] Letter from Karl Jaspers to Hannah Arendt from April 25, 1964, in: AJC, pg. 554.

[800] KSP, pg. 114; cf. Ph 1, pg. 204f..

[801] Cf. KSP, pp. 107 and 110.

[802] KSP, pg. 112.

could only be approached through individual "philosophizing" by means of "existence becoming transparent".[803]

As in *Man in the Modern Age*, Jaspers' concept is grounded in a rigorous distinction of spheres of knowledge which is justified by a narrow interpretation of scientific value freedom. In the self-contained lecture entitled *Insight and Value Judgment* (*Erkenntnis und Werturteil*), held on the occasion of Max Weber's one-hundredth birthday, he expresses these thoughts once more.[804] Jaspers accentuates the strict self-restriction of the sciences to "empirically and logically derived general and compelling insights"[805], particularly in the case of such empirically oriented "humanities" as psychology and sociology, interpreting Weber's postulate of value freedom almost positivistically. The reason for this is the existence-philosophical tendency to shield individual self-reflection almost hermetically from scientific interpretation. Jaspers posits:

> They [the humanities] are concerned with the freedom of the human being but for science there is no freedom. Because freedom cannot be proved empirically, the humanities, insofar as they are sciences, lack the essential aspect which makes them relevant for us.[806]

This statement places Jaspers squarely in the context of the "dispute on positivism in German sociology", as a work which documents this controversy is called.[807] In our context, Jürgen Habermas' discussion of the problematics of value freedom is interesting in that his interpretation of Weber's theses is based not so much on Weber's as on Jaspers' concept of value freedom. As Habermas argues, Weber inaugurated the practice of distinguishing between a factual point of departure, alternative means of action and hypothetical goals, and he only approved of value judgments made in terms of purpose, calling, in general, for "value-free" investigation of the "if-then-relationship" in question.[808] In arguing in this way, Habermas does not take Weber's postulate of constitutive theoretical value judgments into account. This allows him to ascribe to Weber a questionable kind of "value neutrality", with Habermas claiming that Weber had not reflected on the value motives which are connected with initial situations and possibilities for action, having instead concealed them.

Habermas' reading of Weber coincides with the scientific notion of value neutrality propagated by Jaspers as late as 1964. In order for this concept to gain validity, Jaspers had to play down the pathogenetic relevance of the biographical conditions which accompany mental disorders, as such factors could not be allowed to become problems of scientific medicine. Only in this way was it possible to make a scientific case for the position that statements made by the physician on personal life conduct should not constitute a component of medical treatment, this being a

---

[803] Cf. KSP, pp. 114 and 116.
[804] Cf. KSP, pp. 93-105.
[805] KSP, pg. 95.
[806] KSP, pp. 96 and 99.
[807] Adorno et al. (1972).
[808] Habermas (1963a), pg. 187.

position motivated by the attempt to prevent patients from being influenced in terms of their individual life decisions.

In another context, Habermas credits Mitscherlich with having pointed out the "positivistic reduction of the concept of science".[809] With his psychosomatic concept, Mitscherlich had offered a substantial alternative to the conservative aims of science in the Federal Republic which expressly invested "empirico-analytical research" with a normative perspective, Habermas contends, maintaining that this view had made it possible for individuals in "fragmented" modernity to form a "fragile identity".[810]

Habermas mentions Jaspers indirectly when he designates "philosophical belief" as a questionable compromise intended to resolve the issue of value judgments which equivocally fluctuated between rationalistic, dogmatic and decisionist positions.[811] Habermas reproaches Jaspers for subscribing to "unarticulated metaphysics".[812] Considering Jaspers' apprehension of objectifiable value statements, this seems quite plausible. In his *Short School of Philosophy*, Jaspers follows the consequences of his philosophizing in rejecting a normative "Catholicity of the one mutually recognized truth".[813] For him there is only generally valid, value-neutral science and individually interpreted philosophy, albeit a philosophy which allies itself with tradition against modernity and its purely inner-worldly orientation. Thus, it is argued, "philosophical belief" was confronted with the reproach – rightly leveled – of having promoted conservative forces through its rationally equivocal position. Adorno's *The Jargon of Authenticity* (*Jargon der Eigentlichkeit*) repeats this reproach in a polemical, ironic fashion.[814]

Freud and "Society Without a Father"

The friendship between Jürgen Habermas and Alexander Mitscherlich played no small role in the definitive incorporation of Mitscherlich's concept of psychoanalytic medicine into the large stream of socio-scientific theory formation during the 1960's which is now known as the Frankfurt School or Critical Theory.[815] As early as 1963, Habermas affirmed the way in which Mitscherlich elucidated his notion of

---

[809] Habermas (1978), pg. 191.

[810] Habermas (1964), pg. 263f..

[811] Habermas (1963a), pg. 172.

[812] Habermas (1963a), pg. 173.

[813] KPS, pg. 102f.

[814] Adorno (1964), pg. 59.

[815] In 1953 Mitscherlich, as Director of the Psychosomatic Clinic in Heidelberg, officially applied for membership in the reestablished Frankfurt Institute for Social Research. For various reasons, his application was initially unsuccessful, however. Not until 1956, when he collaborated with Horkheimer in planning the festivities to be held in Frankfurt and Heidelberg on the occasion of Freud's one-hundredth birthday were more favorable conditions for establishing closer contacts with the institute created. Through the foundation of the Sigmund Freud Institute in Frankfurt in the year 1960 and the professorship for social philosophy at the University of Frankfurt, closer collaboration became possible. Mitscherlich's intensifying friendship with Habermas from the early 1960's on was decisive. Cf. Wiggershaus (1986), pp. 514 and 604.

psychoanalysis as a guiding theory of societal emancipation in his study entitled *Society without a Father (Auf dem Weg zur vaterlosen Gesellschaft)*.[816] Habermas is particularly impressed by Mitscherlich's analysis of modernity. As Mitscherlich argues, civilizational rationalization processes promoted the erosion of "a culture of fathers" but they also made it harder to establish a "successful identity, i.e. to 'come of age'", this constituting the "positive potential of a fatherless society as something which still harbors risks". Like Mitscherlich, Habermas views all restorative impulses to look for a solution to the conflict in pre-modern structures of authority as wrong in light of the situation at hand. As he maintains, the times are over when the attempt could be made to "set old Adam on a reliable course by invoking fixed behavior codexes, strict norms, blind institutions and accustomed reflexes".[817]

If one studies *Society without a Father*, it is remarkable to note that Mitscherlich rejects educative dogmatism of all kinds in the sense that Jaspers does,[818] turning to the Protestant tradition when he calls for "critical freedom of thought" in resistance to "the compulsion to conform".[819] In keeping with Critical Theory, Mitscherlich primarily opposes what he sees as the attempts of Western societies to repress their citizens, writing:

> Does a society practice, i.e. demand of its members acts of a critical search for truth in the process of social formation: against their own affects, against magic, against mega-lomania, or does it make them afraid to keep them in check, to keep them obedient?[820]

According to Mitscherlich, society could take this emancipatory course most effectively if it utilized psychoanalytic insights. He wanted to inaugurate a "methodology for unmasking questionable claims to authority (and equally questionable meditativeness in consolatory worlds)" which made room for "lots of critical ego", knew how to "detect defense mechanisms" and put "obedience to the ego" before "tabus".[821] Here "obedience to the ego" acted as a kind of guiding notion for the self- and socio-critical individual who had emancipated himself from the customary "obedience to morals" set down by authoritative tradition.[822]

Within the framework of this concept, Mitscherlich attempts to introduce psy-choanalysis as a necessary medium for emancipation by citing Freud's dictum con-cerning the three mortifications. Just as Copernicus had robbed human beings of the illusion that the earth was the center of the universe and Darwin had demonstrated that we originate from the apes, robbing mankind of its exclusive status in creation, "proof of unconscious psychic activity" had contested the "dominion of reason over the self".[823] The authority left to mankind after all these relativizing insights is thus, in Mitscherlich's terms, that of individual self-authorization within a "society

---

[816] Cf. Habermas (1963b) and Mitscherlich (1963).

[817] Habermas (1963b), pg. 184.

[818] Mitscherlich (1963), pg. 31.: "All dogmatic certainty is the end of education."

[819] Mitscherlich (1963), pg. 66.

[820] Mitscherlich (1963), pg. 46.

[821] Mitscherlich (1963), pg. 298.

[822] Mitscherlich (1963), pg. 348.

[823] Mitscherlich (1963), pg. 307.

without a father" which has "matured" in society insofar as it has succeeded in divorcing itself from obsolete fatherly authorities.[824]

Apart from criticizing traditional sources of authority, Mitscherlich also indirectly casts aspersions on the existence-philosophical concept of modernity as a form of restorative compensation for narcissistic mortifications in that he posits a "divide" between knowledge of nature and the "philosophical self-elevation of human existence".[825] For Mitcherlich, there is no alternative to the psychological "road to society without a father".[826]

It is not until he comes to the afterword that Mitscherlich lays out in any detail his notion of psychoanalysis as a practical instrument which can be used to deal with the theoretically derived diagnosis therapeutically. As he argues, individual neuroses serve as indicators of societal malconditions:

> Persons with neurotic disorders suffer more than well-adapted people do; but in many respects they suffer from the same things which adaptation has rendered dumb. This vegetative speechlessness to which life in society regresses as a result of structures of dominion is a central matter of fact worthy of investigation, for it is the large obstacle for emancipation.[827]

As in the dispute with Jaspers in 1950, medicine as it was practiced at the time is charged with attempting to copy the successful natural sciences and of excluding psychosomatic interpretations on the basis of their apparently inexact nature.[828] As Mitcherlich contends, psychoanalysis had been the only discipline to heed "humankind's ability to articulate itself" and know how to promote it with the help of the "distanced but participatory relationship which was established in the therapeutic situation", making it possible to "return to experiences". In his perspective, the "genesis" of the neurotic condition could be understood as a compromise between "demands made by the social environment" and the "psychic" or "psychosomatic organization" of the individual. As Mitscherlich argues, such insights could lead to a possible "emancipation in two respects", first of all in terms of the "nature of society", and secondly as concerned the seemingly fixed nature of one's own character. Through his unavoidably socio-critical interpretations the psychoanalyst becomes – in Mitscherlich's eyes – an educative "model" in the emancipatory battle for more autonomy.[829] His postulate of the extensive socio-critical applicability of psychosomatic and psychoanalytic thought culminates in the hope that his "ideas on social psychology" could now be applied in "the sociological realm, the pedagogical realm, in legislation and the political sciences".[830]

---

[824] Mitscherlich (1963), pg. 309.
[825] Mitscherlich (1963), pg. 307.
[826] Mitscherlich (1963), pg. 359.
[827] Mitscherlich (1963), pg. 378.
[828] Mitscherlich (1963), pg. 364.
[829] Mitscherlich (1963), pg. 364.
[830] Mitscherlich (1963), pg. 366.

Jürgen Habermas' Utopia of Psychoanalytic "Self-Enlightenment"

With *Knowledge and Human Interests*, Habermas attempts, for one, to integrate Freudian thought into his philosophical concept, thus complying in a paradigmatic fashion with Mitscherlich's desire that psychoanalysis be applied interdisciplinarily. For this reason his appropriation of psychoanalytic thought will be analyzed relatively extensively, particularly considering the fact that he addresses the question of psychoanalytic treatment and the issue of training analysis. In doing so Habermas succeeded – like no other philosopher in Germany after 1968 – in promoting psychoanalysis as an appealing guiding theory of individual self-understanding among intellectuals who were not themselves members of the medical profession.

Habermas agrees with Mitcherlich's claim, made in *Society without a Father*, that a "psychoanalytic construction of progress" based on altered "drive constellations and conflicts" in human society could be successful in the absence of an "uncontested fatherly authority figure".[831]

In *Knowledge and Human Interest*, psychoanalysis is presented as the "only tangible example of a science incorporating methodical self-reflection".[832] As he contends, it alone could emancipatorily promote "the self-formative process"[833] because one had been compelled by repressive societal conditions to pay for the preservation of public interference-free communication by limiting privating attempts to communicate.[834] Thus for him the task of the psychoanalyst consists in making the individual aware of the public repression of his "own language". Habermas writes:

> The analyst instructs the patient in reading his own texts, which he himself has mutilated and distorted, and in translating symbols from a mode of expression of public communication.[835]

One of Habermas' aims was to prove that despite the seemingly dominant role played by the analyst in the emancipatory process it is ultimately he who is looking for help who decides whether the psychoanalytic interpretations hold true or not. Like Mitscherlich in *Critique or Politics?*, Habermas attempted to convince Jaspers that the emancipatory function of the psychoanalyst consists in helping the patient to free himself from inappropriate attitudes so as to effect meaningful self-realization.[836] Thus Habermas tries to free the interpretative process from the suspicion of heteronomous paternalism by foregrounding the "technique of free association" – as opposed to hypnosis – as an eminently anti-repressive aspect of psychoanalysis. As Habermas elucidates,

> [t]he 'basic rule of analysis' formulates the conditions of a reserve free from repression in which the 'serious situation' *(Ernstsituation)*, that is the pressure of social sanctions,

---

[831] Habermas (1963b), pg. 184f..
[832] Habermas (1972), pg. 214; cf. Habermas (1968), pg. 262.
[833] Habermas (1972), pg. 228; cf. Habermas (1968), pg. 280.
[834] Habermas (1972), pg. 228; cf. Habermas (1968), pg. 279.
[835] Habermas (1972), pg. 228; cf. Habermas (1968), pg. 280.
[836] Cf. this study, pp. 121-124.

can be suspended as credibly as possible for the duration of the communication between doctor and patient.[837]

According to Habermas, the fact that interpretations were only offered as possibilities in reaction to the associations of the patient guaranteed the non-repressive character of psychoanalytic communication. As he argues:

> [the physician] makes interpretive suggestions for a story that the patient cannot tell. Yet they can be verified in fact only if the patient adopts them and tells his own story with their aid.[838]

Thus in Habermas' account the patient has the last word as concerns the validity of the interpretation. "[A]nalytic insights possess validity for the analyst only after they have been accepted as knowledge by the analysand himself."[839] When formulated quite dialectically this notion reads as follows: "The subject cannot obtain knowledge of the object unless it becomes knowledge for the object – and unless the latter thereby emancipates itself by becoming a subject."[840]

Habermas looks upon psychoanalytic "case studies" as the "successful continuation of an interrupted self-formative process".[841] In doing so he views the interpretations given by psychoanalysts as "systematic generalization[s]" of "hermeneutic experiences which are relatively apriori to application".[842] In Habermas' scheme, their "hermeneutic application" in the psychoanalytic process involved providing the patient with the "narrative background of a general interpretation" for him to complete, making it his own "narrative", his own "individual history".[843] As Habermas contends, "the experience of reflection is the only criterion for the corroboration or failure of hypotheses"; the patient had to decide on his own whether the relatively abstract concepts could be connected with the story of his life and education to reconstruct a meaningful whole in the process of remembering.[844] But in regard to possible resistance to interpretation, Habermas follows Freud in making the success or failure of the psychoanalytic treatment the ultimate criterion for assessing the validity of interpretations. He writes:

> Freud is right in insisting that only the further course of analysis can decide a construction's usefulness or lack of it. Only the context of the self-formative process as a whole has confirming and falsifying power.[845]

---

[837] Habermas (1972), pg. 251; cf. Habermas (1968), pg. 305f..

[838] Habermas (1972), pg. 260; cf. Habermas (1968), pg. 318.

[839] Habermas (1972), pg. 261; cf. Habermas (1968), pg. 318.

[840] Habermas (1972), pg. 262; cf. Habermas (1968), pg. 319.

[841] Habermas (1972), pg. 260; cf. Habermas (1968), pg. 318.

[842] Habermas (1972), pg. 264; cf. Habermas (1968), pg. 322.

[843] Habermas (1972), pg. 265f.; cf. Habermas (1968), pg. 324.

[844] Habermas (1972), pg. 266; cf. Habermas (1968), pg. 325.

[845] Habermas (1972), pg. 269; cf. Habermas (1968), pg. 328. He refers concretely to Freud, Works XXIII, pg. 265: „In short, we conduct ourselves on the model of a familiar figure in one of Nestroy's farces – the manservant who has a single answer on his lips to every question or objection: 'It will all become clear in the course of future developments.'"

Habermas does not mention that Freud had applied other criteria for verifying interpretative hypotheses besides the judgment of the patient, feeling that the patient's ability to remember was a less than reliable criterion.[846]

This statement inevitably implies that Habermas holds a position on the doctrine of neurosis which, as opposed to Jaspers' view, practically excludes "causality of nature". Habermas speaks instead of the "causality of fate", for, as he argues, psychodynamic disorders are not caused by any "invariance of nature" but rather by the "invariance of life histor[ies]", which could be resolved through reflection therapeutically.[847] With this emphatically articulated hope for the potential of the psychoanalytic process to effect change, Habermas demonstrates a close affinity to Mitscherlich, who had described the "scope of psychosomatic medicine" as a utopian project with practically unfathomed limits as early as 1949.

And yet Mitscherlich oriented himself towards Freud's definition of psychoanalysis as an empirical science. One of Habermas' main intentions is to relativize this "scientist self-misunderstanding". For him psychoanalytic hermeneutics – like other humanities – is subject to a "transcendental" condition of insight which suspends it from the nomothetic claims of the natural sciences and corresponds to the historical character of its field of insight.[848]

In light of the assumption that repressive conditions of dominion were primarily responsible for the "mutilated text"[849] of psychic identity, the confident statements made about the immanent validation of the psychoanalytic process immediately take on a socio-critical line of attack, of course. As Habermas argues, the "analytic situation" is the "unity of observation and emancipation" or "insight and liberation from dogmatic dependency".[850] Habermas defines psychoanalysis as a social philosophy with an Enlightenist political orientation, he must place Freud's primarily medical concern in a wider context, and Freud's theory on culture supplies the necessary approach for doing so. Habermas writes:

> Meditating on the historical relativity of the standards for what counts as pathological led Freud from pathological compulsion at the individual level to the pathology of society as a whole.[851]

To be sure, as concerns its culture-critical ambitions, the 'maieutics of the physician' as envisioned by Habermas extends far beyond what Freud vouched for because Habermas' judgment of general culture as decidedly pathogenic exceeds anything which Freud contends in his *Culture and its Discontents*. Habermas veritably idealizes the individual in his ability to form a socially compatible identity, whereas he ossifies the hostile notion of society as repressive. He stylizes the communicative alliance between the psychoanalyst and the patient within this framework

---

[846] Cf. Freud, Works XXIII, pg. 265; Freud (1937), pg. 52f..

[847] Cf. Habermas (1972), pg. 271; cf. Habermas (1968), pg. 330.

[848] Cf. Habermas (1972), pg. 271; cf. Habermas (1968), pg. 330.

[849] Habermas (1972), pg. 216; cf. Habermas (1968), pg. 268.

[850] Habermas (1972), pg. 290f.; cf. Habermas (1968), pg. 352.

[851] Habermas (1972), pg. 287f.; cf. Habermas (1968), pg. 349.

as the *conditio sine qua non* for "progressive, critical-revolutionary, but *tentative* realization of the major illusions of humanity".[852]

This important excursus would not be complete without taking a look at the way in which Habermas attempts to connect obligatory training analysis with his notion of emancipatory reason in psychoanalysis. Since he ascribes potential self-objectivization to the hermeneutic circle of psychoanalytic communication, this expressing itself, as he contends, in the confirmative interplay of 'human knowledge' and 'interest', he must have a vested interest in seeing that the physician, as an "instrument of knowledge", engage in "controlled employment" of "his subjectivity".[853] For only in this way could one assure that the interpretations suggested by the physician were free of "'sources of error from personal comparison'".[854] Thus Habermas completely follows Mitscherlich in demanding of the analyst that he adopts the role of the patient in training analysis in order to "free himself from the very illnesses that he is later to treat as an analyst". Without this kind of self-enlightenment, Habermas argues, the physician would inevitably "miss[...] the right constructions" in his "work of psychoanalytic interpretation" with the patient. Thus Habermas declares training analysis to be an integral component of the hermeneutic circle of successful self-enlightenment through psychoanalysis.[855]

Critical self-doubt about the "empirical cogency" of the "right constructions" is not to be found in his text. On the contrary: the analyst is declared to be the indispensible pace-maker for successful emancipation, and in turn the apparent heteronomy of the psychoanalytic process is interpreted as the path towards ultimate autonomy on the part of the patient. Habermas writes:

> Self-reflection is not a solitary movement; it is tied to the intersubjectivity of linguistic communication with an other. In the end, self-consciousness is constituted only on the basis of mutual recognition.[856]

For one, the asymmetry of this relationship of recognition is practically declared to be necessary, namely insofar as the psychoanalyst is depicted as the superior partner by virtue of his completed training analysis and is seen as indispensible if the patient is to 'work up to' his level of self-reflection. On the other hand, the text suggests that at the end of analysis, the physician releases the now 'autonomous' patient from the heteronomous situation of treatment, a symmetrical relationship of recognition having been obtained between them in which the

> subjects [...] define themselves in relation to one another in such a way that the former patient knows that the identity of his ego is only possible through the identity of an other who recognizes him and whose identity in turn is dependent on his recognition.[857]

---

[852] Habermas (1972), pg. 288; cf. Habermas (1968), pg. 350.
[853] Habermas (1972), pg. 237; cf. Habermas (1968), pg. 290.
[854] Habermas (1972), pg. 236; cf. Habermas (1968), pg. 289.
[855] Habermas (1972), pg. 236; cf. Habermas (1968), pg. 289.
[856] Habermas (1972), pg. 344; cf. Habermas (1968), pg. 290.
[857] Habermas (1972), pg. 345; cf. Habermas (1968), pg. 290.

Without a doubt, this is an appealing utopia but it cannot be brought into correlation with Freud's thought and has been aptly referred to by Adolf Grünbaum as a "philosophical ideology".[858]

If one asks oneself why Habermas reads Freud's oeuvre in such an abbreviated way, as Grünbaum demonstrates, the answer is certainly not to be found in any intellectual deficiency but rather in the "preliminary decision" that psychoanalytic interpretations should be verified by the "self-reflection" of the analysand.[859] In order to be able to clearly present the psychoanalytic situation as the emancipatory vehicle on the way to a society free of repression, contradictory arguments of a theoretical as well as a practical nature must be interpreted short-sightedly by Habermas or ignored altogether. This euphoric evaluation of the psychoanalytic setting is in part understandable if one assumes that Habermas' motive for exaggerating psychoanalytic competence lies in real suffering caused by pressing conditions in society. The justified wish for a more fair-minded and humanitarian society which allows the individual to sublimate his drives in a satisfying manner should not allow the political will to effect change to absolve the real conditons of psychoanalytic treatment from its aporias in such a way, however, especially when 'critical thinking' is championed as proof of intellectual existence in the way it is by Habermas. Moreover, it seems necessary to candidly point out in medico-ethical terms the awkward power relations in psychotherapeutic treatment situations, in particular when it comes to psychoanalysis, whether we are talking about training analysis or regular analysis.

The remarks on Habermas have shown that the philosopher appropriated Mitscherlich's psychoanalytical concept for his own socio-psychological utopia informed by a critical theory of society. In this way, psychoanalysis became a leading theory of life conduct for the intellectual avantgarde in the Federal Republic, impacting it to an immeasurable degree. Unlike Mitscherlich, Habermas does not let the normative implications disappear behind what he deems to be the empirico-objective claims of medicine but rather argues his case in the sense of Critical Theory, championing a consciously value-oriented kind of social science, the value of whose insights evidenced themselves in the hermeneutic argument and its conclusions without the socio-critical intention having to be objectivized as part of the hermeneutic circle beforehand. As late as 1983, Habermas follows Mitscherlich in describing psychoanalytic therapy as a form of "intersubjectively activated self-reflection" which developed an "emancipatory meaning" in the clinical framework.[860]

---

[858] Grünbaum (1984), pg. 42.
[859] Cf. Grünbaum (1984), pp. 22-24 and Habermas (1968), pg. 319.
[860] Habermas (1983), pg. 356.

CHAPTER 9

SUMMARY AND PROSPECTIVE VIEW

> No, I am not looking for answers; they make me suspicious.
> Günter Eich[861]

In the beginnings of Jaspers' critique of psychoanalysis formulated from the perspective of the *Psychopathology* around 1913, Jaspers is relatively well-disposed to Freud's psychology. He appreciates it as an innovative element of descriptive hermeneutics in psychiatry and to some degree, he approves of certain attempts to understand aetiologies in the sense practiced by members of the Swiss School who were involved in the research on schizophrenia led by Eugen Bleuler and C.G. Jung. The *General Psychopathology* of 1920 relativizes this tendency considerably however, introducing existence-philosophically accentuated arguments. In Jaspers' eye, Freud, as a proponent of a psychology of understanding, no longer lived up to the models of Kierkegaard and Nietzsche. Jaspers now approves exclusively of the unspecific talking praxis described in *Studies on Hysteria* of 1895, rejecting the theoretical and practical characteristics of psychoanalysis as it developed from then on. After initially showing interest in the psychoanalytic technique of working with the concepts of resistance and transference, Jaspers eventually distances himself from it, calling instead for a symmetrical relationship of communication without the physician being invested with authority to offer interpretations concerning issues of the patient's inner self-understanding. Jaspers deems suggestive-manipulative psychotherapy to be purposeful in less differentiated forms of communication alone, – forms which, as Ellenberger points out, characterize the transitional phase from the first to the second phase of psychodynamic psychiatry and which Jaspers is impressed by due to the fact that they are not used by Freud alone, but also, if not to say primarily, by Janet in his research on hysteria. From a theoretical perspective, Jaspers rejects Freud's accentuation of sexuality as the aetiological backbone of his theory of neurosis after 1900 and comes to associate psychoanalysis pejoratively with *fin-de-siècle* culture.

In the *General Pathology* of 1941/42, Jaspers' existence-philosophical convictions are more clearly articulated. The concept of psychopathology itself now ascribes to psychological hermeneutics a purely descriptive, orientative function for symptomatology. Free self-determination is introduced as an independent aspect

---

[861] Eich (1959), pg. 448.

alongside what are viewed as for the most part unknown causal determinants of disease. Existential self-reflection now constitutes a central component of the psychopathological conception, whereas psychological hermeneutics is banished to the symptomatological periphery. This new focus also manifested itself in Jaspers' idea of school-independent psychology as a discipline which actually only envisioned unspecific treatment methods, tolerating "depth-psychological" methods for pragmatic reasons alone and looking upon existential communication as a rare possibility for true understanding. Because psychoanalysis claimed to be able to gain rational access to unconscious components of the personality, it was affected most acutely by the apodictic exclusion of the medical potential for understanding. At this time Jaspers still holds the biographically oriented psychosomatics developed by Viktor von Weizsäcker to be plausible to a certain degree because it demanded of the physician that he engage with the patient by providing subjective interpretations but without making any claims to scientific validity. In part, this approach evidenced an affinity to the individualistic orientation of existential communication. Before 1933, von Weizsäcker had been a proponent of psychoanalysis, however, and as Jaspers claims, he had, in this function, demanded the "disappropriation of the psyche's private property". This was something no longer called for in the texts discussed by Jaspers, however.[862]

But when von Weizsäcker and Mitscherlich initiated efforts to establish a psychoanalytically oriented psychosomatics in Heidelberg in the year 1946 which clearly propagated an ascription of psychic causes to somatic symptoms, Jaspers changed his view of von Weizsäcker's psychosomatics. Furthermore, his *Psychopathology* of 1941/1942 had reduced psychoanalysis to an historically illuminating ideotype for dogmatic, sectarian forms of psychotherapy. At the same time, Jaspers became a witness to the reinstitutionalization of psychoanalysis in Heidelberg in the post-war years after it had appeared to dissolve its institutional ties altogether during National Socialism. Jaspers' support of the plan to institutionalize psychoanalytic psychosomatics, albeit within certain limits, was based solely on his high personal esteem for Mitscherlich, which dated back to the years of National Socialism. In 1949 Mitscherlich demanded obligatory training analysis and at the same time, von Weizsäcker began to champion an anti-traditionalistic form of psychotherapy which undoubtedly provoked Jaspers. Beginning in 1950, Jaspers brought forth various polemically articulated arguments against psychoanalysis in a number of articles which were addressed to his colleagues as well as a wider public. More rigidly than before, he negated the pathogenetic competence of all psychological hermeneutic approaches, in particular psychoanalytic psychosomatics. In keeping with this view, he criticized their aim to ascribe psychological meaning to the expanded life context of the patient in the course of interpreting the patient's disorder. He based his criticism on a polarizing interpretation of the postulate of value freedom as it had been formulated for the first time in his 1931 *Man in the Modern Age*. According to this work, medicine constitutes a scientific, fact-based discipline which, as a value-neutral science, should lay no claim to hermeneutic authority as concerns what were

---

[862] Cf. von Weizsäcker (1927), pg. 170 and this study, pg. 93.

imputed to be biographically determined factors of disease. Moreover, Jaspers spoke out vigorously against the planned obligatory training analysis. He was of the opinion that scientific psychotherapeutic training should not aim to effect the kind of socialization which, as Ellenberger, contends, psychoanalysis attempted to achieve following the model of schools of philosophy in antiquity. In concrete terms, Jaspers feared that through its academic institutionalization, psychoanalysis would assert itself as a generator of socio-psychological patterns of meaning in society and influence the intellectual elite in West Germany as it had influenced the intellectual elite in the USA. The developments of the 1960's, during which Alexander Mitscherlich and Jürgen Habermas promoted psychoanalysis and its socio-critical concepts as crucial aspects of emancipatory theory and practice, confirmed such apprehensions.

Jaspers' seismographic sensitivity as regarded efforts made on the part of psychoanalysis to structure self-reflection and thus also the life conduct of the intellectual elite socio-psychologically is no doubt to be attributed to his own interest in providing this target group with existence-philosophical orientation. This implication of Jaspers' thought for modern society manifests itself in *Man in the Modern Age* for the first time, and the author's political philosophy after 1945 squarely places itself in this tradition. Existence-philosophical life orientation proves to be modern insofar as Jaspers conceives of secularization – not unlike Max Weber – sociologically as a withdrawal of ultimate cultural patterns and norms from the public sphere to the realm of private life conduct. Decisions on values and life conduct which are meaningful for the individual become all the more compelling, the more aporetic and meaningless instrumental societal connections appear to be.

But unlike Weber, Jaspers adheres to the pre-modern postulate of transcendence, which he sees as indispensable for the orientation of personal life conduct. Thus the "truthfulness of conscious life conduct"[863] which Jürgen Habermas most recently emphasized in terms of Jaspers' philosophical intentions is inconceivable without this metaphysical premise. In terms of motivation psychology, Jaspers evidences a great affinity to Calvinist notions of standing the test as described by Weber's sociology, – notions which resulted, as Weber argues, from the belief in a concealed but existent transcendence. In subscribing to the postulate of the ciphers of transcendence, Jaspers succeeds in tapping into traditional metaphysical systems without recognizing their norms in a purely conservative sense as being invested with primarily supra-individual, binding authority. For their personal appropriation alone decides their validity. This philosophy must be designated as para-conservative insofar as the pre-modern distinction of transcendence and immanence is implicitly postulated as a collectively valid premise. Jaspers' sobering encounter with Weber's pluralistic thought, whose *Intermediate Reflection* allows purely immanent spheres of meaning to collide with transcendently oriented ones without privileging the one over the other, underscores these connections.

Existence-philosophically founded truthfulness calls for truthfulness in terms of personal life conduct, but not in a moralistic sense. As a cipher, inner-worldy action was to indirectly prove the reality of the conception of transcendence, thus also

---

[863] Habermas (1995).

attesting to the metaphysical motivation of truthful action. That such probity could even help to create more trustworthy and more humane conditions in the private realm as well as the public one is emphasized by Jaspers after 1945 in his political philosophy more clearly. Paying tribute to the transcendent in one's life conduct remains the central, meta-political motive for political action, however. In terms of the existence-philosophical approach, life conduct as it is shaped in the private sphere has primacy over that of the public realm. Dolf Sternberger speaks of an "ethics of intimacy" which he saw as issuing from existence-philosophical "communication" and personal attestments to truthfulness.[864] *Man in the Modern Age* depicts the realms of private life conduct – marriage, family and friendship – as islands of possible trust. Jaspers also viewed the university as a possible realm of communicative probity insofar as it remained untouched by manipulative patronization. Existential self-reflection as it is sketched out in the *General Psychology* of 1941/42 can be described as a charismatic socialization process in which the life conduct to which a person commits himself individually is seen as bearing witness to existence-philosophical belief. It is from this self-understanding that Jaspers' profound reservations against psychoanalysis as a modern form of life conduct in theory and practice derives and is articulated, – reservations which are articulated more pointedly after 1945.

The institutional affinities of existence-philosophical life conduct in particular were impacted by the ideas of von Weizsäcker and Mitscherlich as publicized in an issue of *Psyche* after the 1949 Congress on Internal Medicine. For one, Jaspers had to view Mitscherlich's plan to establish training analysis as an obligatory method of socialization at the university as a direct challenge to the existence-philosophical assertion of self-reflection and its eminent importance. Secondly, von Weizsäcker's provocative statement concerning his intention to illuminate the most personal realms of life (such as marriage) psychoanalytically struck the institutional nerve of Jaspers' existence-philosophical concept. The idea of a psychoanalytically structured concept of personality and life conduct, brought forth with such self-confidence by von Weizsäcker before 1933, was reanimated in 1949 and even boosted by Alexander Mitscherlich's idea of obligatory training analysis. Jaspers formulated a wholesale rejection of the claims to private life conduct staked out by psychoanalysis.

The reproach which Jaspers made to psychoanalysis in the 1950's, namely that it was totalitarian in nature, can be explained in existence-philosophical terms. He was bent on preventing public institutions from launching a scientifically legitimized invasion into the realm of the personality, its formation and the individual form of life conduct which derived from it. He wanted the private sphere to remain intact. The controversial debate which raged around 1950 presents us with the publicly staged culmination, and, in a certain sense, termination of Jaspers' and von Weizsäcker's divergent approaches, whereas Mitcherlichs's psychoanalytic aims only begin to take shape during this time. They will find widespread resonance in the 1960's.

---

[864] Sternberger (1963), pg. 13.

On the occasion of the founding of the Sigmund Freud Institute in 1960, Mitscherlich formulates quite clearly the goal of psychoanalytically oriented life conduct for modern society. Mitscherlich writes:

> However one assesses what is inevitably a time-bound theoretical justification of insights which are not bound to time, there can be no doubt about one fact, namely that the genius of Sigmund Freud revealed a new dimension of self-recognition and established a method of critical inquiry into human behavior and desire. What is important today is to continue scientific research and expand the theoretical foundation of his insights, aiming primarily to act on them in our life conduct.[865]

Let us compare a contention made by Jaspers at the end of his critique of psychoanalytic psychosomatics in 1953. He writes: "Wanting to entrust a physician with the prescription of one's life conduct is an escape from seriousness to convenience on the part of some modern human beings."[866] Jaspers propagates his existence-philosophical alternative via the radio in 1953, proclaiming:

> The will to cultivate philosophical life conduct issues from the abandon which results from being spent by enterprise, when [the individual] suddenly awakes, is startled and asks himself: who am I, what am I missing, what should I do? [...] To philosophize is to decide to let the origin awaken, to find oneself again and to muster up all the power one can to help oneself through inner action.[867]

Both the psychoanalytic and the existence-philosophical concepts of life conduct demand self-reflection on the part of the modern individual with an aim toward leading society out of the modern-day crisis of orientation. As a philosopher, Jaspers' intention was ultimately to help shape societal life politically. By 1946 at the latest, when the question of culpability posed itself, this intention had become clear. Existential self-reflection leads from a moral to a metaphysical recognition of culpability, however. The political writings of the 1950's and 1960's structure their arguments along similar lines in terms of societal crises which Jaspers wanted to remedy by forming an existence-philosophically oriented elite.[868] The fact that Jaspers had practically no reputation as a socio-political thinker after his death despite the considerable dissemination of his political writings in the 1960's is documented by a letter written by Jürgen Habermas in 1979 and addressed to various intellectuals requesting that they deliver new "reflections on 'man in the modern age'". In this document he depicts Jaspers as being invested with the "pathos of a teacher of the nation", commenting on his "obsolete" "holistic approach" and likening him to an astonishing figure from the cabinet of the "great German mandarins". Habermas deems the title which Jaspers had chosen for his book – *Man in the Modern Age* (*Die geistige Situation der Zeit*) – to be useful enough to serve as a stimulating title for what was planned as a collective form of social criticism, however.[869] Independent of Habermas' perfectly clear assessment, Reiner Wiehl and Dominic Kaegi – whose

---

[865] Argelander (1989), pg. 295.

[866] Jaspers (1953a), pg. 38.

[867] Jaspers (1950a), pg. 92f..

[868] Cf. Jaspers (1951b), Jaspers (1958a), Jaspers (1958b), Jaspers (1960), Jaspers (1966) and Jaspers (1967a). Kadereit treats Jaspers as a political philosopher, discussing the role he played in the new Federal Republic. Cf. Kadereit (1999).

[869] Habermas (1979), pg. 9.

aim was to stimulate a critical inquiry into Jaspers' work – confirm the "negligible resonance" of Jaspers' political thought.[870] In the 1960's his political judgments, founded on the tenets of existence philosophy, were viewed as provocative, but for the most part they were treated as detached from societal reality.[871] Like representatives of the Frankfurt School, among them Mitscherlich and Habermas, Jaspers was an intellectual presence conveyed by mass media, i.e. radio and television, but he played an insignificant role in the ongoing "intellectual foundation of the Federal Republic".[872] The turning point in 1968 led to the development of a critical form of pedagogy which derived some decisive elements of its socio-psychological method in theory and practice from psychoanalysis.[873] The existence-philosophical socialization process as proposed by Jaspers for the academic elite led only a shadowy existence and was usually suspected of aiming to support conservative, restorative forces.

In contrast, Mitscherlich not only succeeded in joining forces with other university policy-makers to establish university-based psychoanalytical psychosomatics in 1970. Furthermore, he had previously created a framework in which to carry out psychoanalytic research; the Sigmund Freud Institute in Frankfurt was founded in the interests of "mutually" investigating "societal and inner-psychic processes".[874] His two large studies *Society without a Father*[875] and *The Inability to Mourn* (*Die Unfähigkeit zu trauern*)[876] are an inextricable part of the collective memory of the Federal Republic. The publisher Siegfried Unseld, whose "Suhrkamp culture" shaped the intellectual change of climate in the 1960's to a significant degree, referred to Mitscherlich after his death in 1982 as having been the "mind doctor of our Republic".[877] The essayist Jean Améry described the function which psychology, as the mixture of a "scientistic" and a "humanist utopia", was credited with and expected to fulfill in the early 1970's. His eccentric, leftist view of "modern psychology" and in particular psychoanalysis as it was developed by Mitscherlich ascribes to it the status of a guiding theory of modernity in its belated Federal-Republican form.[878]

Habermas' *Knowledge and Human Interests*, which contains a chapter on psychoanalysis, was also a standard work in the libraries of the intellectual avantgarde in the 1970's. His utopia of psychoanalytically guided self-reflection, fed since the 1950's by the anti-repressive spirit of Herbert Marcuse, provided Mitscherlich, as it

---

[870] Cf. Wiehl/Kaegi (1999), pg. 9.

[871] Kurt Sontheimer aptly attributes this to the fact that Jaspers' "philosophical radicality" had not allowed him to pragmatically put himself in the place of the politically active while taking into account the concrete circumstances. For the goal of his "wholesale critique" had been moral "reserval". But as Sontheimer argues, the persistent demand for a morally consistent politics driven by ethos invests Jaspers' political thought with a classic strain. Cf. Sontheimer (1988).

[872] Cf. Albrecht *et al.* (1999), pp. 230-238.

[873] Cf. Albrecht *et al.* (1999), pp. 448-497.

[874] Mitscherlich-Nielsen/Michaelis (1984), pg. 583.

[875] Mitscherlich (1963).

[876] Mitscherlich/Mitscherlich-Nielsen (1967).

[877] Unseld (1982), pg. 315.

[878] Améry (1970b), pg. 57f..

were, with a philosophical foundation. The "scientific self-enlightenment" of psychoanalysis replaced existential self-reflection after its heyday in the post-war years as a personal modus for orientation among bourgeois individuals in modern society. Questions of personal life conduct in particular were shaped to no small degree by the socio-psychological implications of psychoanalysis as it was understood by Mitcherlich and Habermas during late West-German modernity well into the 1980's. The history of their influence exceeds the intentions of this study, however. These cursory remarks are merely meant to make Jaspers' exceptionally fervent critique of psychoanalysis around 1950 more comprehensible.

In 1946 Jaspers had been wrong in thinking that Mitscherlich would be the one to develop psychoanalysis as a medically limited theory.[879] Although Mitscherlich had assured that he intended to use psychoanalysis only "therapeutically", and not as a "world view", this intention was coupled with an empirical understanding of science which differed completely from that of Jaspers despite a high degree of congruence in terms of the concepts they employed. Mitscherlich violated Weber's postulate of value freedom insofar as he believed he had the capacity to authorize normative premises in an empirico-objective fashion. On the other hand, Jaspers' value-neutral interpretation of empirical science did not do justice to Weber and medical reality either. The discrepant interpretations of science and value freedom are attributable to their intention to answer questions of life conduct for modern individuals in purely psychoanalytic or existence-philosophical terms respectively. Jaspers propagated a kind of science which restricted itself to "objective" facts in the realm of psychotherapy as well, whereas he wanted biographical aspects of life to be treated in the purely subjective sphere of existential communication between the patient and the physician. With his socio-psychological concept of psychoanalysis, Mitscherlich persistently and self-confidently overstepped the natural-scientific boundaries of medicine in the direction of individual and collective questions of life conduct.[880]

Jaspers' critique of psychoanalysis had issued from the psychiatric discussion on the pathogenetic significance of psychodynamic interpretations. His existence-philosophical interest influenced his conception of psychopathology in the decades to come to an ever increasing degree. His debate with von Weizsäcker and Mitscherlich on the self-understanding of the personality and individual life conduct gained force in 1946 during the process which led to the establishment of the Psychosomatic Clinic in Heidelberg. It seems improbable that Jaspers would have formulated such an increasingly pointed position on psychoanalysis after 1950 without this contingent event. One cannot contend that he altered the position he held in the *General Psychopathology* of 1941/42 in any truly fundamental way, however. Jaspers' arguments against psychoanalysis were in place before the developments which ensued in 1946 took their course. His critique was only waiting to be brought to the fore in the concrete situation which posed itself after 1945, a situation which came to a head around 1950 in the course of the debate on totalitarianism, adopting a

---

[879] Copy of letter from Karl Jaspers to Alexander Mitscherlich from July 20, 1946, JLE-GLA.
[880] König (1989), pg. 213f..

political and polemical character. If we look at these developments from the perspective of a history of mentalities, the confrontation with Mitscherlich around 1950 constitutes the attempt on the part of Jaspers to prevent a development from gaining force in the Federal Republic of Germany analogous to that observed and conveyed to Jaspers by Hannah Arendt in the USA, namely the growing pan-societal influence of psychoanalysis. Mitscherlich was the one to reestablish transatlantic contacts in the 1950's – for the most part with exiled psychoanalysists. In this way he promoted the reception of psychoanalysis in Germany in the direction which Jaspers had rejected. The ramifications were inestimable.

Beyond the concrete findings at hand, this study offers room for inquiry in various directions. In medico-ethical terms, issues are raised which connect with more recent discussions on instrumental and ultimate goals of psychotherapy. And difficult processes which involve weighing the principles of patient autonomy and the responsibility of the physician, in particular in the area of psychiatry and psychotherapy, can be illuminated by the issues which Jaspers' critique of psychoanalysis raises.[881] In psychiatric terms, the discussion as to which position should be adopted between the poles of a strictly biological and a psychodynamic approach to disease is not yet conclusive. In any case, many arguments are prefigured by the historical discussions which took place between Jaspers, Mitscherlich and von Weizsäcker.[882] An investigation into Jaspers' critique of psychoanalysis invites the reader to follow Max Weber in preserving an awareness of the normativity of every scientific procedure and clarifying the specific premises which guide the inquiry in question. It would also be desirable if this study could keep alive the Weberian interest in a liberal notion of life conduct for which we are individually answerable.

---

[881] Cf. this study, pp. 90-92 and 128-131.

[882] Heimann points out paradigmatically that the biological and the psychodynamic perspective need not necessarily be mutually exclusive but rather evidence a high degree of correlation. Cf. Heimann (1987).

BIBLIOGRAPHY

Abbreviations

AJB   *Hannah Arendt - Karl Jaspers. Briefwechsel 1926-1969*, edited by Lotte Köhler and Hans Saner, Munich 1985.

AJC   *Hannah Arendt - Karl Jaspers. Correspondence 1926-1969*, edited by Lotte Köhler and Hans Saner, New York 1992.

AP 1   Karl Jaspers, *Allgemeine Psychopathologie. Ein Leitfaden für Studierende, Ärzte und Psychologen*, Berlin 1913.

AP 2   Karl Jaspers, *Allgemeine Psychopathologie. Für Studierende, Ärzte und Psychologen*. Second, revised edition, Berlin 1920.

AP 3   Karl Jaspers, *Allgemeine Psychopathologie. Für Studierende, Ärzte und Psychologen*. Third, expanded and improved edition, Berlin 1923.

AP 4   Karl Jaspers, *Allgemeine Psychopathologie* (1946; fourth, completely revised edition), 9th ed. Berlin 1973.

ATZ   Karl Jaspers, *Der Arzt im technischen Zeitalter. Technik und Medizin, Arzt und Patient, Kritik der Psychotherapie*, Munich 1986.

GLA   Germany Literary Archives (Deutsches Literaturarchiv Marbach a.N.).

GP 4   Karl Jaspers, *General Psychopathology*, translated by J. Hoenig and Marian W. Hamilton with a new foreword by Paul R. McHugh, 2nd ed. Baltimore 1997.

EU   Karl Jaspers, *Erneuerung der Universität. Reden und Schriften 1945/46*. Afterword: Renato de Rosa, "Politische Akzente im Leben eines Philosophen. Karl Jaspers in Heidelberg 1901-1946", Heidelberg 1986.

FA   Family archives

FGW   Sigmund Freud, *Gesammelte Werke* (1948). Vols. 1-18, edited by Anna Freud, 6th ed. Frankfurt a.M. 1976.

GSZ   Karl Jaspers, *Die geistige Situation der Zeit* (1931) (Fifth, revised edition 1932), 3rd ed. Berlin 1953.

GSP   Karl Jaspers, *Gesammelte Aufsätze zur Psychopathologie*, Berlin 1963.

KSP   Karl Jaspers, *Kleine Schule des philosophischen Denkens* (1965), 6th ed. Munich 1977.

MGS   Alexander Mitscherlich, *Gesammelte Schriften*. Vols. 1-10, edited by Klaus Menne, Frankfurt a.M. 1983.

MMA   Karl Jaspers, *Man in the Modern Age,* by Eden and Cedar Paul, 3rd ed. London 1959.

MW   Karl Jaspers, *Max Weber. Gesammelte Schriften*. With an introduction by Dieter Henrich, Munich 1988.

JLE   Jaspers' literary estate

PA   Personnel files

Ph   Karl Jaspers, *Philosophie*. 3 volumes (1932), 3rd ed. Berlin 1956.

PhA   Karl Jaspers, *Philosophische Autobiographie* (new, expanded edition 1977), 2nd ed. Munich 1984. Original: "Philosophical Autobiography", in: Schilpp (1957), pp. 1-94.

PhW   Karl Jaspers, *Philosophie und Welt. Reden und Aufsätze*, Munich 1958.

PW   Karl Jaspers, *Psychologie der Weltanschauungen* (1919), 5th ed. Berlin 1960.

RA   Karl Jaspers, *Rechenschaft und Ausblick* (1951), 2nd ed. Munich 1958.

RAR   Karl Jaspers, *Reason and Anti-Reason in Our Time*, London 1952.

RS   Max Weber, *Gesammelte Aufsätze zur Religionssoziologie* (1920). Vols. 1-3, 5th ed. Tübingen 1963.

UA   University archives

W   Karl Jaspers, *Von der Wahrheit. Philosophische Logik.* vol. 1, Munich 1947.
WF   Karl Jaspers, *Das Wagnis der Freiheit. Gesammelte Aufsätze zur Philosophie,* edited by Hans Saner, Munich 1996.
WG   Max Weber, *Wirtschaft und Gesellschaft. Grundriss der verstehenden Soziologie* (1922). Fifth, revised edition (*Studienausgabe*), edited by Johannes Winkelmann, Tübingen 1980.
WL   Max Weber, *Gesammelte Aufsätze zur Wissenschaftslehre* (1922). Sixth, newly revised edition, edited by Johannes Winkelmann, Tübingen 1985.
ZfgNP   *Zeitschrift für die gesamte Neurologie und Psychiatrie*

Unpublished texts

Letters

Letter from Hannah Arendt to Mrs. Decker, May 18, 1966, Arendt's literary estate, Library of Congress, Washington D.C.
Correspondance between Karl Jaspers and Ludwig Binswanger, JLE-GLA and Binswanger's literary estate, UA Tübingen.
Correspondance between Karl Jaspers and Hans W. Gruhle, JLE-GLA and Gruhle's literary estate, Max Planck Institute for Psychiatry, Munich.
Correspondance between Karl Jaspers and Kurt Kolle, JLE-GLA and Kolle family archives.
Correspondance between Karl Jaspers and Karl Löwith, Löwith's literary estate, GLA.
Correspondance between Karl Jaspers and Alexander Mitscherlich, JLE-GLA and Mitscherlich's literary estate, UA Frankfurt a.M.
Correspondance between Karl Jaspers and Rudolf Nissen, JLE-GLA.
Correspondance between Karl Jaspers and Curt Oehme, JLE-GLA.
Correspondance between Karl Jaspers and Oskar Pfister, JLE-GLA.
Correspondance between Karl Jaspers and Kurt Schneider, JLE-GLA and Kurt Schneider's literary estate, GLA.
Correspondance between Karl Jaspers and Manfred Thiel, JLE-GLA.
Correspondance between Karl Jaspers and Carl Friedrich v. Weizsäcker, JLE-GLA.
Correspondance between Karl Jaspers and Viktor v. Weizsäcker, JLE-GLA.
Letters from Max Weber to Karl Jaspers, JLE-GLA.
Letters from Alexander Mitscherlich to Felix Schottländer, Mitscherlich's literary estate, UA Frankfurt a.M.
Letter from Curt Oehme to Dean Ernst Enkelking, June 8, 1946, PA Mitscherlich, UA Heidelberg.
Copy of letter from Kurt Schneider to Dean Ernst Enkelking, May 6,1946, JLE-GLA.
Letters from Kurt Schneider to Dean Ernst Engelking, PA Mitscherlich, UA Heidelberg.
Letter from Richard Siebeck to Dean Ernst Enkelking, PA Mitscherlich, UA Heidelberg.
Letter from Viktor v. Weizsäcker to Dean Ernst Enkelking, May 25, 1946, Viktor v. Weizsäcker, UA Heidelberg.
Letter from Viktor v. Weizsäcker to the Ministery of Culture in Württemberg and Baden, April 4, 1946, PA Mitscherlich, UA Heidelberg.
Letter from Viktor v. Weizsäcker to Alexander Mitscherlich, July 28, 1945, Mitscherlich's literary estate, UA Frankfurt a.M.
Letter from Paul Vogel to Dean Ernst Enkelking, July 8, 1946, PA Mitscherlich, UA Heidelberg.

Manuscripts

Jaspers, Karl, *In der Heilkunde,* Folder "Arzt und Patient", JLE-GLA.
Jaspers, Karl, *Über die Errichtung eines Instituts für Psychotherapie,* JLE-GLA.
Mitscherlich, Alexander, *Exposé to Dean Ernst Enkelking,* May 3, 1946, PA Mitscherlich, UA Heidelberg.
Mitscherlich, Alexander, *Vorschlag zur Errichtung eines Institutes für biographische Medizin,* March 6, 1946, PA Mitscherlich, UA Heidelberg.

Cited references

Ackerknecht, Erwin H. (1985): *Kurze Geschichte der Psychiatrie* (1957), 3rd ed. Stuttgart.
Ackerknecht, Erwin H. (1943): "Problems of Primitive Medicine" in: *Bulletin of the History of Medicine* 14 (1943), pp. 30-67.
Ackermann, Ulrike (2000): *Sündenfall der Intellektuellen. Ein deutsch-französischer Streit von 1945 bis heute*, Stuttgart.
Adorno, Theodor W. (1964): *Jargon der Eigentlichkeit. Zur deutschen Ideologie*, Frankfurt a.M.
Adorno, Theodor W., Ralf Dahrendorf, Harald Pilot, Hans Albert, Jürgen Habermas, and Karl R. Popper (eds.) (1972): *Der Positivismusstreit in der deutschen Soziologie*, Darmstadt.
Albrecht, Clemens, Günter C. Behrmann, Michael Bock, Harald Homann, and Friedrich H. Tenbruck (eds.) (1999): *Die intellektuelle Gründung der Bundesrepublik. Eine Wirkungsgeschichte der Frankfurter Schule*, Frankfurt a.M.
Améry, Jean (1970b): "Weiterleben - aber wie?", Bavarian Broadcasting Company, October 8, 1970, printed in: Améry (1982), pp. 46-58.
Améry, Jean (1982): *Weiterleben - aber wie? Essays 1968-1978*, edited with an afterword by Gisela Lindemann, Stuttgart 1982.
Arendt, Hannah (1948): *Sechs Essays*, Heidelberg.
Arendt, Hannah (1976): *Die verborgene Tradition. Acht Essays*, Frankfurt a.M.
Arendt, Hannah (1955) *Elemente und Ursprünge totaler Herrschaft*. Translated and revised by the author, Frankfurt a.M. 1955. Original: *The Origins of Totalitarianism*, New York 1951 and cited as Arendt, *Elemente und Ursprünge totaler Herrschaft,* second, revised edition, Frankfurt a.M. 1958.
Arendt, Hannah (1957): "Was ist Autorität?", in: ibid., *Fragwürdige Traditionsbestände im politischen Denken der Gegenwart*, Frankfurt a.M., pp. 117-168.
Arendt, Hannah (1979): *Vom Leben des Geistes. Das Denken*. Vol. 1, Munich. Original: *The Life of the Mind*. vol. 1.: *Thinking*, London 1978.
Argentinian Psychoanalytic Society (1949): "Ausbildungsverordnung für Psychoanalytiker", in: *Psyche* 3 (1949), pg. 399.
Bachmann, Ingeborg (1979): "Der Fall Franza", Munich 1979, quoted in: ibid., *Werke*, vol. 3, 2nd ed. Munich 1982, pp. 341-482.
Bally, Gustav (1934): "Deutschstämmige Psychotherapie", in: *Neue Zürcher Zeitung,* February 27, 1934.
Bartels, Jeroen (1999): "Totalität", in Sandkühler (1999), pp. 1632-1638.
Baumgarten, Eduard (1964): *Max Weber. Werk und Person*, Tübingen 1964.
Bay, E. (1980): "Paul Vogel (1900 - 1979)", in: *Journal of Neurology* 222 (1980), pp. 139-144.
Bayer, Walter v. (1979): "Resonanz und Nachwirkung Heidelberger Ansätze in der internationalen Psychiatrie", in: Janzarik (1979), pp. 171-177.
Benzenhöfer, Udo (ed.) (1994): *Anthropologische Medizin und Sozialmedizin im Werk Viktor von Weizsäckers*, Frankfurt a.M.
Bering, Dieter (1978): *Die Intellektuellen. Geschichte eines Schimpfwortes*, Stuttgart.
Berlin, Isaiah (1981): "Igel und Fuchs", in: ibid., *Russische Denker*, Frankfurt a.M. 1981, pp. 51-123.
Berlin, Isaiah (1995): *Freiheit. Vier Versuche*, Frankfurt a.M.. Original: *Four Essays on Liberty*, London 1969.
Birnbacher, Dieter and Leonore Kottje-Birnbacher (1998): "Ethische Aspekte bei der Setzung von Therapiezielen", in: Ambühl, Hansrudi and Bernhard Strauß (eds.), *Therapieziele*, Göttingen 1998, quoted in abridged reprint in: Wiesing (2000), pp. 184-188.
Blankenburg, Wolfgang (1991): "Karl Jaspers", in: Engelhardt, Dietrich v. and Fritz Hartmann (eds.), *Klassiker der Medizin*. Vol. 2, Munich, pp. 350-365.
Bleuler, Eugen (1911): "Dementia praecox oder Gruppe der Schizophrenien", in: Gustav Aschaffenburg (ed.), *Handbuch der Psychiatrie*. Special Section, 4th chapter, 1st half, Leipzig.
Bleuler, Eugen (1914): "Psychische Kausalität und Willensakt", in: *Zeitschrift für Psychologie und Physiologie der Sinnesorgane* 69 (1914), pg. 30.
Bollnow, Otto-Friedrich (1938): "Existenzerhellung und philosophische Anthropologie. Versuch einer Auseinandersetzung mit Karl Jaspers", in: *Blätter für deutsche Philosophie*, 11 (1938), quoted in: Saner (1973), pp. 185-223.

Bonhoeffer, Karl (1910): *Die symptomatische Psychose im Gefolge von akuten Infektionen und inneren Erkrankungen*, Leipzig.

Bormuth, Matthias (1996): "Das Verhältnis von Karl Jaspers und Kurt Kolle im Spiegel ihres Diskurses um Psychotherapie", in: *Jahrbuch der Österreichischen Karl-Jaspers-Gesellschaft* 9 (1996), pp. 71-89.

Bormuth, Matthias (2000): "Karl Jaspers zur Aufklärung über Medizin und Psychiatrie im Nationalsozialismus", in: *Schriftenreihe der deutschen Gesellschaft zur Geschichte der Nervenheilkunde* 6 (2000), pp. 75-91.

Bormuth, Matthias (2002): *Lebensführung in der Moderne. Karl Jaspers und die Psychoanalyse*, Stuttgart.

Bormuth, Matthias (2004): "Karl Jaspers als Pathograph", in: *Fundamenta Psychiatrica* 18 (2002), pp. 154-159.

Bormuth, Matthias (2004): "'Schrei nach Erlösung' – Otto Gross und Max Weber. Luzifer-Amor", in: *Zeitschrift zur Geschichte der Psychoanalyse* 17 (2004), pp. 138-163.

Bormuth, Matthias (2004): "Pathographie als Zeitkritik – Anmerkungen zu Jaspers' *Strindberg und van Gogh*", in: Gockel, Bettina und Michael Hagner (eds.), *Die Wissenschaft vom Künstler. Körper, Geist und Lebensgeschichte des Künstlers als Objekte der Wissenschaften, 1880-1930*. Max Planck Institute for the History of the Sciences and Humanities, Berlin 2004, pp. 101-115.

Bormuth, Matthias (2004): "Lebensführung in der Moderne. Karl Jaspers und Max Weber", in: Weidmann, Bernd (ed.), *Zur philosophischen Ethik von Karl Jaspers*, Würzburg 2004, pp. 119-150.

Bormuth, Matthias (2005): "'Ärztliche Seelsorge' in der entzauberten Welt – Karl Jaspers als Kritiker des frühen Viktor E. Frankl", in: Batthyany, Dominik and Otto Zsok (eds.), *Viktor E. Frankl und die Philosophie*, Vienna 2005, pp. 213-236.

Bracher, Karl Dietrich (1984): *Zeit der Ideologien. Eine Geschichte politischen Denkens im 20. Jahrhundert*. Expanded, revised edition, Stuttgart.

Bräutigam, Walter (1967): "Die Beziehungen zwischen Psychiatrie und Psychoanalyse in Deutschland", in: *Der Nervenarzt* 38 (1967), pp. 394-397.

Bräutigam, Walter (1984): "Rückblick auf das Jahr 1942. Betrachtungen eines psychoanalytischen Ausbildungskandidaten des Berliner Instituts der Kriegsjahre", in: *Psyche* (1984), pp. 905-914.

Bräutigam, Walter and Christian, Paul (1961): "Klinische Psychotherapie bei psychosomatischen Krankheiten", in: *Der Nervenarzt* 32 (1961), pp. 347-354.

Bräutigam, Walter and Paul Christian (1985): *Psychosomatische Medizin. Ein kurzgefaßtes Lehrbuch* (1973), 4th ed. Stuttgart 1985.

Carus, Carl Gustav (1846): *Psyche. Zur Entwicklungsgeschichte der Seele*, Pforzheim.

Cocks, Geoffry C. (1983): "Psychoanalyse, Psychotherapie und Nationalsozialismus", in: *Psyche* 37 (1983), pp. 1057-1106.

Cocks, Geoffry C. (1985): *Psychotherapy in the Third Reich*, Oxford.

Cremerius, Johannes (1978): *Zur Theorie und Praxis der Psychosomatischen Medizin*, Frankfurt a.M.

Cremerius, Johannes (ed.) (1981a): *Die Rezeption der Psychoanalyse in der Soziologie, Psychologie und Theologie im deutschsprachigen Raum bis 1940*, Frankfurt a.M.

Dilthey Wilhelm (1894), "Ideen über eine beschreibende und zergliedernde Psychologie", Berlin. Quoted in: ibid., *Wilhelm Dilthey - Eine Auswahl aus seinen Schriften*, edited by Hermann Nohl, Stuttgart 1961, pp. 131-229.

Walter Sparn (1996): "Die Moderne: Kulturkrise und Konstruktionsgeist", in: Drehsen, Volker and Walter Sparn (eds.), *Vom Weltbildwandel zur Weltanschauungsanalyse. Krisenwahrnehmung und Krisenbewältigung um 1900*, Berlin.

Droysen, Johann Gustav (1867): *Historik. Vorlesungen über Enzyklopädie und Methodologie der Geschichte*, edited by Rudolf Hübner, 4th ed. Munich 1960.

Eich, Günter (1959): "Rede zur Verleihung des Georg-Büchner-Preises (1959)", in: ibid., *Gesammelte Werke* vol. 4, edited by Heinz F. Schafroth, Frankfurt a.M. 1973.

Ellenberger, Henri F. (1973): *The Discovery of the Unconscious: The History and Evolution of Dynamic Psychiatry*, New York 1970.

Engelhardt, Dietrich v. and Fritz Hartmann (1991): *Klassiker der Medizin*, 2 vols., Munich.

Erdheim, Mario (1986): "Das Verenden einer Institution", in: *Psyche* 40 (1986), pp. 1092-1104.

Frank, Ludwig (1913): *Affektstörungen. Studien über ihre Ätiologie und Therapie*, Berlin.

Freud, Sigmund and Joseph Breuer (1895): *Studien über Hysterie*, Leipzig, quoted in: FGW 1, pp. 75-312. English translation: *Studies on Hysteria*. Standard Edition, vol. 2.

Freud, Sigmund (1900): *Die Traumdeutung*, Leipzig, quoted in: FGW 2/3. English translation: *The Interpretation of Dreams*. Standard Edition, vols. 4/5.

Freud, Sigmund (1905a): "Bruchstücke einer Hysterieanalyse", in: *Monatsschrift für Psychiatrie und Neurologie* 22 (1905), also in: Freud (1909), quoted in: FGW 5, pp. 161-286. English translation: "Fragment of an Analysis of a Case of Hysteria". Standard Edition, vol. 7, pp. 7-122.

Freud, Sigmund (1905b): *Der Witz und seine Beziehung zum Unbewußten*, Leipzig 1905, quoted in: FGW 6. English translation: *Jokes and Their Relation to the Unconscious*. Standard Edition, vol. 8.

Freud, Sigmund (1905c): *Drei Abhandlungen zur Sexualtheorie*, Leipzig, quoted in: FGW 5, pp. 27-145. English translation: *Three Essays on the Theory of Sexuality*. Standard Edition, vol. 7, p. 130-243.

Freud, Sigmund (1906a): "Meine Ansichten über die Rolle der Sexualität in der Ätiologie der Neurosen", in: Freud (1906b), quoted in: FGW 5, pp. 147-159. English translation: "My Views on the Part Played by Sexuality in the Aetiology of the Neurosis". Standard Edition, vol. 7, pp. 271-279.

Freud, Sigmund (1906b): *Sammlung kleiner Schriften zur Neurosenlehre 1893-1906*, Leipzig.

Freud, Sigmund (1907): *Der Wahn und die Träume in W. Jensens `Gradiva'*, Vienna, quoted in: FGW 7, pp. 29-125. English translation: *Delusions and Dreams in Jensen's Gradiva*. Standard Edition, vol. 9, pp. 7-95.

Freud, Sigmund (1909): *Sammlung kleiner Schriften zur Neurosenlehre. Neue Folge*, Leipzig.

Freud, Sigmund (1910a): *Eine Kindheitserinnerung des Leonardo da Vinci*, Leipzig, quoted in: FGW 8, pp. 127-211. English translation: *Leonardo da Vinci and a Memory of his Childhood*. Standard Edition, vol. 11, pp. 63-137.

Freud, Sigmund (1910b): *Über Psychoanalyse. Fünf Vorlesungen gehalten zur zwanzigjährigen Gründungsfeier der Clark University*. 1909, Leipzig, quoted in: FGW 8, pp. 3-60. English translation: *Five Lectures on Psycho-Analysis*. Standard Edition, vol. 11, pp. 3-55.

Freud, Sigmund (1912): "Ratschläge für den Arzt bei der psychoanalytischen Behandlung", in: *Zentralblatt für Psychoanalyse* 2 (1912), quoted in: FGW 8, pp. 375-387. English translation: "Recommendations to Physicians Practising Psycho-Analysis". Standard Edition, vol. 12, pp. 111-120.

Freud, Sigmund (1914): "Zur Geschichte der psychoanalytischen Bewegung", in: *Jahrbuch für psychoanalytische und psychopathologische Forschungen* Bd. 6, Leipzig, quoted in: FGW 10, pp. 41-113. English translation: "On the History of the Psycho-Analytic Movement". Standard Edition, vol. 14, pp. 7-66.

Freud, Sigmund (1915): "Trieb und Triebschicksal", in: *Zeitschrift für Psychoanalyse* 2 (1915), quoted in: FGW 10, pp. 209-232. English translation: "Instincts and Their Vicissitudes". Standard Edition, vol. 14, pp. 117-140.

Freud, Sigmund (1917): *Vorlesungen zur Einführung in die Psychoanalyse*, Leipzig, quoted in: FGW 11. English translation: *Introductory Lectures on Psycho-Analysis*. Standard Edition, vols. 15/16.

Freud, Sigmund (1919): *Wege der analytischen Therapie*, quoted in: FGW 12, pp. 81-94. English Translation: "Lines of Advance in Psycho-analytic Therapy". Standard Editon vol. 17, pp. 157-168.

Freud, Sigmund (1920): *Jenseits des Lustprinzips*, Leipzig, quoted in: FGW 13, pp. 1-69. English translation: *Beyond the Pleasure Principle*. Standard Edition, vol. 18, pp. 7-64.

Freud, Sigmund (1923): *Das Ich und das Es*, Leipzig, quoted in FGW 8, pp. 235-289. English translation: *The Ego and the Id*. Standard Edition, vol. 19, pp. 12-66.

Freud, Sigmund (1925): "Selbstdarstellung", in: L.R. Grote (ed.), *Die Medizin der Gegenwart in Selbstdarstellungen* Bd. 4, Leipzig, quoted in: FGW 14, pp. 31-96. English translation: "An Autobiographical Study". Standard Edition, vol. 20, pp. 7-74.

Freud, Sigmund (1926): *Zur Frage der Laienanalyse*, Leipzig, quoted in: FGW 14, pp. 207-296. English translation: *The Question of Lay Analysis*. Standard Edition, vol. 20, pp. 183-258.

Freud, Sigmund (1930): *Das Unbehagen in der Kultur*, Leipzig, in: FGW 14, pp. 417-506. English translation: *Civilization and its Discontents*. Standard Edition, vol. 21, p. 64-145.

Freud, Sigmund (1933): *Neue Vorlesungen zur Einführung in die Psychoanalyse*, Leipzig 1933, quoted in: FGW 15. English translation: *New Introductory Lectures on Psycho-Analysis*. Standard Edition, vol. 22, pp. 5-182.

Freud, Sigmund (1937): "Konstruktionen in der Analyse", in: *Internationale Zeitschrift für Psychoanalyse* 23 (1937), quoted in: FGW 16, pp. 41-56. English translation: "Constructions in Analysis". Standard Edition, vol. 23, pp. 255-269.

Freud, Sigmund (1986): *Briefe an Wilhelm Fließ 1887-1904*. Unabridged edition edited by Jeffrey Moussaieff Masson; German edition by Michael Schröter with transcriptions by Gerhard Fichtner,

Frankfurt a.M.. English translation: *The Complete Letters of Sigmund Freud to Wilhelm Fliess. 1887-1904*, edited by. J.M. Masson, Cambridge 1985.

Freud, Sigmund and Oskar Pfister (1963): *Sigmund Freud - Oskar Pfister. Letters 1909-1939*, edited by Ernst. L. Freud and Heinrich Meng, Frankfurt a.M.

Freud, Sigmund and Abraham, Karl (1965): *Sigmund Freud - Karl Abraham. Letters 1907-1926*, edited by Hilda S. Abraham and Ernst L. Freud, Frankfurt a.M. English translation: *A Psycho-analytic dialoque: The Letters of Sigmund Freud and Karl Abraham 1907-1926*, edited by H. Abraham and Ernst L. Freud, New York 1965.

Freud, Sigmund and Carl Gustav Jung (1974): *Sigmund Freud - CG. Jung. Briefwechsel*, edited by William McGuire and Wolfgang Sauerländer, Frankfurt a.M.. English translation: *The Freud-Jung-Letters: The Correspondance between Sigmund Freud and C.G. Jung*. Edited by William McGuirre, London 1974.

Freud, Sigmund and Ludwig Binswanger (1992): *Sigmund Freud - Ludwig Binswanger. Correspondance 1908 - 1938*, edited by Gerhard Fichtner, Frankfurt a.M.

Frommer, Jörg and Sabine Frommer (1990): "Max Webers Bedeutung für den Verstehensbegriff in der Psychiatrie", in: *Der Nervenarzt* 61 (1990), pp. 397-401.

Frommer, Sabine (1990): "Der Begriff des psychologischen Verstehens bei Max Weber", in: *Psychologie und Geschichte* 2 (1990), pp. 37-44.

Frommer, Sabine (1994): "Bezüge zu experimenteller Psychologie, Psychiatrie und Psychopathologie in Max Webers methodologischen Schriften", in: Gerhard Wagner and Heinz Zipprian (eds.)*, Max Webers Wissenschaftslehre. Interpretationen und Kritik*, Frankfurt a.M., pp. 239-258.

Frommer, Jörg and Sabine Frommer (1999): "Psychotherapie als Beruf", in: Tress/Langenbach (1999), pp. 50-71.

Frühmann, Renate and Hilarion Petzold (1994): *Lehrjahre der Seele. Lehranalyse, Selbsterfahrung, Eigentherapie in den psychotherapeutischen Schulen*, Paderborn.

Fügen, Norbert (1995): *Max Weber*, Reinbek bei Hamburg.

Furet, Francois (1996): *Das Ende der Illusion. Der Kommunismus im 20. Jahrhundert*, Munich.

Gadamer, Hans Georg (1960): *Wahrheit und Methode. Grundzüge einer philosophischen Hermeneutik*, 4th ed. Tübingen 1975.

Gadamer, Hans Georg (1977): *Philosphische Lehrjahre. Eine Rückschau*, Frankfurt a.M.

Gay, Peter (1988): *Freud: A Life for Our Time,* London 1988.

Gerst, Thomas (1994): "Nürnberger Ärzteprozeß´ und ärztliche Standespolitik. Der Auftrag der Ärztekammern an Alexander Mitscherlich zur Beobachtung und Dokumentation des Prozeßverlaufes", in: *Deutsches Ärzteblatt* (1994) Heft 22/23, pp. B 1200-1210.

Gombrowicz, Witold (1988): *Tagebuch 1953-1969*, Munich.

Greiffenhagen, Martin (1986): *Das Dilemma des Konservatismus in Deutschland*. Expanded edition, Frankfurt a.M.

Green, Martin (1974): *Else und Frieda, die Richthofen-Schwestern*, Stuttgart 1980.

Griessinger, Wilhelm (1861): *Die Pathologie und Therapie der psychischen Krankheiten*. Second, revised and greatly expanded edition (1841), Stuttgart.

Grimm, Dieter (1987): *Recht und Staat der bürgerlichen Gesellschaft*, Frankfurt a.M.

Gross, Otto (1913): "Die Überwindung der kulturellen Krise", in: *Die Aktion* 3 (1913), Col. 387, quoted in: ibid., *Von geschlechtlicher Not zur sozialen Katastrophe*, edited and annotated by Kurt Kreiler, Frankfurt a.M. 1980, pp. 13-16.

Grünbaum, Adolf (1984): *The Foundations of Psychoanalysis. A Philosophical Critique.* Berkeley.

Grünbaum, Adolf (1987): *Psychoanalyse in wissenschaftstheoretischer Sicht. Zum Werk Sigmund Freuds und seiner Rezeption*, Konstanz.

Gruhle, Hans W. (1953): "Psychopathologie und akademischer Unterricht", in: Piper (1953), pp. 155-168.

Habermas Jürgen (1963): "Eine psychoanalytische Konstruktion des Fortschritts" [Review of Alexander Mitscherlich (1963)] in: *Merkur* 17 (1963), pp. 1105-1109, quoted in: Habermas (1981), pp. 180-185.

Habermas, Jürgen (1968): *Erkenntnis und Interesse*, Frankfurt a.M. 1968. English translation: *Knowledge and Human Interest*, translated by Jeremy J. Shapiro, London (1972).

Habermas, Jürgen (1978): "Arzt und Intellektueller. Alexander Mitscherlich zum 70. Geburtstag", in: *Die Zeit*, Sept. 22, 1978, quoted in: *Philosophisch-politische Profile*. Expanded edition, Frankfurt a.M. 1981.

Habermas, Jürgen (1979): "Einleitung", in ibid.: *Stichworte zur `Geistigen Situation der Zeit´*, vol. 1 (*Nation und Republik*), Frankfurt a.M. 1979, pp. 7-35.

Habermas, Jürgen (1982): "In memoriam Alexander Mitscherlich", in: *Psyche* 36 (1982), pp. 1060-1063.

Habermas, Jürgen (1995): "Wahrheit und Wahrhaftigkeit. Rede zur Verleihung des Karl-Jaspers-Preises der Universität Heidelberg 1995", in: *Die Zeit*, Dec. 8, 1995.

Hadot, Pierre (2002): *What is Ancient Philosophy?*, Cambridge.

Hattingberg, Hans v. (1933): "Neue Richtung, Neue Bindung", in: *Zentralblatt für Psychotherapie* (1933), pp. 98-107.

Heimann, Hans (1950): "Der Einfluß von Karl Jaspers auf die Psychopathologie", in: *Monatsschrift für Psychiatrie und Neurologie* 120 (1950), pp. 1-19.

Heimann, Hans (1956): "K.W. Idelers *Versuch einer Theorie des religösen Wahnsinns* – nach 100 Jahren". Summary in: *Schweizer Archiv für Neurologie und Psychiatrie*, 78 (1956), pg. 394.

Heimann, Hans (1976): "Psychiatrie und Menschlichkeit", in: *Confinia Psychiatrica* 19 (1976), pp. 24-34.

Heimann, Hans (1980): "Nosologie und Pathophysiologie in der Psychiatrie - Aspekte der Krankheitslehre Kraepelins heute", in: *Convinia Psychiatrica* 23 (1980), pp. 262-274.

Heimann, Hans (1988): "Wilhelm Griesinger und Lehre und Forschung in der modernen Psychiatrie", in: *Fet al.lmenta Psychiatrica* 2 (1988), pp. 124-129.

Heimann, Hans (1989): "Die Psychiatrie zwischen Naturwissenschaft und Geisteswissenschaft", in: Dietrich Rössler and Hans Dierck Waller (eds.), *Medizin zwischen Geisteswissenschaft und Naturwissenschaft*, Tübingen.

Heimann, Moritz (1966): *Die Wahrheit liegt nicht in der Mitte. Essays*, Frankfurt a.M.

Heinroth, Johann Christian August (1818): *Lehrbuch der Störungen des Seelenlebens oder der Seelenstörungen*. 2 vols., Leipzig.

Heinroth, Johann Christian August (1827): *Die Psychologie als Selbsterkenntnislehre*, Leipzig.

Henkelmann, Thomas (1986): *Viktor v. Weizsäcker. 1886-1957. Materialien zu Leben und Werk*, Berlin.

Henkelmann, Thomas (1992): "Zur Geschichte der Psychosomatik in Heidelberg. Viktor von Weizsäcker und Alexander Mitscherlich als Kliniksgründer", in: *Zeitschrift für Psychotherapie, Psychosomatik und medizinische Psychologie* 42 (1992), pp. 175-188.

Hennis, Wilhelm (1987): *Max Webers Fragestellung*, Tübingen.

Hennis, Wilhelm (1996): *Max Webers Wissenschaft vom Menschen*, Tübingen.

Henrich, Dieter (1952): *Die Einheit der Wissenschaftslehre Max Webers*, Tübingen.

Henrich, Dieter (1986): "Denken im Blick auf Max Weber", in: Hersch *et al.* (1986), pp. 207-231, quoted in: MW, pp. 7-31.

Hersch, Jeanne (1957): "Is Jaspers´ Conception of Tradition Adequate For Our Times?", in: Schilpp (1957), pp. 593-610.

Hersch, Jeanne, Jan Milic Lochmann and Reiner Wiehl (eds.) (1986): *Karl Jaspers. Philosoph, Arzt, politischer Denker*, Munich.

Hochgeschwender, Michael (1998): *Freiheit in der Offensive? Der Kongreß für kulturelle Freiheit und die Deutschen*, Munich.

Hölderlin, Friedrich (1969): *Gedichte*, edited and annotated by Jochen Schmidt, Frankfurt a.M.

Hoff, Paul (1985): "Zum Krankheitsbegriff bei Emil Kraepelin", in: *Der Nervenarzt* 56 (1985), pp. 510-513.

Hoff, Paul (1989): "Erkenntnistheoretische Vorurteile in der Psychiatrie. Eine kritische Reflexion 75 Jahre nach Karl Jaspers' *Allgemeiner Psychopathologie* (1913)", in: *Fet al.lmenta Psychiatrica* 3 (1989), pp. 141-150.

Hoff, Paul (1994): *Emil Kraepelin und die Psychiatrie als klinische Wissenschaft. Ein Beitrag zum Selbstverständnis psychiatrischer Forschung*, Berlin.

Hoffmann, Sven Olaf *et al.* (eds.) (1999): *Psychosomatische Medizin und Psychotherapie. Denkschrift zur Lage des Faches an den Hochschulen der Bundesrepublik Deutschland*, Stuttgart.

Hurwitz, Emanuel (1979): *Otto Gross. Paradies-Sucher zwischen Freud und Jung*, Zürich.

Ideler, Karl Wilhelm (1835): *Grundriß der Seelenheilkunde*. 2 vols., Berlin.

Isserlin, Max (1910): "Die psychoanalytische Methode Freuds", in: *ZfgNP* 1 (1910), pp. 53-80.

Isserlin, Max (1912b): "Methoden der Psychotherapie?", in: *Ergebnisse der Neurologie und Psychiatrie* 1 (1912).

Jaeger, Friedrich (1994): *Bürgerliche Modernisierungskrise und historische Sinnbildung. Kulturgeschichte bei Droysen, Burckhardt und Max Weber*, Göttingen.

Janet, Pierre (1889): *L`Automatisme Psychologique*, Paris.

Janet, Pierre (1898): *Néuroses et idées fixes*, Paris.

Janet, Pierre (1906): "Un cas de délire systématisé dans la paralysie générale", in: *Journal de Psychologie* 3 (1906), pp. 329-331.

Janz, Curt Paul (1978): *Friedrich Nietzsche*. 3 vols., Munich.

Janzarik, Werner (1974): *Themen und Tendenzen der deutschsprachigen Psychiatrie*, Berlin.

Janzarik, Werner (1976): "Die Krise der Psychopathologie", in: *Der Nervenarzt* 47 (1976), pp. 73-80.

Janzarik, Werner (1979a): "Die klinische Psychopathologie zwischen Griesinger und Kraepelin im Querschnitt des Jahres 1878", in: Janzarik (1979b), pp. 51-61.

Janzarik, Werner (1979b): "100 Jahre Heidelberger Psychiatrie", in: Janzarik (1979c), pp. 1-18.

Janzarik, Werner (ed.) (1979c): *Psychopathologie als Grundlagenwissenschaft*, Stuttgart.

Janzarik, Werner (ed.) (1985): *Psychopathologie und Praxis*, Stuttgart.

Janzarik, Werner (1986): "Jaspers, Kurt Schneider und die Heidelberger Psychopathologie", in: Hersch *et al.* (1986), pp. 112-126.

Jaspers, Karl (1909): *Heimweh und Verbrechen*, Leipzig 1909; reprint in: *Gross Archiv für Kriminal-Anthropologie* 35 (1909), quoted in: GSP, pp. 1-84.

Jaspers, Karl (1910a): "Die Methoden der Intelligenzprüfung und der Begriff der Demenz. Kritisches Referat", in: *ZfgNP. Referate und Ergebnisse* 1 (1910), pp. 402-452, quoted in: GSP, pp. 142-190.

Jaspers, Karl (1910b): "Eifersuchtswahn. Ein Beitrag zur Frage: 'Entwicklung einer Persönlichkeit' oder 'Prozeß'?" in: *ZfgNP* 1 (1910), pp. 567-637, quoted in: GSP, pp. 85-141.

Jaspers, Karl (1911): "Zur Analyse der Trugwahrnehmungen (Leibhaftigkeit und Realitätsurteil)", in: *ZfgNP* 6 (1911), pp. 460-535, quoted in: GSP, pp. 191-251.

Jaspers, Karl (1912a): "Die phänomenologische Methode in der Psychopathologie", in: *ZfgNP* 9 (1912), pp. 391-408, quoted in: GSP, pp. 314-328. English translation: "The Phenomenological Approach in Psychopathology, in: *The British Journal of Psychiatry* 114 (1968), pp. 1313-1323.

Jaspers, Karl (1912b): "Die Trugwahrnehmungen, Kritisches Referat" in: *ZfgNP. Referate und Ergebnisse* 4 (1912), pp. 289-354, quoted in: GSP, pp. 252-313.

Jaspers, Karl (1913a): *Allgemeine Psychopathologie. Ein Leitfaden für Studierende, Ärzte und Psychologen*, Berlin (AP 1).

Jaspers, Karl (1913b): "Kausale und 'verständliche' Zusammenhänge zwischen Schicksal und Psychose bei der Dementia Praecox (Schizophrenie)", in: *ZfgNP. Originalien* 14 (1913), pp. 158-263, quoted in: GSP, pp. 329-412.

Jaspers, Karl (1913c): Review [Carl Gustav Jung, *Wandlungen und Symbole der Libido. Zweiter Teil*, in: *Jahrbuch für psychoanalytische und psychopathologische Forschungen* 4 (1912)], in: *ZfgNP* 6 (1913), pp. 548-550.

Jaspers, Karl (1914): Review [Carl Gustav Jung, *Versuch einer Darstellung der psychoanalytischen Theorie*, in: *Jahrbuch für psychoanalytische und psychopathologische Forschungen* 5 (1913)], in: *ZfgNP* 8 (1914), pp. 582-583.

Jaspers, Karl (1915): Review [Eugen Bleuler, *Psychische Kausalität und Willensakt*, in: *Zeitschrift für Psychologie und Physiologie der Sinnesorgane* 69 (1914), in: *ZfgNP* 11 (1915), pp. 168-169.

Jaspers, Karl (1918): Review [Ernst Kretschmer, *Der sensitive Beziehungswahn. Ein Beitrag zur Paranoiafrage und zur psychiatrischen Charakterlehre*, Berlin 1918], in *ZfgNP*, pp. 123-124.

Jaspers, Karl (1919): *Psychologie der Weltanschauungen*, 5th ed. Berlin 1960 (PW).

Jaspers, Karl (1920): *Allgemeine Psychopathologie. Für Studierende, Ärzte und Psychologen*, 2nd, revised edition, Berlin (AP 2).

Jaspers, Karl (1921): "Max Weber. Rede bei der von der Heidelberger Studentenschaft am 17. Juli 1920 veranstalteten Trauerfeier", Tübingen, quoted in: MW, pp. 32-48.

Jaspers, Karl (1923a): *Allgemeine Psychopathologie. Für Studierende, Ärzte und Psychologen*. 3rd, expanded and improved edition, Berlin (AP 3).

Jaspers, Karl (1926): *Strindberg und van Gogh. Versuch einer pathographischen Analyse unter vergleichender Heranziehung von Swedenborg und Hölderlin* (1922). 2nd, expanded edition, Berlin.

Jaspers, Karl (1931): *Die geistige Situation der Zeit*. 5th, revised edition 1932, 3rd ed. Berlin 1953.

Jaspers, Karl (1932a): *Max Weber. Deutsches Wesen im politischen Denken, im Forschen und Philosophieren*, Bremen, quoted in: MW, pp. 49-114.

Jaspers, Karl (1932b): *Philosophie*. Vols. 1-3, 3rd ed. Berlin 1956 (Ph).

Jaspers, Karl (1936): *Nietzsche. Einführung in das Verständnis seines Philosophierens*, 3rd ed. Berlin 1950.

Jaspers, Karl (1938): *Existenzphilosophie. Drei Vorlesungen, gehalten am Freien Deutschen Hochstift in Frankfurt a.M.*, 2nd ed. Berlin 1956.

Jaspers, Karl (1946): *Allgemeine Psychopathologie* (1946; fourth, completely revised edition), 9th ed. Berlin 1973 (AP 4). English Translation: *General Psychopathology*, translated by J. Hoenig and Marian W. Hamilton with a   new foreward by Paul R. McHugh, 2nd ed. Baltimore 1997 (GP 4).

Jaspers, Karl (1947b): *Von der Wahrheit. Philosophische Logik.* vol. I, Munich.

Jaspers, Karl (1949/50): "Über Gefahren und Chancen der Freiheit", in: *Der Monat* 2 (1949/50), pp. 396-406, quoted in: RA, 345-369.

Jaspers, Karl (1950a): *Einführung in die Philosophie. Zwölf Radiovorträge*, Zürich, quoted in: Munich 1971.

Jaspers, Karl (1950b): "Marx und Freud", in: *Der Monat* 3 (1950), pp. 141 - 150.

Jaspers, Karl (1950c): *Vernunft und Widervernunft in unserer Zeit*, Munich 1950 (VW). English translation: *Reason and Anti-Reason in Our Time*, London 1952 (RAR).

Jaspers, Karl (1950d): "Zur Kritik der Psychoanalyse", in: *Der Nervenarzt* 31 (1950), pp. 465-468, quoted in: ATZ, pp. 59-67.

Jaspers, Karl (1951a): "Freiheit und Autorität", in: *Protokoll der Konferenz schweizerischer Gymnasial-Rektoren* 1950, Lucerne 1951, quoted in: PhW, pp. 357-376.

Jaspers, Karl (1951b): *Rechenschaft und Ausblick*, 2nd ed. Munich 1958 (RA).

Jaspers, Karl (1952a): "Lebenslauf Ernst Mayers", in: *Ärztliche Mitteilungen* 37 (1952), pp. 543f.

Jaspers, Karl (1952b): "Von den Grenzen pädagogischen Planens", in: *Basler Schulblatt* 13 (1952), pp. 72-77, quoted in: PhW, pp. 28-38.

Jaspers, Karl (1953) "Arzt und Patient", in: *Studium Generale* 6 (1953), quoted in: ATZ, pp. 19-38.

Jaspers, Karl (1954a): "Die Aufgabe der Philosophie in der Gegenwart. Radiovortrag im Studio Basel 1953", in: Klaus Piper (ed.), *Nach 50 Jahren. Almanach*, Munich, pp. 153-163, quoted in: PhW, pp. 9-20.

Jaspers, Karl (1954b): "Im Kampf mit dem Totalitarismus", orginally as "The Fight Against Totalitarianism", in: *Confluence* 3 (1954), S 251-266, translated in: *Kontinente* 8 (1955), pp. 1-8 and quoted in: PhW, pp. 76-96.

Jaspers, Karl (1955): *Wesen und Kritik der Psychotherapie*, Munich.

Jaspers, Karl (1956): "Das Kollektiv und der Einzelne. Radiovortrag", in: *Mensch und Menschlichkeit*, Stuttgart, pp. 65-76, quoted in: PhW, pp. 65-75.

Jaspers, Karl (1957): "Antwort", in: Schilpp (1957), pp. 750-852. Original: "Reply To My Critics", in Schilpp (1957a), pg. 748-869.

Jaspers, Karl (1958a): *Die Atombombe und die Zukunft des Menschen. Politisches Bewußtsein in unserer Zeit*, Munich (AZM).

Jaspers, Karl (1958b): *Philosophie und Welt. Reden und Aufsätze*, Munich (PhW).

Jaspers, Karl (1958c): "Vorwort", in: Malvin J. Lasky, *Die ungarische Revolution. Ein Weißbuch. Die Geschichte des Oktober-Aufstandes nach Dokumenten, Meldungen, Augenzeugenberichten und dem Echo der Weltöffentlichkeit*. Published for the *Kongreß für die Freiheit der Kultur*, Berlin, pp. 11-13.

Jaspers, Karl (1962): "Max Webers politisches Denken", in: E. Beckerath and Heinrich Popitz (eds.), *Antidoron. Edgar Salin zum 70. Geburtstag*, Tübingen, pp. 200-214, quoted in: MW, pp. 115-127.

Jaspers, Karl (1963): *Gesammelte Aufsätze zur Psychopathologie*, Berlin (GSP).

Jaspers, Karl (1965c): *Kleine Schule des philosophischen Denkens. Vorlesungen, gehalten im 1. Trimester des Studienprogramms des Bayrischen Rundfunks 1964*, Munich (KSP).

Jaspers, Karl (1966). *Wohin treibt die Bundesrepublik? Tatsachen - Gefahren - Chancen*, Munich.

Jaspers, Karl (1967a): *Antwort. Zur Kritik meiner Schrift 'Wohin treibt die Bundesrepublik?'*, Munich.

Jaspers, Karl (1967b): "Ein Selbstportrait" (1966/67), in: Jaspers (1967c), pp. 15-38.

Jaspers, Karl (1967c): *Schicksal und Wille. Autobiographische Schriften*, edited by Hans Saner, Munich.

Jaspers, Karl (1977): *Philosophische Autobiographie*. Expanded, revised edition, 2nd ed. Munich 1984 (PhA).

Jaspers, Karl (1978): *Notizen zu Martin Heidegger*, edited by Hans Saner, Munich.

Jaspers, Karl (1983): "Einsamkeit", edited by Hans Saner in: *Revue Internationale de Philosophie, Revue Trimestrielle. Bruxelles* 37 (1983), pp. 390-409, quoted in: WF.

Jaspers, Karl (1986): *Der Arzt im technischen Zeitalter. Technik und Medizin, Arzt und Patient, Kritik der Psychotherapie*, Munich (ATZ).

Jaspers, Karl (1986): *Erneuerung der Universität. Reden und Schriften 1945/46*. Afterword: Renato de Rosa, "Politische Akzente im Leben eines Philosophen. Karl Jaspers in Heidelberg 1901-1946", Heidelberg (EU).

Jaspers, Karl (1990): *Martin Heidegger - Karl Jaspers. Briefwechsel 1920-1963*, edited by Walter Biemel and Hans Saner, Munich 1990. Translation: *The Heidegger-Jaspers Correspondence (1920-1963)*, ed. by Walter Biemel and Hans Saner, New York 2003.

Jaspers, Karl (1996): *Das Wagnis der Freiheit. Gesammelte Aufsätze zur Philosophie*, edited by Hans Saner, Munich 1996 (WF).

Johnson, Uwe (1981): *Skizze eines Verunglückten*, Frankfurt a.M.

Kadereit, Ralf (1999): *Karl Jaspers und die Bundesrepublik Deutschland. Politische Gedanken eines Philosophen*, Paderborn.

Kippenberg, Hans G. (1989): "Intellektuellen-Religion", in: Peter Antes and Donate Pahnke (eds.), *Die Religionen von Oberschichten. Religion-Profession-Intellektualismus*, Marburg, pp. 181-201.

Kirkbright, Suzanne (2004): *Karl Jaspers. A Biography. Navigations in Truth*, New Haven.

Kittel, Ingo-Wolf (1988): *Arthur Kronfeld 1886-1941. Ein Pionier der Psychologie, Sexualwissenschaft und Psychotherapie*, Konstanz.

Kolle, Kurt (1949): "Diskussionsbeitrag auf der 55. Tagung der Deutschen Gesellschaft für Innere Medizin in Wiesbaden", in: *Psyche*, 3 (1949), pp. 377-384.

Kolle, Kurt (1955): "Karl Jaspers". in: Kurt Kolle (ed.), *Große Nervenärzte*, vol. 1, 2nd ed. Munich 1970, pp. 145-152.

Kolle, Kurt (1957): "Karl Jaspers als Psychopathologe". in: Schilpp (1957a), pp. 436 - 464. Original: "Karl Jaspers as Psychopathologist", in: Schilpp (1957), pp. 437-466.

Kolle, Kurt (1974): "Karl Jaspers als Lehrer eines Psychiaters", in: Piper/Saner (1974): pp. 53-58.

Kommerell, Max (1943): *Gedanken über Gedichte*, 4th ed. Frankfurt a.M. 1985.

Koselleck, Reinhart (1976): "Krise", in: Gerhard Ritter et al. (ed.), *Historisches Wörterbuch der Philosophie*, vol. 4, Darmstadt, Col. 1239.

Koselleck, Reinhart (1985): "Zeitverkürzung und Beschleunigung. Eine Studie zur Säkularisierung", in: ibid., *Zeitschichten*, Frankfurt a.M. 2000, pp. 177-202.

Koselleck, Reinhart (1986): "Jaspers, die Geschichte und das Überpolitische", in: Jeanne Hersch *et al.* (1986), pp. 291-302.

Kracauer, Siegfried (1920): "Rezension [Georg von Lukács, Theorie des Romans. Ein geschichtsphilosophischer Versuch über die Formen der großen Epik", Berlin 1920], in: KS Jan. 5, pp. 117-123.

Kracauer, Siegfried (1922): "Die Wartenden", in: Kracauer (1990), vol. 1, pp. 160-170.

Kracauer, Siegfried (1924): "Psychologie der Weltanschauungen", in: Kracauer (1990), vol. 1, pp. 260-262.

Kracauer, Siegfried (1948): "Psychiatry for Everything and Everybody. The present Vogue - and What is Behind It," in: *Commentary* 5 (1948), pp. 222-228, quoted in: ibid., "Psychiatrie für alles und Jeden. Die gegenwärtige Mode und ihre Hintergründe", in: Kracauer (1990), vol. 3, pp. 319-331.

Kracauer, Siegfried (1990): *Schriften 5. Aufsätze*, 3 vols., edited by Inka Mülder-Bach, Frankfurt a.M.

Kraepelin, Emil (1896): *Psychiatrie. Ein Lehrbuch für Studierende und Ärzte*, 5th, completely revised edition, Leipzig.

Kraepelin, Emil (1905): "Fragestellungen der klinischen Psychiatrie", in: *Zentralblatt für Nervenheilkunde und Psychiatrie* 28 (1905), pp. 573-590.

Kretschmer, Ernst (1918): *Der sensitive Beziehungswahn. Ein Beitrag zur Paranoiafrage und zur psychiatrischen Charakterlehre*, Berlin.

Kronfeld, Arthur (1912): "Über die psychologischen Theorien Freuds und verwandte Anschauungen. Systematik und kritische Erörterung", in: *Archiv für die gesamte Psychologie* 22 (1912), pp. 130-248.

Kronfeld, Arthur (1920): *Das Wesen der psychiatrischen Erkenntnis. Beiträge zur Allgemeinen Psychiatrie I*, Berlin.

Krüger, Gerhard (1958): *Grundfragen der Philosophie. Geschichte - Wahrheit - Wissenschaft*, Frankfurt a.M.

Laplanche, J. and Pontalis, J.-B. (1973): *The Language of Psycho-Analysis*, New York.

Leonhard, Joachim-Felix (ed.) (1983): *Karl Jaspers in seiner Heidelberger Zeit*, Heidelberg.

Lockot, Regine (1985): *Erinnern und Durcharbeiten. Zur Geschichte der Psychoanalyse und Psychotherapie im Nationalsozialismus*, Frankfurt a.M.

Lockot, Regine (1994): *Die Reinigung der Psychoanalyse. Die Deutsche Psychoanalytische Gesellschaft im Spiegel von Dokumenten und Zeitzeugen (1933-1951)*, Tübingen.

Löwith, Karl (1932): "Max Weber und Karl Marx", in: ibid., *Sämtliche Schriften* 5, Stuttgart 1988, pp. 324-407.

Löwith, Karl (1933): "Die geistige Situation der Zeit", in: *Neue Jahrbücher für Wissenschaft und Jugendbildung* 9 (1933), pp. 1-10, quoted in ibid.: *Sämtliche Schriften* 8, Stuttgart 1984, pg. 20f.

Löwith, Karl (1939/40): "Max Weber und seine Nachfolger", in ibid.: *Sämtliche Schriften* 5, Stuttgart 1988, pp. 408-418.

Löwith, Karl (1953): *Weltgeschichte und Heilsgeschehen. Die theologischen Voraussetzungen der Geschichtsphilosophie* (1949/1953), Stuttgart, quoted in ibid.: *Sämtliche Schriften* 2, Stuttgart 1983, pp. 7-239. Original: *Meaning in History. The Theological Implications of the Philosophy of History*, Chicago 1949.

Löwith, Karl (1964): "Max Webers Stellung zur Wissenschaft", in ibid.: *Sämtliche Schriften* 5, pp. 419-447, Stuttgart 1988.

Löwith, Karl (1986): *Mein Leben in Deutschland vor und nach 1933. Ein Bericht*, Stuttgart. English translation: *My Life in Germany Before and After 1933: A Report*, London 1994.

Lohmann, Hans-Martin (1987): *Alexander Mitscherlich*, Reinbek bei Hamburg.

Lohmann, Hans-Martin (1998): *Sigmund Freud*, Reinbek bei Hamburg.

Luckmann, Thomas (1980): *Lebenswelt und Gesellschaft*, Paderborn.

Maeder, Alphonse (1910): "Untersuchungen an Dementia-praecox-Kranken", in: *Jahrbuch für psychoanalytische und psychopathologische Forschung* 2 (1910).

Martin, Marco (ed.) (2000): *Ein Fenster zur Welt. Die Zeitschrift 'Der Monat'. Beiträge aus vier Jahrzehnten*, Weinheim.

Mies, Thomas (1999): "Weltanschauung", in: Hans Jörg Sandkuhler (ed.*)*, *Enzyklopädie Philosophie*, vol. 2, Hamburg, pp. 1734.

Milosz, Czeslaw (1953): *Verführtes Denken*. With a foreward by Karl Jaspers, Cologne.

Mitscherlich, Alexander (1947): *Vom Ursprung der Sucht. Eine pathogenetische Untersuchung des Vieltrinkens*, Stuttgart 1947, quoted in: MGS 1, pp. 139-382.

Mitscherlich, Alexander (1949): "Über die Reichweite psychosomatischen Denkens. Referat auf dem 55. Kongreß der Deutschen Gesellschaft für Innere Medizin in Wiesbaden 1949", in: *Psyche* 3 (1949/50), pp. 342-358, quoted in: MGS 2, pp. 32-51.

Mitscherlich, Alexander (1951): "Kritik oder Politik?", in: *Psyche* 4 (1951), pp. 241-254, quoted in: MGS 7, pp. 164-183.

Mitscherlich, Alexander (1963): *Auf dem Weg zur vaterlosen Gesellschaft. Ideen zur Sozialpsychologie*, Munich 1963, quoted in: MGS 3, pp. 15-369.

Mitscherlich, Alexander (1982): *Ein Leben für die Psychoanalyse*, Frankfurt a.M. 1982.

Mitscherlich, Alexander (1983a): *Gesammelte Schriften*. Vols. 1-10, edited by Klaus Menne, Frankfurt a.M. (MGS).

Mitscherlich, Alexander and Mielke, Fred (eds.) (1947): *Das Diktat der Menschenverachtung. Der Nürnberger Ärzteprozeß und seine Quellen*, Heidelberg.

Mitscherlich, Alexander and Fred Mielke (ed.) (1949): *Wissenschaft ohne Menschlichkeit. Medizinische und eugenische Irrwege unter Diktatur Bürokratie und Krieg. Mit einem Vorwort der Arbeitsgemeinschaft westdeutscher Ärztekammern*, Heidelberg.

Mitscherlich, Alexander and Fred Mielke (1960): *Medizin ohne Menschlichkeit. Dokumente des Nürnberger Ärzteprozesses*, Frankfurt a.M.

Mitscherlich, Alexander and Margarethe Mitscherlich-Nielsen (1967): *Die Unfähigkeit zu trauern. Grundlagen kollektiven Verhaltens*, Munich.

Mommsen, Wolfgang J. (1959): *Max Weber und die deutsche Politik. 1890-1920*, Tübingen 1959.

Mommsen, Wolfgang J. (1985): "Max Weber - Persönliche Lebensführung und gesellschaftlicher Wandel in der Geschichte", in: Peter Alter, Wolfgang J. Mommsen and Thomas Nipperdey (eds.), *Geschichte und politisches Handeln*, Stuttgart, pp. 261-281.

Mommsen, Wolfgang J. (1988): "Einleitung", in ibid. and Wolfgang Schwendtker (eds.), *Max Weber und seine Zeitgenossen*, Göttingen.

Nietzsche, Friedrich (1986): *Sämtliche Briefe. Kritische Studienausgabe*, vols. 1-8, Berlin.

Nietzsche, Friedrich (1973): *Sämtliche Werke. Kritische Studienausgabe*, vols. 1-15, edited by Giorgio Colli and Mazzino Montinari, Berlin.

Nissen, Rudolf (1962): "Der hippokratische Eid in unserer Zeit", in: E. Beckerath and Heinrich Popitz (eds.): *Antidoron. Edgar Salin zum 70. Geburtstag*, Tübingen, pp 196-198.

Peter, Jürgen (1994): *Der Nürnberger Ärzteprozeß im Spiegel seiner Aufarbeitung anhand der drei Dokumentensammlungen von Alexander Mitscherlich und Fred Mielke*, Münster.

Peters, Uwe Henrik (1992): *Psychiatrie im Exil. Die Emigration der dynamischen Psychiatrie aus Deutschland 1933-1939*, Düsseldorf.

Peters, Uwe Henrik (2000): *Lexikon Psychiatrie, Psychotherapie, Medizinische Psychologie*, Munich.

Peukert, Detlev, J.K. (1987): *Die Weimarer Republik. Krisenjahre der Klassischen Moderne*, Frankfurt a.M.

Peukert, Detlev, J.K. (1989): *Max Webers Diagnose der Moderne*, Göttingen.

Piper, Klaus (1953): *Offener Horizont. Festschrift für Karl Jaspers*, Munich.

Piper, Klaus (1963): *Karl Jaspers. Werk und Wirkung*, Munich.

Piper, Klaus and Saner, Hans (eds.) (1974); *Erinnerungen an Karl Jaspers*, Munich.

Pitsch, Benedikt (1983*): Zur Methodologie des Verstehens in der Psychopathologie von Karl Jaspers.* Univ. Diss. Freiburg.

Pfister, Oskar (1952): "Karl Jaspers als Sigmund Freuds Widersacher", in: *Psyche* 6 (1952), pp. 241-275.

Popper, Karl R. (1979): *Ausgangspunkte. Meine intellektuelle Entwicklung*, Hamburg.

Popper, Karl R. (1992): *Die offene Gesellschaft und ihre Feinde* (1945). 2 vols., 7th, revised edition, Tübingen 1992. Original: *The Open Society and its Enemies*. 2 vols., London 1980.

Raaflaub, Walter (1986): *Ernst Mayer 1983-1952*, Bern.

Rabanus, Christian (ed.) (2000): *Primärbibliographie der Schriften Karl Jaspers'*, Tübingen.

Ringer, Fritz K. (1969): *The Decline of the German Mandarins. The German Academic Community, 1890-1933*, Cambridge 1969.

Rosa, Renato de (1986): "Politische Akzente im Leben eines Philosophen. Karl Jaspers in Heidelberg 1901-1946", in: *EU*, pp. 301-423.

Salamun, Kurt (1985): *Karl Jaspers*, Munich.

Salamun, Kurt (1988): "Moral Implications of Karl Jaspers' Existentialism", in: *Philosophy and Phenomenological Research* 49 (1988), pp. 317-323.

Sandkühler, Hans Jörg (ed.) (1999): *Enzyklopädie Philosophie*, 2 vols., with the collaboration of Detlev Pätzold, Arnim Regenbogen and Pirmin Stekeler-Weithofer, Hamburg.

Saner, Hans (1970): *Karl Jaspers*, Reinbek bei Hamburg.

Saner, Hans (ed.) (1973): *Karl Jaspers in der Diskussion*, Munich.

Saner, Hans (2000): "Philosophie beginnt zu zweit", in: Hannah Arendt: "Mut zum Politischen!", in: *DU. Die Zeitschrift für Kultur* Nr. 710 ((2000), pp. 14-15.

Sarkowski, Heinz (1982): Karl Jaspers, in: ibid., *Autorenbriefe aus dem Springer-Archiv*, Heidelberg, pp. 32-34.

Schaub, Norbert (1973): *Die Beurteilung der Psychoanalyse im psychiatrischen Werk von Jaspers.* Univ. Diss. Freiburg.

Scheidt, Carl Eduard (1986): *Die Rezeption der Psychoanalyse in der deutschsprachigen Philosophie vor 1940*, Frankfurt a.M.

Schiller, Friedrich v. (1962): *Sämtliche Werke*, Munich.

Schilpp, Paul Oskar (ed.) (1957): *Karl Jaspers*, Stuttgart. Original: *The Philosophy of Karl Jaspers.* Augmented edition with new section on Martin Heidegger in the "Philosophical Autobiography" (1957), La Salle 1981.

Schluchter, Wolfgang (1988): *Religion und Lebensführung*. 2 vols., Frankfurt a.M.

Schluchter, Wolfgang (1996): "Polytheismus der Werte. Überlegungen im Anschluß an Max Weber", in: ibid., *Unversöhnte Moderne*, Frankfurt a.M., pp. 223-255.

Schmid, Wilhelm (1998): *Philosophie der Lebenskunst. Eine Grundlegung*, Frankfurt a.M.

Schmidt-Degenhard, Michael (1983): *Melancholie und Depression. Zur Problemgeschichte der depressiven Erkrankung seit Beginn des 19. Jahrhunderts*, Stuttgart.

Schmidt-Degenhard, Michael (1997): "Zur Standortbestimmung einer anthropologischen Psychiatrie", in: *Fortschritte der Neurologie und Psychiatrie* 65 (1997), pp. 473-480.

Schmidt-Degenhard, Michael (2000): "Anthropologische Aspekte psychiatrischer Erkrankungen", in: Hans Jürgen Möller et al. (eds.), *Psychiatrie und Psychotherapie*, Berlin, pp. 259-270.

Schmitt, Wolfram (1979): "Karl Jaspers und die Methodenfrage in der Psychiatrie", in: Janzarik (1979c), pp. 74-82.

Schmitt, Wolfram (1980): "Die Psychopathologie von Karl Jaspers in der modernen Psychiatrie", in: Uwe Hendrik Peters (ed.): *Kindlers Psychologie des 20. Jahrhunderts,* vol. 10, pp. 46-62.

Schmitt, Wolfram (1983): "Karl Jaspers als Psychiater und sein Einfluß auf die Psychiatrie", in: Leonhard (1983), pp. 23-38.

Schneider, Kurt (1938): "25 Jahre *Allgemeine Psychopathologie*", in: *Der Nervenarzt*, 11 (1938), pp. 281-283, quoted in: Saner (1973), pp. 13-16.

Schneider, Kurt (1952): *Psychiatrie heute*, Stuttgart.

Schwentker, Wolfgang (1988): "Leidenschaft als Lebensform. Erotik und Moral bei Max Weber und im Kreis um Otto Gross", in: Mommsen/Schwendtker (1988), pp. 661-681.

Schwinn, Thomas (1998): "Wertsphären, Lebensordnungen und Lebensführungen", in: Agathe Bienfait and Gerhard Wagner (eds.), *Verantwortliches Handeln in gesellschaftlichen Ordnungen. Beiträge zu Wolfgang Schluchters 'Religion und Lebensführung'*, Frankfurt a.M., pp. 270-319.

Seidler, Eduard, Hildburg Kindt, and Norbert Schaub (1978): "Jaspers und Freud", in: *Sudhoffs Archiv* 62 (1978), pp. 37-63.

Simmel, Georg (1907): *Die Probleme der Geschichtsphilosophie*, 3rd edition, Berlin, quoted in: ibid., *Die Probleme der Geschichtsphilosophie. Complete Writings*, vol. 9, pp. 227-420.

Simmel, Georg (1908): *Soziologie*, Berlin, quoted in: ibid., *Complete Writings*, vol. 11, Frankfurt a.M. 1992, pp. 383-414.

Spitzer, Manfred (1985): *Allgemeine Subjektivität und Psychopathologie*, Frankfurt a.M.

Sternberger, Dolf (1963): "Jaspers und der Staat", in: Piper (1963), pp. 133-141.

Sternberger, Dolf (1985): "Karl Jaspers. 1883-1969", in: *Semper Apertus. Sechshundert-Jahre Ruprecht-Karls-Universität 1386-1986*. Vol. III: *Das zwanzigste Jahrhundert 1918-1985*, edited by Wilhelm Doerr, Berlin, pp. 286-298.

Taylor, Charles (1989): *Sources of the Self. The Making of the Modern Identity*, Cambridge 1989.

Tellenbach, Hubertus (1987): "Karl Jaspers' Konzeption einer geistigen Psychiatrie. Ein Nachwort zum 7. Jahrzehnt *Allgemeine Psychopathologie*", in: *Der Nervenarzt* 58 (1987), pp. 468-470.

Tenbruck, Friedrich (1999): *Das Werk Max Webers. Aufsätze zu Max Weber*, edited by Harald Homann, Tübingen.

Tölle, Rainer (1980): "Die Entwicklung der deutschen Psychiatrie im 20. Jahrhundert", in: *Kindlers Psychologie des 20. Jahrhunderts*, vol. 10, edited by Uwe Henrik Peters, Zürich, pp. 13-23.

Unseld, Siegfried (1982): "Versuch die Welt besser zu verstehen", in: *Psyche* 37 (1982), pp. 311-321.

Warsitz, Rolf Peter (1985): *Das zweifache Selbstmißverständnis der Psychoanalyse. Die Psychoanalysekritik von Karl Jaspers in immanenter Kritik*. Univ. Diss. Marburg.

Warsitz, Rolf Peter (1990): *Zwischen Verstehen und Erklären. Die widerständige Erfahrung der Psychoanalyse bei Karl Jaspers, Jürgen Habermas und Jacques Lacan*, Würzburg.

Weber, Marianne (1926): *Max Weber. Ein Lebensbild*, Tübingen.

Weber, Max (1903/06): "Roscher und Knies und die logischen Probleme der historischen Nationalökonomie", in: *Schmollers Jahrbuch* 27, 29, 30 (1903/6), pp. 1181-1221, pp. 1323-1384, pp. 81-120, quoted in: WL, pp. 1-145.

Weber, Max (1904): "Die 'Objektivität' sozialwissenschaftlicher und sozialpolitischer Erkenntnis", in: *AfSS* 19 (1904), pp. 22-87, quoted in: WL, pp. 146-214. English translation in: Max Weber (1949), pp. 49-112.

Weber, Max (1904/05): "Die protestantische Ethik und der 'Geist' des Kapitalismus", in: *AfSS* 20, 21 (1904/05), pp. 1-54 and pp. 1-110, quoted in: RS 1, pp. 17-206. English translation: The Protestant Ethic and the Spirit of Capitalism, translated by Talcott Parsons, London 1976.

Weber, Max (1906a): "Die protestantischen Sekten und der Geist des Kapitalismus", originally as: "'Kirchen' und 'Sekten'" in: *Frankfurter Zeitung*, April 13, 1906 and April 15, 1906, quoted in: RS 1, pp. 207-236. English translation in: Max Weber (1991), pp. 302-322.

Weber, Max (1906b): "Kritische Studien auf dem Gebiet der kulturwissenschaftlichen Logik", in: *AfSS* 22 (1906), pp. 143-207, quoted in: WL, pp. 215-290. English translation in: Max Weber (1949), pp. 113-188.

Weber, Max (1907): "R. Staemmlers 'Überwindung' der materialistischen Geschichtsauffassung", in: *AfSS* 24 (1907), pp. 94-151, quoted in: WL, pp. 291-359.

Max Weber (1910): "Geschäftsbericht und Diskussionsreden auf den deutschen soziologischen Tagungen (1910, 1912)", in: *GASS*, pp. 431-491.

Weber, Max (1917): "Der Sinn der 'Wertfreiheit' der soziologischen und ökonomischen Wissenschaften", in: *Logos* 7 (1917), pp. 40-88, quoted in: WL, pp. 489-540. English translation in: Max Weber (1949), pp. 1-47.

Weber, Max (1919a): *Politik als Beruf.* In the series *Geistige Arbeit als Beruf. Vorträge vor dem Freistudentischen Bund. Zweiter Vortrag,* Munich, quoted in: Weber (1992), pp. 113-252. English translation in: Max Weber (1991), pp. 77-128.

Weber, Max (1919b): *Wissenschaft als Beruf.* In the series *Geistige Arbeit als Beruf. Vorträge vor dem Freistudentischen Bund. Erster Vortrag,* Munich 1919, quoted in: WL, pp. 582-613. English translation in: Weber (1989), pp. 3-31.

Weber, Max (1920a): *Die Wirtschaftsethik der Weltreligionen. Vergleichende religionssoziologische Versuche.* Introduction: "1. Konfuzianismus und Taoismus; Zwischenbetrachtung: Theorie der Stufen und Richtungen religiöser Weltablehnung", quoted in: RS 1, pp. 237-573. English translation in: Max Weber (1991), pp. 276-301 and 323-359.

Weber, Max (1920b): *Gesammelte Aufsätze zur Religionssoziologie.* vol. 1, 5th ed. Tübingen 1963 (RS).

Weber, Max (1920c): "Vorbemerkung", quoted in: RS 1, pp. 1-16.

Weber, Max (1922a): *Gesammelte Aufsätze zur Wissenschaftslehre.* 6th, newly revised edition, edited by Johannes Winkelmann, Tübingen 1985 (WL).

Weber, Max (1922b): *Wirtschaft und Gesellschaft. Grundriss der verstehenden Soziologie,* 5th, revised edition (Studienausgabe), edited by Johannes Winkelmann, Tübingen 1980 (WG). English translation: Max Weber (1968).

Weber, Max (1949): *The Methodology of the Social Sciences,* ed. by Edward A. Shils and Henry A. Finch, New York.

Weber, Max (1968): *Economy and Society. An Outline of Interpretative Sociology,* 3 vols., edited by Guenther Roth and Claus Wittich, New York.

Weber, Max (1989): *Max Weber's 'Science as a Vocation',* ed. by Peter Lassmann and Irving Volody, London, pp. 3-31.

Weber, Max (1990): *Letters 1906-1908,* edited by M. Rainer Lepsius and Wolfgang J. Mommsen in collaboration with Birgit Rudhard and Manfred Schön, Tübingen.

Max Weber (1991): *Essays in Sociology,* ed. by H.H. Gerth and S. Wright Mills, London.

Weber, Max (1992): *Wissenschaft als Beruf 1917/1919. Politik als Beruf 1919,* edited by Wolfgang J. Mommsen and Wolfgang Schluchter, Tübingen.

Weil, Simone (1974): *Zeugnis für das Gute. Traktate, Letters, Aufzeichnungen,* edited by Friedhelm Kemp, Munich 1990.

Wein, Martin (1988): *Die Weizsäckers. Geschichte einer deutschen Familie,* Stuttgart.

Weiß, Johannes (1992): *Max Webers Grundlegung der Soziologie,* Munich.

Weizsäcker, Viktor v. (1934): *Ärztliche Fragen. Vorlesungen über Allgemeine Therapie,* Leipzig, quoted in: WGS 5, pp. 259-342.

Weizsäcker, Viktor v. (1935): *Studien zur Pathogenese,* Leipzig, quoted in: WGS 6, pp. 253-330.

Weizsäcker, Viktor v. (1949): "Psychosomatische Medizin", in: *Psyche* 3 (1949), pp. 331-331, quoted in: WGS 6, pp. 451-464.

Weizsäcker, Viktor v. (1954): *Natur und Geist,* Göttingen, quoted in: WGS 1, pp. 9-190.

Wiehl, Reiner (1999): "Jaspers' Bestimmung des Überpolitischen", in: Wiehl/Kaegi (1999), pp. 81-96.

Wiehl, Reiner and Kaegi, Dominic (eds.) (1999): *Karl Jaspers - Philosophie und Politik,* Heidelberg.

Wiehl, Reiner and Kaegi, Dominic (1999): Foreward, in: Wiehl/Kaegi (ed.) (1999), pp. 9-12.

Wiesing, Urban (ed.) (2000): *Ethik in der Medizin. Ein Reader,* Stuttgart.

Wiggershaus, Rolf (1986): *Die Frankfurter Schule. Geschichte, Theoretische Entwicklung und Bedeutung,* Munich 1988.

Wilmans, Karl (1910): "Zur klinischen Stellung der Paranoia", in: *Zentralblatt für Nervenheilkunde,* pp. 207.

Windelband, Wilhelm (1894): "Geschichte und Naturwissenschaft", in: *Stiftungsfest der Kaiser-Wilhelm-Universität Strassburg, 1890-1902,* Strassburg (year not given), pp. 17-41.

Young-Bruehl, Elisabeth (1982): *Hannah Arendt. For Love in the World,* New Haven 1982.

INDEX

CPSIA information can be obtained
at www.ICGtesting.com
Printed in the USA
LVOW03*1111220816

501182LV00009BB/104/P